D1206113

Fighting for Foreigners

FIGHTING FOR FOREIGNERS

*Immigration and Its Impact
on Japanese Democracy*

APICHAI W. SHIPPER

CORNELL UNIVERSITY PRESS
ITHACA AND LONDON

Cornell University Press gratefully acknowledges receipt of a
subvention from the University of Southern California, which helped
in the publication of this book.

First published 2008 by Cornell University Press
Printed in the United States of America

Library of Congress Cataloging-in-Publication Data

Shipper, Apichai W. (Apichai Wongsod), 1968–
    Fighting for foreigners : immigration and its impact on Japanese
democracy / Apichai W. Shipper.
        p. cm.
    Includes bibliographical references and index.
    ISBN 978-0-8014-4715-0 (cloth : alk. paper)
    1. Immigrants—Japan—Political activity. 2. Aliens—Japan—Political
activity. 3. Illegal aliens—Japan—Political activity. 4. Alien labor—
Japan. 5. Japan—Emigration and immigration—Government policy.
6. Emigration and immigration law—Japan. 7. Democracy—Japan.
I. Title.
    DS832.7.A1S55   2008
    320.952—dc22   2008015708

Cornell University Press strives to use environmentally responsible
suppliers and materials to the fullest extent possible in the publishing of
its books. Such materials include vegetable-based, low-VOC inks and
acid-free papers that are recycled, totally chlorine-free, or partly composed
of nonwood fibers. For further information, visit our website at www.
cornellpress.cornell.edu.

Cloth printing   10 9 8 7 6 5 4 3 2 1

For my parents,
Ranoo and Sander Shipper

Contents

PREFACE

At the beginning of the third millennium, the development of capitalism has reached a point where capital, ideas, and people move readily across national boundaries. Globalization, as this stage of capitalism is now called, poses a challenge for many thinkers in the new millennium. It challenges us not only to understand how globalization positively or negatively affects societies but also to find imaginative rules and institutions to ensure that globalization works justly for those 200 million people who live and work in a country other than the one they were born in. Japanese capitalism, which is known for its innovative business practices and institutions, can be expected to offer new ideas on such rules and institutions to students of comparative immigration politics. This book explores Japan's immigration laws and institutions and their impact on its democracy.

This project originated at Massachusetts Institute of Technology (MIT) where I received my graduate training. I greatly appreciate the guidance of my thesis committee: Richard Samuels, Michael Piore, Benedict Anderson (from Cornell), and the late Myron Weiner. They have shown me a path to my becoming a committed scholar as well as a caring teacher and a decent human being. Loren King and Robert Pekkanen, whose academic paths crossed mine in Cambridge, have witnessed and deeply influenced the development of this project, both theoretically and empirically, from its initial stage to the final product. They tirelessly offered critical, new challenges to my idea, and I cherish our long friendship and their continued intellectual support.

I also benefited greatly from scholars who have read and commented on portions of this book in earlier forms. I would like to thank John Dower, David Gartner, Andrew Gordon, Norma Field, Wolfgang Herbert, Higuchi Naoto, Peter Hill, Horiuchi Yusaku, the late Kajita Takamichi, Anthony Kammas, Hyung Gu Lynn, Peter Nosco, Susan Pharr, T. J. Pempel, Kim Reimann, Frank Schwartz, Jefferey Sellers, Tanno Kiyoto, Tsujinaka Yutaka, Tsunekawa Kei'ichi, and Watanabe Hiroaki. I am also grateful to the two anonymous reviewers for helpful comments on earlier versions and appreciate the enthusiasm and professionalism of Roger Haydon of Cornell University Press. Finally, I thank Barbara Gartner and Ange Romeo-Hall for helping to improve the writing of the manuscript.

I acknowledge the financial and institutional support from the United Nations University Institute of Advanced Studies, the Matsushita International Foundation, the University of Tokyo Institute of Social Science, the Hitotsubashi University Department of Social Studies, the Harvard–MIT MacArthur Fellowship on Transnational Security, the MIT Industrial Performance Center, the Harvard University Program on U.S.–Japan Relations, the Japan Foundation, and the University of Southern California (USC) Center for International Studies. I am grateful to the USC Department of Political Science and the School of International Relations for providing me with great research assistants: Jeany Choi, Christine Jun, Nadejda Marinova, Abigail Ruane, and Laura Sjoberg.

Part of this book draws from my earlier work: "Criminals or Victims? The Politics of Illegal Foreigners in Japan," reprinted by permission of *Journal of Japanese Studies* 31, no. 2 (2005): 299–327; and "Foreigners and Civil Society in Japan," reprinted by permission of *Pacific Affairs* 79, no. 2 (2006): 269–289.

I owe a great debt to the foreigners, social activists, and government officials with whom I have interacted over the years. They have been generous in sharing time, stories, ideas, and documents with me.

I thank my partner, Akiko, for allowing me to indulge in my other love and for making numerous sacrifices. I also am grateful to my children, Karuna and Lui, for not following through on their threats to destroy my manuscript. Finally, I thank my parents. They brought me out of the rice fields of Thailand to a suburb in America and raised me in an environment surrounded by union activism and political volunteerism. It is to them, who made me a "foreigner" and first taught me about "democracy," that this book is dedicated.

APICHAI W. SHIPPER

Los Angeles, California

ABBREVIATIONS

AFVKN	Association of Families of Victims Kidnapped by North Korea
AMDA	Association of Medical Doctors of Asia
ANPO	US–Japan Security Treaty (*anzen hoshō jōyaku*)
APFS	Asian Peoples Friendship Society
AUN	[Burmese] Association of United Nationalities in Japan
Āyus	Network of Buddhist Volunteers on International Cooperation
CBCJ	Catholic Bishops' Conference of Japan
Chōsen Sōren	General Association of Korean Residents in Japan (*zainihon chōsenjin sōrengokai*); also Ch'ongryŏn
CLAIR	Council of Local Authorities for International Relations
CTIC	Catholic Tokyo International Center
DPJ	Democratic Party of Japan
DPP	Democratic Progressive Party (Taiwan)
EPA	Economic Promotion Agreement

FLU	Foreign Laborers' Union
FTUB	Federation Trade Union of Burma—Japan
FTA	Free Trade Agreement
FWBZ	Foreign Workers' Branch of Zentōitsu
HELP	House in Emergency of Love and Peace
IMADR	International Movement against All Forms of Discriminations and Racism
ILO	International Labor Organization
IOM	International Organization for Migration
JCLU	Japan Civil Liberties Union
JCP	Japan Communist Party
JET	Japan Exchange and Teaching
JITCO	Japan International Training Cooperation Organization
JNATIP	Japan Network Against Trafficking in Persons
KCIA	[South] Korean Central Intelligence Agency
KMT	Kuomintang of China
KOSHC	Kanagawa Occupational Safety and Health Center
LAFLR	Lawyers' Association for Foreign Laborers Rights
LAFOCC	Lawyers' Association for Foreign Criminal Cases
LDB	League for Democracy in Burma
LDP	Liberal Democratic Party
LSIO	Labor Standards Inspection Office
MEXT	Ministry of Education, Culture, Sports, Science, and Technology
MF-MASH	Minatomachi Foreign Migrant Workers' Mutual Aid Scheme for Health
MHLW	Ministry of Health, Labor, and Welfare
MIC	Ministry of Internal Affairs and Communications
Mindan	Korean Residents Union in Japan (*zainihon daikan minkoku mindan*)
Minsen	Democratic Front for Unification of Koreans in Japan (*zainichi chōsen tōitsu minshu sensen*)
Mintōren	Council for Combating Discrimination against Ethnic People in Japan (*minzoku sabetsu to tatakau renraku kyōgikai*)
MITI	Ministry of International Trade and Industry (currently Ministry of Economy, Trade, and Industry, or METI)
MOFA	Ministry of Foreign Affairs

MOJ	Ministry of Justice
MOL	Ministry of Labor (currently part of MHLW)
NARKIN	National Association for the Rescue of Japanese Kidnapped by North Korea
NCC/J	National Christian Council in Japan
NDF	National Democratic Front (Burma)
NGO	Nongovernmental organization
NHI	National Health Insurance (*kokumin kenkō hoken*)
NLD-LA	National League for Democracy—Liberated Area (Burma)
NPA	National Police Agency
NPO	Nonprofit Organization
OCA	Overseas Chinese Association (*kakyo sōkai*)
OC-Net	Ōta Citizen's Network for Peoples' Togetherness
OECD	Organization for Economic Cooperation and Development
OSHC	Occupational Safety and Health Centers
PACEM	Pastoral Center for Migrants
PFB	People's Forum on Burma
PRC	People's Republic of China
Rengō	Japanese Trade Union Confederation
SDP	Social Democratic Party
SHARE	Services for Health in Asian and African Regions
SMJ	Solidarity Network with Migrants in Japan
Sōhyō	General Council of Trade Unions of Japan
SOL	Yokohama Diocese: Solidarity Center for Migrants
SSI	Supplemental Security Income
TAN	Transnational advocacy network
TANF	Temporary Assistance to Needy Families
TELL	Tokyo English Life Line
TIP	Technical Internship Program
TOSHC	Tokyo Occupational Safety and Health Resource Center
WCTU	Women's Christian Temperance Union
YOKE	Yokohama Association for International Communication and Exchange
Zai-a-kyō	Society to Struggle Together with Asian Workers in Japan
Zenrōkyō	National Trade Unions Council
Zenrōren	National Confederation of Trade Unions

NOTE ON CONVENTIONS

Japanese names are given in Japanese order (family name followed by given name) except for those individuals who write principally in a Western language. Names and words familiar to Anglophone readers are in their Anglicized form: thus Tokyo, not Tōkyō. Unless otherwise noted, all translations are my own, and Japanese-language newspaper citations refer to morning editions.

FIGHTING FOR FOREIGNERS

1

INTRODUCTION

Associative Activism

The following description by a Filipina missionary of a weekly church gathering of Filipinos in Japan illustrates the undemocratic relationship among foreigners based on their legal and occupational categorization:

> At the front pews you will see the "legitimate" Filipino community—the embassy people, the students on Monbusho scholarships, the spouses of Japanese nationals, then the male migrant workers, who are engaged in "decent back-breaking labor." Crowded by the door are the women who work in the sex industry, the last to arrive and the first to leave. Readers and leaders are almost always the students. Although coffee or tea and cookies are served after mass, for fellowship, only the "legitimate" members of the community remain.[1]

---

1. Published interview with Lisa Go in *Japan Christian Activity News* 711 (winter 1994): 4–7 (5ff).

Such experience is not uncommon among the variety of foreigners from different races and socioeconomic backgrounds. Although Japan has one of the most controlled borders in the industrialized world, the number of foreigners rose from 750,000 in 1975 to 2 million in 2005. Many of these are old immigrants from Korea and China who were born in Japan, but over half are new immigrants from Asia and Latin America, who work in small- or medium-sized manufacturing firms. In addition, approximately 200,000 foreign workers, mostly from Asia, who have overstayed their visas, have low-paying positions as construction workers, factory workers, waitresses, entertainers, and cooks. This recent influx of foreign workers, particularly from Asia and South America, is creating new challenges for Japan's democratic ideals and institutions. The large number of foreigners in Japan is forcing the government to reevaluate basic principles of democracy, a political system that requires agreement among members of the political community on membership rules, entitlements, and a minimum of shared values. The presence of these foreigners is challenging the Japanese government and society to accord new respect to individual and group differences in culture, beliefs, and identity, while guaranteeing equality of social and economic opportunity.

I do not intend to explore salient characteristics that might be required for a system to be a democracy and then evaluate whether Japan is a democratic society. Based on its liberal constitution and existing political institutions that provide essential guarantees, I assume that Japan is already a democracy.[2] Instead, the recent influx of foreigners and their legal distinction raise interesting questions about the direction and quality of Japan's democracy. Scholars generally agree that foreigners have a causal impact on democratic institutions, but they disagree on whether this impact is *positive* (strengthening and transforming democracy and reducing economic inequalities) or *negative* (weakening or undermining democracy and increasing economic inequalities). I aim to clarify this relationship by examining how foreigners have advanced (or hindered) democracy in

---

2. These guarantees include freedom to form and join organizations, freedom of expression, right to vote, right of political leaders to compete for support, alternative sources of information, free and fair elections, and institutions for making government policies depend on votes and other expressions of preference. For a discussion of these guarantees, see Robert A. Dahl, *Polyarchy: Participation and Opposition* (New Haven: Yale University Press, 1971), 1–9.

Japan. Which type of foreign workers and their organizations best promotes Japan's democratic institutions and processes that aim to protect individual freedom and basic liberties as well as to improve social and economic equality? This question is addressed through a discussion of the efforts of immigrant rights activists to protect foreigners at the local level and to provide alternative sources of information on foreigners at the national level. I then explore the responses of local governments to the demands or preferences of these activists and the government efforts to provide wider and more egalitarian representation even for nonresidents. These efforts of nonstate institutions and local governments are important and inherently good for democracy because humane treatment of the worst-off populations, including foreigners, as well as wider and more egalitarian representation even for noncitizens are crucial aspects of this model of democracy.[3]

Despite its antiforeigner image of the past, Japan has achieved a surprisingly high degree of civility in its accommodation of foreign workers, including illegal ones. This achievement, which advances more inclusive democracy in Japan, is credited not to government efforts but to the initiatives of certain Japanese citizens and their organizations to support foreigners. This book explains how this process takes place.

Foreigners and Democracy in Theoretical Perspective

As modern technology facilitates the movement of capital, people, and ideas across national boundaries and socioeconomic conditions propel migration from underdeveloped to wealthy countries, the impact of foreigners on democratic institutions and ideals has generated increasing scholarly interest. Some scholars, including democratic theorists and critical legal scholars, see the participation of immigrants in the civil society and pressure on institutions to respond to their needs as driving democracy

---

3. On hospitality to foreigners, see Seyla Benhabib, *The Rights of Others: Aliens, Residents, and Citizens* (Cambridge: Cambridge University Press, 2004); on foreigners' representation, see Iris Marion Young, *Inclusion and Democracy* (New York: Oxford University Press, 2000), and Melissa S. Williams, *Voice, Trust, and Memory: Marginalized Groups and the Failings of Liberal Representation* (Princeton: Princeton University Press, 1998).

forward. Others, such as nationalist theorists and certain labor scholars, have argued that the presence of foreigners undermines democratic ideals such as worker rights and equality and weakens citizen commitment to the common good. This section discusses the debate on the impact of foreigners on democracy before turning to an explanation of Japan's institutional arrangement for foreigners.

Strengthening or Weakening Civil Society and Democracy?

During a hot summer night in Kotobuki-chō of Yokohama, a young Korean man stood on the stairs of the Labor and Welfare Center listening to the free summer concert. The Asian economic crisis had interrupted his third year of law studies in a university in Seoul and brought him to Kotobuki-chō in search of work. Below him in front of the stage, a group of happy Bangladeshis gathered. Next to this group of foreign workers stood a few staff and volunteers from the Kalabaw-no-kai, a support group for foreign workers in Kotobuki-chō. They had helped organize this annual event with various volunteer groups from the area and operated a *yatai* (stall) selling barbeque meat all afternoon. One Kalabaw staff had also helped another volunteer group handing out food to homeless residents during the festival (earlier in the week, homeless residents were given a coupon to receive free food during the festival). These foreign workers and members of the foreigners support group were immersed in this community festival and the beautiful music.

Foreigners participate in the creation and maintenance of a variety of institutions, such as cultural or religious associations, immigrant ethnic associations, hometown associations, or homeland language schools. These institutions generate a vibrant civic life and political awareness among their members, while functioning as transnational agents of social capital and trust. Through these institutions, foreigners organize festivals, cultural activities, and other events that bring together foreigners and natives in the community while preserving certain features of the immigrants' culture. These institutions can promote public discussion about immigrant and local issues through public meetings and the mass media. All these activities aim to improve multicultural understanding. This associational involvement by foreigners, who appear particularly zealous in their community-sustaining activities, has led some democratic theorists such as

Michael Walzer to view new American immigrants as a major source that reinvigorates civil society and democracy.[4]

In contrast, others have observed that foreigners are less likely than natives to volunteer for public service and to participate in the political and civic activities of their *host* societies. They are not required to participate in civic duties, such as jury service, or to serve in the military. Where foreigners are allowed to vote at local elections, they tend to have lower rates of voter turnout than that of citizens.[5] In addition, foreign workers in most industrialized countries have lower levels of participation in and hold different attitudes toward their unions than do native workers.[6] This division between natives and foreigners undermines working-class solidarity and can weaken labor-backed political parties.[7] Furthermore, the presence of immigrant workers typically reduces the political and economic bargaining power of organized labor. Their growing number provides firms—domestic and transnational—with a valuable tool to suppress wages and benefits, thereby disempowering labor. During periods of economic recession when organized labor hopes to exert its leverage against business, business often responds by scapegoating and repatriating foreign workers rather than by making concessions to native workers.[8]

Transformation or Retrenchment?

Scholars also disagree on whether foreigners offer opportunities for democratic transformation or encourage democratic retrenchment. Critical legal scholar Roberto Mangabeira Unger sees "hidden opportunities for democratic transformation in the rich democracies" as a result of the

---

4. Michael Walzer, *What It Means to Be an American: Essays on the American Experience* (New York: Marsilio, 1996).

5. Tomas Hammer, *Democracy and the Nation State* (Aldershot: Avebury, 1990).

6. See Julie Watts, *Immigration Policy and the Challenge of Globalization: Unions and Employers in Unlikely Alliance* (Ithaca: Cornell University Press, 2002), 62–73; Santina Bertone et al., "Immigrant Workers and Australian Trade Unions: Participation and Attitudes," *International Migration Review* 24, no. 4 (1995): 723–744.

7. Mark Miller, *Foreign Workers in Western Europe: An Emerging Political Force* (New York: Praeger, 1981), 2–5.

8. Ibid.

gradual movement of labor from developing countries to rich countries. He believes that immigration generates "involuntary or half-conscious institutional experimentalism" in host countries.[9] In Unger's view, this institutional experimentalism by state actors in rich countries drives democracy forward in these countries. Bonnie Honig adds that, historically, the foreigner, as an "agent of refounding," has helped a society to define and shape its national community, thereby further advancing democracy.[10] Foreigners may induce a modern society to redefine the criteria for membership and entitlements as well as to rethink the status of natives, thereby reconceptualizing its own ideal of justice. For Honig, "democracy is always about living with strangers, [and] being mobilized into action periodically with and on behalf of people who are surely opaque to us and often unknown to us."[11] Will Kymlicka concurs that foreigners propel liberal democracies to experiment with and to establish new institutions for multicultural representation that guarantee justice.[12] However, he cautions that certain types of immigration organizations promote the development of democratic citizenship better than others.[13]

Others have argued that foreigners can lead a country down the dark path toward democratic retrenchment. Because he believes that foreigners lack national loyalty and do not share the same notion of the common good, David Miller argues that foreigners will undermine the community's interests and even national security.[14] In the United States, the 9/11 terrorist acts raised such a concern over national security and Muslim foreigners who are seen as not sharing similar values and ideals as Americans. Viewed as purveyors of antinational ideas and potential threats to national security, many Arabs and Muslims living in the United States were required to register with the government, and many were imprisoned

9. Roberto Mangabeira Unger, *Democracy Realized: The Progressive Alternative* (London: Verso, 1998), 27.

10. Bonnie Honig, *Democracy and the Foreigner* (Princeton: Princeton University Press, 1998).

11. Ibid., p. 39.

12. Will Kymlicka, *Multicultural Citizenship* (New York: Oxford University Press, 1995).

13. Will Kymlicka, "Ethnic Associations and Democratic Citizenship," in Amy Gutmann, ed., *Freedom of Association* (Princeton: Princeton University Press, 1998).

14. David Miller, "Bounded Citizenship," in Kimberly Hutchings and Roland Dannreuther, eds., *Cosmopolitan Citizenship* (London: Macmillan, 1999), 60–80.

without charges or legal representation.[15] The subsequent passage of the Uniting and Strengthening America by Providing Appropriate Tools Required to Intercept and Obstruct Terrorism (USA PATRIOT) Act of 2001 curtailed civil liberties (e.g., by relaxing the restrictions on phone tapping), for *citizens* as well as foreigners.[16] Significantly, an official view of foreigners as a subversive force and threat to national security promotes racism and xenophobia among citizens, as occurred with the Nativism movement in the United States during the late nineteenth and early twentieth century. Similarly in Japan during the 1920s and 1930s, some officials worried that certain Korean residents were harboring ill-will toward Japan and its citizens. These officials spread horrifying rumors about Koreans in Japan, following the Great Kanto Earthquake on September 1, 1923, that Koreans were setting fires, looting, and poisoning wells in a planned attempt to attack the Japanese. The Home Ministry then instructed the local authorities to take strong measures to prevent any Korean subversion in their areas.[17] It helped to organize vigilante corps, comprised of both army reservists and civilian volunteers, to search the streets for Koreans and acted brutally against them. At least two thousand innocent Koreans died at the hands of these vigilantes.

Increasing or Reducing Economic Inequalities?

Foreigners, through the migration of labor from poor to rich countries, have been viewed as both a solution and a source of world economic inequality. Building on philosopher John Rawls's well-known "difference principle" of distributive justice, which states that inequality is allowed to exist if it benefits the least advantaged in society, supporters such as Joseph Carens stress the importance of a commitment to freedom of movement as

---

15. Such government actions against Middle Easterners are similar to those against Japanese-Americans after Japan attacked Pearl Harbor. Because the U.S. government feared that Japanese-Americans would be involved in espionage and sabotage for the Japanese government during wartime, they were distrusted and subjected to registering with the government and held in either detention centers or jailed.

16. For details of the Patriot Act, which President George W. Bush signed into law on October 26, 2001, see Public Law 107-56, 115 Stat. 272 (2001).

17. Richard M. Mitchell, *The Korean Minority in Japan* (Berkeley: University of California Press, 1967), 39n.

both an important liberty in itself and as a prerequisite for other freedoms.[18] While Rawls's theory of justice, in its original form, is confined within a given society, Carens applies Rawls's conception universally across societies. That is to say, justice requires that the well-off take steps to improve the condition of worse-off groups in the world. For Carens, permitting extensive immigration from poor to affluent countries is one way to accomplish this end. Carens's argument is founded on the neoclassical economic premise that gross economic inequalities exist between states.[19] In the face of such inequality, freedom of movement enables individuals to "avail" themselves of opportunities to improve their income and general well-being. Consequently, international migration leads to a convergence of real wage rates between the home and recipient countries while the overall world economic output increases in the long run.[20] In other words, Carens argues that "freedom of movement [of people] would [lead] to a reduction of political, social, and economic inequalities."[21] In essence, Carens views immigration as a strategy to reduce Third World poverty, global inequality, and, therefore, world tyranny.

By contrast, critics such as labor economists Vernon Briggs and George Borjas view immigration as a force that widens economic inequality. Briggs argues that "immigrants depress wages too low for natives and thereby drive native workers out of their jobs."[22] Borjas adds that immigrants hurt the economic prospects of poor, unskilled native workers such as minorities

18. Joseph H. Carens, "Aliens and Citizens: The Case for Open Borders," *The Review of Politics* 49, no. 2 (1987): 251–273; Carens, "Migration and Morality: A Liberal Egalitarian Perspective," in B. Barry and R. Goodin, eds., *Free Movement: Ethical Issues in the Transnational Migration of People and of Money* (University Park: Pennsylvania State University Press, 1992), 25–47 (25ff).

19. John Harris and Michael Todaro argue that given the high and institutionally rigid wages of industrialized areas, workers from low-income underdeveloped regions would be attracted in numbers much larger than the labor market demands, based on the chance that they would luck into a job. In other words, an economic person from poor countries finds it advantageous to migrate to rich countries even if employment is not ensured. See their "Migration, Unemployment, and Development: A Two Sector Analysis," *American Economic Review* 60, no. 1 (1970): 126–142.

20. See Julian Simon, *The Economic Consequences of Immigration* (Cambridge: Basil Blackwell, 1989).

21. Carens, "Migration and Morality: A Liberal Egalitarian Perspective," 26.

22. Vernon M. Briggs, Jr., *Immigration Policy and the American Labor Force* (Baltimore: Johns Hopkins University Press, 1984), 139; also see Briggs, "The Imperative of Immigration Reform: The Case for an Employment-based Immigration Policy," in Vernon M. Briggs, Jr., and Stephen Moore, *Still an Open Door? U.S. Immigration Policy and the American Economy* (Washington, D.C.: American University Press, 1994), 3–73 (51ff).

and high school dropouts.[23] The debate on the level of impact on the native labor force continues to be highly contested among economists, but empirical data from the United States suggest that immigrant workers are widening economic inequality.[24] Immigrants have depressed wages and employment opportunities of unskilled native workers by an insignificant amount, but they have raised the income of average native workers.[25] For democratic theorists, this finding is troubling because many believe that economic inequality is the source of domination and injustice, which impede the development of democracy.[26] David Miller raises the further concern that foreigners may weaken citizen commitment to such common goods as welfare services.[27] Recent studies of U.S. public opinion consistently support the view that citizen attitudes toward welfare policies are adversely affected by community heterogeneity, especially racial differences, particularly in metropolitan areas.[28] Immigrants have been blamed for overloading social welfare programs and many public institutions.[29] Immigration in some metropolitan areas, such as Los Angeles, has created serious problems

---

23. Gorge J. Borjas, *Heaven's Door: Immigration Policy and the American Economy* (Princeton: Princeton University Press, 1999); Borjas, *Friends or Strangers: The Impact of Immigration on the U.S. Economy* (New York: Basic Books, 1990); Borjas, "The Economics of Immigration," *Journal of Economic Review* 32 (1994): 1667–1717; George J. Borjas and Richard Freeman, eds., *Immigration and the Work Force: Economic Consequences for the United States and Source Areas* (Chicago: University of Chicago Press, 1992).

24. For a succinct summary of this debate, see Roger Lowenstein, "The Immigration Equation," *New York Times,* July 9, 2006.

25. See John M. Abowd and Richard B. Freeman, eds., *Immigration, Trade, and the Labor Market* (Chicago: University of Chicago Press, 1991); Gregory DeFreitas, "Hispanic Immigration and Labor Market Segmentation," *Industrial Relations* 27 (1988): 195–214; Richard Mines and Jeffrey Avina, "Immigration and Labor Standards: The Case of California Janitors," in Jorge A. Bustamante et al., *US–Mexico Relations: Labor Market Interdependence* (Stanford: Stanford University Press, 1992), 429–448.

26. Michael Walzer, *Spheres of Justice: A Defense of Pluralism and Equality* (New York: Basic Books, 1983).

27. David Miller, *On Nationality* (Oxford: Oxford University Press, 1995). Recently, economists have suggested some cautionary implications from the U.S. experience for the future of the welfare state in Europe; see Alberto Alesina and Edward Glaeser, *Fighting Poverty in the US and Europe: A World of Difference* (Oxford: Oxford University Press, 2004).

28. See J. Eric Oliver, *Democracy in Suburbia* (Princeton: Princeton University Press, 2001); Dora L. Costa and Matthew E. Kahn, "Civic Engagement and Community Heterogeneity: An Economist's Perspective," *Perspectives on Politics* 1, no. 1 (2003): 103–111.

29. See James Woodward, "Commentary: Liberalism and Migration," in B. Barry and R. Goodin, eds., *Free Movement: Ethical Issues in the Transnational Migration of People and of Money* (University Park: Pennsylvania State University Press, 1992), 59–84.

for some public schools and public health institutions.[30] This was the argument behind California's controversial Proposition 187, which aimed to exclude undocumented immigrants from public education at all levels and from all health care except emergency room visits. Gary Freeman observes that foreigners have eroded the standards of welfare provision in Europe to the level of those in the United States.[31]

An Institutional Approach

In light of this debate, I sort out which type of institutions for foreigners better promote *civil society* (civic engagement, public discussion, and trust), *institutional experimentation* (self-help groups, support groups, and deliberative organizations), and *democratic governance* (political participation of marginalized groups) while preventing the worsening of *economic and social inequality* (wage gap and provision of welfare services). I highlight how government policies and state institutions shape organizational logics and decisions of immigrant groups. Specifically, I explore how Japan's immigration control policy without integration efforts limits the activities and institutional development of immigrant ethnic associations and how the passage of the 1998 Nonprofit Organization (NPO) Law (Law for the Promotion of Specified Nonprofit Activities) affects the operation of immigrant rights nongovernmental organizations (NGOs).

Through this approach, I find that most ethnic associations for legal foreigners in Japan mainly promote political awareness of their homelands and fail to promote trust between Japanese and foreigners, which does not significantly strengthen Japanese civil society. Surprisingly, it is the immigrant rights NGOs, which were established to assist illegal foreigners, that have contributed greatly to democratic citizenship and Japan's democratic development during the past two decades. This finding suggests that considering the kinds of groups or institutions involved would lead to a more nuanced debate over the impact of foreigners on democractic governance.

---

30. See Los Angeles County Board of Supervisors, *Impact of Immigrants on County Services* (Los Angeles: Los Angeles County Board of Supervisors, 1992).
31. Gary P. Freeman, "Migration and the Political Economy of the Welfare State," *The Annals* 485 (1986): 51–63.

Associative Activism

To explain organized local Japanese support for illegal foreign workers, I interpret the recent history of Japanese activism in light of a model of *associative activism*. According to this model, local actors seek to transform inflexible and relatively unresponsive political institutions through coordinated local activities aimed at resolving a particular problem that, while not directly conflicting with prevailing government policies, nonetheless challenges the broader political status quo. I consider activism to be associative when (1) like-minded activists form a range of NGOs to address specific problems and (2) local governments increasingly cooperate with activists and their organizations, forming novel and flexible institutions.

Alone, such associations are unlikely to be perceived by established political actors as a significant threat to the status quo; for instance, the work of a small group of doctors who provide informal medical services to illegal workers is likely be perceived (if noticed at all at the regional and national levels) as a harmless humanitarian effort. Such efforts may perhaps be in tension with prevailing immigration requirements, but they do not pose a serious threat to the standing laws or to the credibility of officials charged with their enforcement. But when a number of these local task-specific associations begin to exchange information and publicize their work, the stage is set for transformation of the social meanings associated with these groups and their activities.

What is striking about these activities, wherever they are found, is that they generally take place almost entirely in the informal public sphere, by which I mean to include much of what is generally referred to as "civil society" and to exclude the formal political institutions of the democratic state. Insofar as associative activism does impact governing institutions, they are almost always local offices and agencies. This is certainly the case in Japan, where local governments are increasingly eager to embrace the NGOs established by activists, especially since the passage of the NPO Law in 1998.

My interpretation addresses two theoretical concerns: (1) how the political motivations of Japanese activists change as deliberative exchanges occur across organizations in various localities; and (2) how these networks transform both local institutions and dominant social meanings.

My model is *dynamic:* Political motivations are clarified and elaborated through a deliberative process of exchanges among activists. Activism is initially local; it is often motivated by a general commitment to abstract religious or philosophical principles, which in turn motivates a desire to solve specific problems. Problem solving often involves improvisation, which takes place not only in action but also in the way an institution develops, as group decision making continually takes place. This active engagement and improvisation constitute a major strength of associative activism. At this stage, broader yet distinctly political goals may be present, but they are inchoate. As social networks are established among specific activists and activist communities, information is exchanged, situations compared, and strategies evaluated. Through these exchanges, specific goals become identified with shared beliefs about broader social and political problems; communities of interest form around shared problems, and solutions are sought that go beyond the specific issue at hand. A coherent political agenda emerges from the interplay of abstract ideals and specific problem-solving activities across the networks that link activists and their organizations. In other words, associative activism finds broader political meaning and motivation *after* engaging in local, narrowly circumscribed action, particularly problem-solving action.

Thus, my account is also *pragmatic,* in that broader social and political goals emerge out of the efforts of activists to solve very specific local problems. Pragmatic action may or may not be rational in the economic sense: activists' supportive actions may in some respects threaten their settled interests or contradict their stated preferences. For example, members of community workers' unions in Tokyo often voice opposition to admittance of unskilled foreign workers into Japan, yet they support illegal foreigners against corporate exploitation. Similarly, antiprostitution activists help foreign prostitutes. In this sense, associative activism seems to be a largely *unintended* consequence of the activities of local groups. It is a by-product of their efforts to help illegal foreign workers. As others have observed, this lack of clear motivation prior to activism is not limited to Japanese society.[32] Some students of social movements may find this explanation of

---

32. Hanspeter Kriesi, "The Organizational Structure of New Social Movements in a Political Context," in Doug McAdam, John D. McCarthy, and Mayer N. Zald, eds., *Comparative*

pragmatic motivation to be troublesome, as they interpret this as activists responding to political opportunities that open up with the migration
of foreigners into the country.[33] From this perspective, illegal foreigners,
who cannot exercise any real agency independent of their appeal for help,
represent an opportunity for local activists to vent their own objections
to Japanese society in a way that they cannot with legal aliens and with
Japanese themselves. Illegal foreigners in this sense become the vessels
through which activists lodge their complaints against Japanese society.
Counter to this perspective, however, I argue that initially, actors are not
opportunistic. Instead, they begin by solving problems, and only afterward
interpret their motivations for these actions in terms of potential political
opportunities.

Furthermore, my account is *deliberative* in that these individuals and
organizations not only exchange information about specific problems but
also evaluate the sources of these problems and the effectiveness of various
solutions. Their deliberations are *representative,* insofar as these activists
effectively represent the needs and interests of marginalized actors—
mine is not, for instance, a story of "directly deliberative" democracy, or
of "empowered participation" by illegal workers themselves.[34] My concept includes *activism* insofar as activists are engaged in (1) transforming
the informal public sphere of democracy, (2) shaping public opinion, and
(3) revealing to fellow citizens certain consequences of the political status
quo that seem inconsistent with widely affirmed values in society. Therefore, associative activism contains an institutional component as well as a
transformative component.

Perspectives on Social Movements: Political Opportunities, Mobilizing Structures, and Cultural Framings
(New York: Cambridge University Press, 1996), 152–184.

33. Sidney Tarrow, *The New Transnational Activism* (New York: Cambridge University Press,
2005); Tarrow, *Power in Movement: Social Movements, Collective Action, and Mass Politics in the Mod-
ern State* (New York: Cambridge University Press, 1994); Tarrow, "States and Opportunities: The
Political Structuring of Social Movements," in Doug McAdam, John D. McCarthy, and Mayer
N. Zald, eds., *Comparative Perspectives on Social Movements: Political Opportunities, Mobilizing
Structures, and Cultural Framings* (New York: Cambridge University Press, 1996), 41–61.

34. The terms are respectively from Joshua Cohen and Charles Sabel, "Directly Deliberative
Polyarchy," *European Law Journal* 3, no. 4 (1997): 313–342, and Archon Fung, *Empowered Participation: Reinventing Urban Democracy* (Princeton: Princeton University Press, 2004).

A Normative Model of Justice for Foreigners

Associative activism offers another normative model of democratic governance that stresses the importance of innovative forms of association for foreigners. Such associations are expected to encourage deliberation and to help citizens scrutinize and criticize existing institutions and popular attitudes and motivations.[35] They should also promote multicultural understanding or national unity and prevent a worsening of inequality and working conditions for both natives and foreigners. As such, this model is "normative" in the Rawlsian sense, in that it describes the mechanisms of democratic governance that promote a more just society. However, whereas John Rawls looks to regulations and state intervention to ensure that inequalities are designed to bring the greatest possible benefit to the least advantaged social class, this normative model of democratic governance relies on the activism of concerned citizens within their own spheres of competence and expertise, without large-scale state action.[36] When associative activists encounter structural impediments in solving local problems, they then make demands for new or improved regulations and government intervention. At that critical moment, they become creators of new values and norms.

This model is based on the premise that legitimate governance demands effective representation of a wide range of interests in society. Democratic theorists, such as Iris Marion Young and Melissa Williams, see possibilities for improving representative democracy through the inclusion

---

35. On deliberation, associations, and democratic governance, see Joshua Cohen and Joel Rogers, *Associations and Democracy* (London: Verso, 1995). On appropriate forms of democratic deliberation and representation under conditions of moral pluralism and social complexity, and given historical legacies of injustice and inequality, see Joshua Cohen, "Procedure and Substance in Deliberative Democracy," in Seyla Benhabib, ed., *Democracy and Difference: Contesting the Boundaries of the Political* (Princeton: Princeton University Press, 1996); Mark E. Warren, "Deliberative Democracy and Authority," *American Political Science Review* 90, no. 1 (1996): 46–60; Philip Pettit, "Republican Freedom and Contestatory Democratization," in Ian Shapiro and Casiano Hacker-Cordón, eds. *Democracy's Value* (Cambridge: Cambridge University Press, 1999); John S. Dryzek, *Deliberative Democracy and Beyond: Liberals, Critics, Contestations* (New York: Oxford University Press, 2000); Robert Goodin, "Democratic Deliberation Within," *Philosophy and Public Affairs* 29, no. 1 (2000): 81–109.

36. See John Rawls, *A Theory of Justice* (Cambridge: Harvard University Press, 1971); Rawls, "Justice as Fairness in the Liberal Polity," in Gershon Shafir, ed., *The Citizenship Debates: A Reader* (Minneapolis: University of Minnesota Press, 1998), 53–74.

of foreigners or their voices in various forms of deliberative institutions. Young explains that group difference, which can create greater disadvantage or oppression for some, exists in all modern complex societies. Young specifically believes that groups have a claim to representation if members of the group are subjected to systematic disadvantage in the political process.[37] In addition to promoting fairness, Young also believes that group representation maximizes public knowledge expressed in discussion, thereby promotes practical wisdom. Young explains, "different groups have different ways of understanding the meaning of social events, which can contribute to the others' understanding if they are expressed and heard."[38]

Williams, who proposes a deliberative, group-based theory of fair representation, points out that the task of institutional design aimed at fair group representation is to focus on institutional changes that would have the effect of moving representatives away from competition and toward more inclusive deliberation (without the expectation that we can ever achieve a "pure" form of deliberative decision making). Williams stresses the importance to fair representation of situations in which "the representative shares his or her constituents' experiences, and consequently shares the cognitive agency that arises out of that experience."[39] Williams is not suggesting that shared experiences are a necessary and sufficient condition for effective representation; that is, that only those with sufficiently similar experiences and attributes can legitimately claim to represent one another. Shared experiences do not amount to an essential attribute according to which representation is authentic, rather than merely approximate. Rather, her point is that, as a practical matter and in some specific cases, legacies of cultural marginalization and institutionalized exclusion from government activities and social benefits can undermine the sort of trust that is essential to a fair and responsive system of democratic representation.

A more fully inclusive democratic society requires that all residents be treated fairly by political institutions, including those residents who may

---

37. Young, *Inclusion and Democracy*.
38. Iris Marion Young, "Polity and Group Difference: A Critique of the Ideal of Universal Citizenship," in Gershon Shafir, ed., *The Citizenship Debates: A Reader* (Minneapolis: University of Minnesota Press, 1998), 277.
39. Williams, *Voice, Trust, and Memory*, 222–223.

not fit the dominant legal and cultural definitions of citizenship, but who nonetheless contribute to society in important ways and who face rigid resource and mobility constraints in host societies. Therefore, such a representative democracy should also grant the right of political representation to foreigners, including illegal foreigners.[40] Because distributive justice requires clear membership rules, direct participation by illegal foreigners in representative institutions will undermine such rules.[41] However, the interests of illegal foreigners can still be represented in deliberative institutions through the participation of immigrant rights activists, who may share similar experience of oppression, have demonstrated a deep understanding of the problems faced by foreigners, and have developed compassion for them.

Clearly, the normative stance that this book is premised on is not uncontentious. Various democratic theorists have noted that prominent formulations of deliberative and associative democracy make stringent informational demands on citizens and institutions and may be vulnerable to a range of behavioral pathologies and exclusionary tendencies along lines of class, race, and gender.[42] In terms of pathologies, the idea of "protecting" the worst off in society, despite good intentions otherwise, can in practice be paternalistic, rather than democratic. These concerns are important, but the value of deliberation as a democratic fundamental cannot be ignored,

---

40. Other and more neutral terms for illegal foreigners include "overstayed," "undocumented," "irregular," and "unauthorized." The term "illegal foreigners" (and, occasionally, "illegals") is used in this discussion because it most adequately captures the meaning of a group which includes both "overstayed" and "undocumented" workers, as well as those with false documents, and is the term used in public discourse (in the media, academic communities, and government circles). However, this should not be read to imply a negative connotation. As later discussion demonstrates, illegal foreigners can have a positive influence on the society in which they live.
41. On the importance of membership rules for distributive justice, see Walzer, *Spheres of Justice.*
42. On these worries, see Jack Knight and James Johnson, "Aggregation and Deliberation: On the Possibility of Democratic Legitimacy," *Political Theory* 22, no. 2 (1994): 277–296; Lynn M. Sanders, "Against Deliberation," *Political Theory* 25, no. 3 (1997): 347–376; James Johnson, "Arguing for Deliberation: Some Skeptical Considerations," in John Elster, ed., *Deliberative Democracy* (Cambridge: Cambridge University Press, 1998); Adam Przeworski, "Deliberation and Ideological Domination," in John Elster, ed., *Deliberative Democracy* (Cambridge: Cambridge University Press, 1998); Cass Sunstein, "Deliberative Trouble? Why Groups Go to Extremes," *Yale Law Journal* 110, no. 1 (2000): 71–121; Brooke Ackerly, *Political Theory and Feminist Social Criticism* (Cambridge: Cambridge University Press, 2000).

especially when there are several cases of deliberative and associative reforms that have made governments more responsive to a wide range of values and interests.[43]

Moreover, because paternalism requires some effort to accommodate a population and to provide for its needs, examination of the Japanese state suggests that the national government is not paternalistic, especially toward foreigners. Rather, the Japanese central government controls foreigners, while treating them in a racialized, hierarchical manner. Instead, it is the local actors (civil society actors and local officials) who accommodate foreigners and provide for their needs in ways that could be interpreted as "paternalistic." However, even if the original intention of local actors is seen as paternalistic, the end result of local activism is emancipatory and empowering, and usually overcomes such paternalistic motivations. This is because the high level of civic engagement promoted by the deep commitment of local officials to their targeted populations often provides local actors the insight into the problems foreigners face, allowing them to be a positive, enabling, and empowering resource for foreign residents. This analysis suggests that the accommodating (or "paternalistic") intentions of these local actors can be transformed by close interactions with foreigners and consequently result in actions that make Japan a more democratic and just society. Such activities at the local level help increase decentralization of government, promote civic engagement of citizens, and provide protection to the worst-off populations. However, these changes are best promoted when immigrant institutions give these populations the opportunity to become directly engaged in civic action, amplifying their voices in an empowering manner, rather than speaking for them in a paternalistic manner. Consequently, this analysis suggests that associative activism can support the importance of the tradition of deliberative democracy while mitigating concerns regarding its potential paternalism. Associative activism succeeds

---

43. See, e.g., James Fishkin, *The Voice of the People: Public Opinion and Democracy* (New Haven: Yale University Press, 1995) on the democratic potential of deliberative citizen assemblies; Peter Medoff and Holly Sklar, *Streets of Hope: The Fall and Rise of an Urban Neighborhood* (Boston: South End Press, 1994) on local coordination and control over land uses in Boston's Dudley Street Neighborhood Initiative; Rebecca Abers, "From Clientelism to Cooperation: Local Government, Participatory Policy, and Civic Organizing in Porto Alegre, Brazil," *Politics and Society* 26, no. 4 (1998): 511–537 on participatory budgeting in Porto Alegre, Brazil; and Fung, *Empowered Participation* on deliberative innovations in school policy and community policing in Chicago.

in making public deliberations more reliably representative of marginalized voices, not so much through direct inclusion of these voices in deliberative assemblies and legislative bodies but through the input of elites who demonstrate their deep commitment to those whom they represent by being highly involved with them and consequently develop a more authentic basis on which to develop their strategies and goals.

Another contentious aspect of this normative model of justice for foreigners deals with rules of citizenship. Even if deliberative and associative reforms (including the more informal representative variant) are feasible and desirable, a contrary view suggests that rules of citizenship should be clearly defined and rigidly enforced, and that the duties associated with citizenship ought not to extend beyond the spatial boundaries and legal categories that define a national community. After all, a clear and widespread sense of national unity arguably promotes a culture of trust, which is vital to implementing redistributive policies demanded by social justice. In this view, a shared national identity fosters "loose reciprocity": citizens accept certain burdens, such as higher taxes for welfare and training programs, without requiring strict reciprocity and close monitoring; and they are willing to make some sacrifices for the sake of shared fundamental interests and widely shared beliefs about what fairness demands of the better-off in their society. If, however, rules of membership and entitlement in a national community are not clearly defined and enforced, then public goods may be seen as being vulnerable to exploitation, and so individuals may not be motivated to make sacrifices for their fellow citizens.[44] Accordingly, one might conclude that the presence of illegal foreign workers is undesirable, especially if they are perceived as benefiting from existing institutions or threatening the livelihood of citizens and legal residents. Governments are then justified in taking aggressive measures to ensure that foreign workers do not overstay their visas and to limit social benefits to citizens and legal residents.[45] One might also favor stringent residency

---

44. Consider, e.g., Walzer, *Spheres of Justice,* who argues for clear boundaries of citizenship, and Miller, *On Nationality,* who argues that national identity is vital to social justice.

45. See Myron Weiner, "Ethics, National Sovereignty and the Control of Immigration," *International Migration Review* 30, no. 1 (1996): 171–197, on whether the state has a moral obligation to respond to the claims of illegal foreigners.

requirements for legal foreigners to ensure that they really are committed to productive membership in the political community.

I acknowledge the intuitive appeal of clear membership rules within a specific territory and the associated idea that social benefits should accrue only to those who contribute to the society in question. But such rules are far from sufficient as the basis for a *realistic* account of democratic citizenship in modern industrial and increasingly plural societies, all of which contain some level of illegal foreigners. Moreover, illegal foreign workers often contribute to the economy. Therefore, even if we think that precise and carefully enforced membership rules are vital to a persuasive account of democratic citizenship and trump more abstract considerations of fairness and desert, the interests of these workers should still be represented in political institutions. More important, the Japanese activists I consider act *as if* they are committed to something like the normative ideal of democracy many endorse, and they engage in activities that seek to challenge prevailing ideas about ethnic identity, legal and socioeconomic status, and Japanese citizenship. Associative activism explains why this might be the case when Japanese politics and society seem inimical to such motives.

While recognizing these concerns of illegal foreigners as valid, this book highlights the less appreciated contribution of such illegal foreigners to more inclusive deliberative democracy. It suggests that illegal immigrants contribute to a more inclusive form of democratic governance, and it proposes a normative model that complicates existing theories by arguing that more inclusive democracy is possible because of organizations characterized by associative activism. By examining the Japanese experience, this book offers a normative model of democratic governance that grants indirect political representation in deliberative institutions to illegal foreigners. This model of indirect political representation demonstrates that it is important to complicate the picture by seeking to understand the kind of organization that emerges from the influx of illegal foreigners before supporting or dismissing wholesale their impact on democratic governance.

Methodology

I focus on various institutions for immigrants, such as immigrant ethnic associations and immigrant rights NGOs. Specifically, I examine how various institutions can contribute to or hinder democratic processes and institutions. What similarities and differences can be observed in different types of institutions for foreigners with respect to promoting democracy? Immigrant institutions can promote political participation through the informal public sphere. For example, they can support various immigrant rights campaigns to provide comprehensive health coverage to illegal foreigners. They can negotiate on behalf of immigrants with local government officials directly or through advisory or consultative committees for the provision of social welfare services. In this way, these institutions can provide a voice to more people and improve deliberative processes as well as multicultural representative institutions. In addition, they can organize protests against a public policy or a political figure that targets immigrants. They make the greatest contribution to civic engagement when their staff and volunteers do not just speak for the ethnic groups they serve but encourage and assist their participants to become directly involved in civic action. Finally, immigrant institutions can also create other civic groups. Such an institutional approach provides an analytical lens to understand the contribution of foreigners to democracy.

As governments in industrialized societies face increasing incompetence and legal restrictions in delivering social welfare services to needy individuals and nonmembers, an overview of the range of services and problem-solving activities provided by immigrant institutions can help us understand the impact of these organizations on social democracy. Furthermore, we can determine to what extent immigration organizations contribute to social and economic equality by examining the number and socioeconomic background of people or immigrants they serve per year. Through a systematic examination of these activities in the informal public sphere and the range and extent of social services to immigrants, we can understand the relationship between immigration organizations and democracy. Because Japan has been traditionally viewed as a highly centralized polity, it represents an "unlikely" case for democratic transformation to occur from the bottom up. As a closed society without established, internalized norms on dealing with outsiders, Japan is also a "crucial" case for the study of foreigners' contribution to democracy. Moreover, Japan is an interesting but not an outlier case of a country that increasingly demonstrates a lack of tolerance for foreigners. Most interesting about Japan is the way in which specific barriers to legal immigration create certain differences between legal and illegal foreign migrants. These barriers have produced some surprising consequences for the quality of Japan's democracy.

The data is based on my fieldwork in Tokyo, Kanagawa, Ibaraki, and Gunma between 1998 and 2007. For the analysis, I conducted over 350 in-depth interviews with Japanese NGO leaders and volunteers, foreign migrants, government officials, and Japanese residents living in foreign communities inside Japan. In addition, I interacted extensively with foreign migrants, activists, natives living in foreigner communities, and government officials at both national and local levels. I also employed various forms of participant observation: participating in NGO activities, attending various organizational meetings, and observing local governments sponsored deliberations. I collected secondary sources such as internal documents from these support groups and local and national governments, newspaper clippings on foreign workers, newsletters from all support groups, and published materials written by or about leaders of these groups.

In the next chapter I discuss the typology of foreigners in Japan with their rights and privileges, framed in the legal, political, and cultural context of Japanese immigration policy. I focus on how government policies have produced differentiated labor entitlements and legal rights across different ethnic groups and demarcated immigrants in Japan into legal and illegal foreigners. Legal foreigners in Japan, who are at the high end of the racial hierarchy, include Chinese and Koreans born in Japan, foreign-born Japanese, wives of Japanese, English language teachers, and foreign trainees. Illegal foreigners are generally Asians—typically from Korea, China, the Philippines, Thailand, Iran, India, Bangladesh, and Pakistan—who have remained in Japan beyond the expiration of their three-month visiting visa. What is striking about this contrast is the way in which Japanese law and public sentiment have divided foreigners from the same ethnic and cultural backgrounds: legal and illegal foreigners in Japan do not share the same life experiences, and a variety of social pressures encourage legal residents to avoid intervening in the plight of illegals, regardless of shared ethnicity, language, and culture. Because of the legalized hierarchy, certain Asian workers are particularly vulnerable or institutionally encouraged to drop into the ranks of illegal workers, where they lose even more rights.

Government institutions for foreign workers in Japan are extensive, but these organizations mainly offer information and interpretation services, and they limit themselves to assisting legal foreigners. The chapter concludes that the division between legal and illegal co-ethnics complicates ethnic strategies of political representation in local and national legislatures because legal foreigners do not share the same interests as their illegal co-ethnics with respect to legal and socioeconomic issues.

In chapter 3 I examine immigrant ethnic associations established by legal foreigners from Korea, China, Thailand, Vietnam, Burma, and the Philippines. Korean and Chinese ethnic associations hold strong ideological views and have preoccupied themselves with political activities in their "home" countries despite the fact that these Korean and Chinese have little, if any, experience with their "home" lands. For them, "home" is more imagined than experienced. Vietnamese and Burmese ethnic associations engage in radical politics, aiming to undermine their undemocratic home governments. In the cases of legal Filipinos and Thais, their legal resident status creates a social distance between them and their illegal compatriots. Legal Asians prefer to maintain their privileged status by not assisting their illegal compatriots. Instead, members of these co-ethnic associations aim to improve the living conditions for only legal foreigners or, basically, themselves. And like the Koreans and Chinese, members of these co-ethnic associations are preoccupied with their own country's politics.

In chapter 4 I discuss the work of Japanese activists and their immigrant rights NGOs in helping illegal foreigners. Whereas legally recognized foreigners can create their own self-help groups to fight for the improvement of their livelihood in Japan, illegal foreigners can form no such groups, for fear of arrest and deportation. As a result, certain Japanese citizens have established NGOs to assist illegal foreigners, fighting for the protection of basic rights and the provision of welfare services. I detail activities of these NGOs, which include Christian groups, community workers unions, women's support groups, lawyers' associations, medical NGOs, and concerned citizen groups. The chapter stresses the point that members of these groups concentrate their activities on solving specific problems that illegal foreign workers bring with them to their institutions. It concludes with a discussion on patterns and shared characteristics of these groups and their activists.

Chapter 5 examines the impact of immigrant rights NGOs (and immigrant ethnic associations) on democratic institutions. Some groups have successfully pressured the government to grant certain overstayed foreigners with "special residence permission"; others have challenged the government to extend National Health Insurance to certain unqualified foreigners. More significant, these groups are pushing some local governments to accept responsibility for caring for all of their residents. The Kanagawa prefectural government, in particular, has responded to the growing importance of these NGOs by establishing an NGO Advisory Council along with its Foreign Residents Council. Such institutional innovation provides a form of democratic deliberation to both marginalized Japanese activists and foreign residents of Japan at the local level and, more impressive, a "voice" to illegal immigrants through Japanese activists. These associative efforts demonstrate how civil society groups in Japan can play a role in redefining membership rules and state responsibilities for its residents—a role that is traditionally monopolized by officials of the central government. Seen in this light, this partnership between civil society organizations and local governments demonstrates the political strength and independence of these small, foreigner support groups.

Chapter 6 discusses the role of NGOs in providing a counter-image of foreigners, particularly illegal foreigners, to that promulgated by the government in the public sphere. It argues that recent public imagination over illegal foreigners in the public sphere is highly contested, as certain political leaders construct negative images of illegal foreigners as "criminals," while Japanese activists try to portray them as "victims." Japanese attitudes toward illegal foreigners during the 1990s were mixed, with an increasing association of illegal foreigners with criminality and a rise in perception of them as victims deprived of basic rights. In the past decade, renewed efforts by state actors have resulted in further inciting xenophobic attitudes toward illegal foreigners. In contrast, NGO activists contribute to the public discourse by providing an alternative, expert source of information about the actual conditions of illegal foreigners and serving as an important counterweight to official Japan's more prejudiced activities.

The conclusion discusses the theoretical implications of the study for comparative immigration politics and the organization of Japan's civil society. First, it examines Japan's policy response to the challenges of the rising number of foreigners to democratic ideals and situates Japan some-where between Western and Asian models. Second, it discusses the extent to which support groups organized by Japanese citizens on behalf of il-legal foreigners can influence state actors. This influence from civil society actors rather than initiatives from politicians promotes a more inclusive democratic governance and makes Japan a more humane and democratic multicultural society.

2

CONTROLLING FOREIGNERS

Japan's Foreign Worker Policy

Japan's immigration policy focuses on controlling foreigners and lacks an active policy to incorporate them into society or to participate in Japan's political life. Recognizing the demand for foreign workers in certain industries, the national government allows selected foreigners to enter and work in Japan without satisfactorily providing for their needs. It treats foreigners unpaternalistically and categorizes them hierarchically by race (or nationality), their function in Japanese society, and, sometimes, gender. This racialized hierarchy—which produces differentiated jobs, wages, rights, and privileges for different groups of foreigners—is a political construction of the Japanese government, rooted in a cultural view that certain races and nationalities are uniquely qualified for certain kinds of labor.[1] At the high end of the racial hierarchy are *zainichi* (Japan-born)

---

1. I first made this argument in "The Political Construction of Foreign Workers in Japan," *Critical Asian Studies* 34 no. 1 (2002): 41–68.

foreigners and *nikkeijin* (foreign-born Japanese), who have better jobs, higher pay, and better working conditions than other foreign workers. At the bottom are South Asians (from Bangladesh, Pakistan, and India), with low-skill jobs, poor pay, and dangerous working environments. Japanese government policies both establish the legal superiority of certain races over others and constrain the livelihood of each tier of foreigners. This racialized hierarchy applies primarily to legal immigrants. However, because of the legalized hierarchy, certain groups (especially Asian workers) are particularly vulnerable or even systematically encouraged to drop into the ranks of illegal workers, where they lose even more rights. As such, although foreigners of the same ethnic and cultural backgrounds exist in both legal and illegal categories, both groups are influenced by this racialized hierarchy.

The Japanese government's view that certain races/nationalities are better qualified to engage in certain jobs is reflected in its historical differentiation in immigration control laws among different ethnic groups. First, officials of the Ministry of Justice (MOJ) rank nikkeijin higher than other Asians based on racial-descent criteria.[2] Nikkeijin are of Japanese descent but of foreign birth and upbringing (frequently Brazilian or Peruvian), and few speak Japanese fluently. As such, nikkeijin are considered to be "foreign" migrants who seek work in Japan, not ethnic immigrants returning to their home country. The Japanese government's decision to allow such foreigners with Japanese blood to work legally and to forbid those with non-Japanese blood from doing the same jobs reflects this belief of racial dominance. This perspective continues to be evident today, for example in the government's decision to launch incorporation policies "in areas where nikkeijin are concentrated."[3] The government is planning to offer specialized Japanese language instructors in schools where *nikkei* (foreign-born, Japanese descent) children attend and to improve social insurance coverage, working environment, and housing condition for nikkeijin.

---

2. Kajita Takamichi explains that Japanese consider racial descent and blood ties to be the primary basis for feelings of ethnic commonality. See his *Gaikokujin rōdōsha to Nihon* [Foreign Workers and Japan] (Tokyo: NHK Books, 1994).

3. Interview with an official of the Cabinet Office International Economic Affairs, July 3, 2006.

At the same time, policies allowing other Asian workers to work legally in Japan in undesirable and specified jobs as trainees but with much lower wages, and restrictive rights and services, also contributed to this racialized hierarchy. Currently, Japan, which experiences a growing elderly population, is engaging in several bilateral negotiations with the Philippines, Thailand, and Indonesia through its Free Trade Agreements (FTA) or Economic Promotion Agreement (EPA) talks to admit Filipina nurses, Thai caretakers and masseuses, and Indonesian caretakers into the country; it is also considering a request by the Indonesian government to open its borders to high-level manufacturing Indonesian workers.[4] This preference for workers from Southeast Asia (despite continued restrictions on the rights and opportunities of illegal workers from these countries) suggests that the government's historical foreign labor system of racialized preferences continues to exist today. As a result, Japanese government policies, which address skilled migrants and declare unskilled work done by foreigners other than zainichi and nikkeijin illegal, support people with "superior" ethnic backgrounds (zainichi or nikkeijin) or abilities (skilled) while constraining people with less desirable ethnic backgrounds (non-Japanese birth or blood) and abilities (unskilled).

The position of zainichi is an exception to the racialized hierarchy. Zainichi are of Japanese birth and upbringing but of foreign (mostly Korean and some Chinese) descent, and most speak Japanese fluently. They are expected to live and die in Japan. As such, zainichi are considered to be "special permanent residents"—a class above Asian wives and foreign migrants (including the "almost Japanese" nikkeijin) but below Japanese citizens. As will be discussed later in this chapter, this status is an unintended result of diplomatic relations and the signing of international treaties protecting refugees that Japan became party to in 1982. Consequently, zainichi gained rights despite Japanese government preferences otherwise.

Despite the exception of the zainichi, the racialized hierarchy constructed by Japanese government policy has a significant and direct influence on the labor entitlements and legal rights among most legal foreigners. This hierarchy impacts illegal foreigners as well: by restricting immigrants

---

4. Interview with an official of the Ministry of Economy, Trade, and Industry Minister's Secretariat, June 28, 2006.

at the bottom of the legal racialized hierarchy the most, this system pushes such migrants (particularly Asian workers) toward becoming illegal workers. Consequently, the racialized hierarchy directly impacts legal foreigners but also indirectly impacts illegal foreigners.

This demarcation of immigrants into legal and illegal foreigners significantly impacts their living and working conditions. Legal foreigners are afforded protections of the law, as well as various institutional means to express their views to the government, and are allowed to form self-help groups to support their own people. In contrast, *illegal foreigners*—those who overstayed their visas or entered Japan illegally—encounter serious labor and family problems. They lack legal protections and have no formal means of expressing their views to the government. Employment brokers and employers take advantage of their underprivileged positions; police and immigration officers abuse them; and society looks down on them and their children.

One striking consequence of this distinction is the way in which Japanese law and public sentiment have created a division between foreigners of the same ethnic and cultural backgrounds. Legal and illegal foreigners in Japan have distinct life experiences, and a variety of social pressures encourage legal foreigners to avoid intervening in the plight of illegals, regardless of shared ethnicity, language, and culture. Because legal and illegal co-ethnics do not share life experiences or, perhaps more important, legal and socioeconomic concerns, the politically constructed division between them significantly constrains ethnic strategies for political representation in local and national legislatures.

Typology of Foreigners in Japan

In 2006, over two million foreigners in Japan registered with their local wards; foreigners from Korea, China, Brazil, the Philippines, Peru, Thailand, Vietnam, and Indonesia constituted 85 percent of these registered foreigners.[5] In addition, the Immigration Bureau estimated that 240,000

---

5. Ministry of Justice, *Shutsunyukoku kanri* [Annual Statistics on Immigration Control] (Tokyo: Ōkurasho Insatsukyoku, 2006).

foreigners who had overstayed their visas or illegally entered the country were still living in Japan. About half of the foreign workers are immigrants who come to work in dirty, difficult, and dangerous (3Ds) jobs that Japanese reject. Officials at the Ministry of Justice (MOJ) construct a racialized and occupational category of foreigners, including zainichi, nikkeijin, foreign students and English language teachers, legal Asian workers, and illegal Asian workers. Zainichi can live and work *permanently* in the country, while nikkeijin can work *temporarily*. Foreign wives, who are supposed to produce offspring with some Japanese blood, belong somewhere in the middle. Foreign students, English language teachers, and legal Asian workers enjoy only *restrictive* temporary living and working conditions. Illegal foreigners have no rights to live and work in Japan. Table 2.1 summarizes Japan's racialized hierarchy of foreigners in terms of occupation and political, civic, and social rights. This section examines each of these groups, including its politically constructed origins and sociological characteristics, working and living environment, and legal rights.

Zainichi

The group of Japan-born foreigners known as zainichi includes approximately 460,000 Koreans and 4,000 Chinese who have lived in Japan for several generations and have chosen not to become naturalized.[6] Their existence is rooted in Japan's colonial policies after Japan annexed Formosa in 1895 and Korea in 1910.[7] The annexation of Korea allowed Japanese firms to bring young Korean men, mostly from depressed regions of southern Korea, to Osaka and Kobe to do simple manual labor. Most worked in mining and railroad construction. During the 1920s, the Japanese government at various levels promoted a plan for public works to help unskilled

---

6. The zainichi population has declined significantly since 1990, as about 10,000 of them choose to naturalize annually.

7. Although communities of Korean potters and Chinese traders existed in Kyushū during the Tokugawa period, their numbers were small. See Changsoo Lee and George de Vos, *Koreans in Japan: Ethnic Conflict and Accommodation* (Berkeley: University of California Press, 1981), 15–16; Andrea Vasishth, "A Model Minority: The Chinese Community in Japan," in Michael Weiner, ed., *Japan's Minorities: the Illusion of Homogeneity* (London: Routledge, 1997), 108–139 (118).

TABLE 2.1. Categories of Foreigners and Their Rights in Japan, 2005

Type of Foreigner and Overall Status	Immigration Status	Occupation	Political Rights	Civic Rights	Social Rights
Zainichi (Japan-born foreigners) 460,000 Koreans 4,000 Chinese *Free to live and work permanently*	"Special permanent residents"	Self-employed; salarymen (with bonuses and lifetime employment)	No rights to vote at national and local elections; no legal protection against racism	No rights of membership in district welfare commission, board of education, or human rights commission	No legal protection against discrimination until mid-1970s; comprehensive social welfare benefits
Asian wives 200,000 Chinese, Koreans, Filipinas, Thais *Free to live and work temporarily*	"Spouses of Japanese"	Self-employed; farm workers; mama-san; foreign firms workers	Same as above	Same as above	Full access to medical care and public health services
Nikkeijin (foreign-born Japanese) 302,000 Brazilians 58,000 Peruvians *Free to live and work temporarily*	"Spouses or children of Japanese" or "long-term residents"	Factory workers in secondary and tertiary subcontractors (with no bonuses or lifetime employment)	Same as above	Same as above	Full access to medical care and public health services, but few subscribe to them

					Full access to medical care and public health services after one year
Foreign students and English language teachers 117,000 Foreign Students (Chinese, Koreans) 26,000 Americans, British, Canadians, etc. *Restrictive living and working situation*	"Pre-college" and "college" "specialist in humanities/international services"; "instructor"	Part-time workers English teachers	Same as above	Same as above	
Asian workers 150,000 Trainees (Chinese, Indonesians, Vietnamese, Filipinos, and Thais) 65,000 Entertainers (Filipinos) *Restrictive living and working situation*	"Designated activities"; "Trainee" "Entertainer"	Work in dying sectors Dancers, singers	Same as above	Same as above No labor protection	None
Illegal Asian workers 224,000 men and women from Korea, China, the Philippines, and Thailand; Men from India, Pakistan, Bangladesh *No rights to live or work*	Overstaying their visas for "temporary visitor," "entertainer," "trainee," "students"; illegal entry	Factory workers in small subcontractors; sex workers; construction workers; restaurant workers	None	None	None

labor, resulting in a seasonal migration of Koreans to Japan.[8] Under this plan, the number of Koreans in Japan increased from 3,635 in 1913 to 690,503 in 1936.

In August 1939, soon after Japan expanded into mainland China, the government passed the Labor Mobilization Act. Under this Act, Korean laborers and military draftees were brought to Japan to fill the labor power vacuum created by the expansion of Japan's military forces and the war economy.[9] Manchurian Chinese were also subject to labor conscription after 1942, although not on the same scale as Koreans. Between 1943 and 1945, the Japanese government transported approximately 42,000 Chinese from the mainland to Japan to complement the 150,000 Taiwanese who had already been recruited to do military labor service. In 1944, the Diet (the national parliament) passed the Korean Labor Conscription Act, under which all Korean men were subject to mobilization. By the end of World War II, more than two million Koreans were residing in Japan, of which 680,000 were requisitioned persons.

After Japan's defeat in World War II, many Koreans and Chinese returned to their homelands. In 1950, only 620,000 Koreans and 40,000 Chinese (mostly from Taiwan) remained in Japan. Those Koreans and Chinese who decided to stay in Japan lost the right to vote along with any legal protection from discrimination. This was despite the fact that before the war, people from the former colonies or "imperial subjects" in Japan were entitled to vote, to be elected, and to assume public office. In fact, several Koreans were actively involved in politics as candidates for public office during the early 1930s. On December 17, 1945, however, Japan's House of Representatives amended the Election Law, suspending suffrage for the nationals of Japan's former colonies in all phases of the electoral

---

8. Many Koreans planned to work in urban centers of Japan only long enough to save some money; others came just for the winter relief projects. Richard H. Mitchell, *The Korean Minority in Japan* (Berkeley: University of California Press, 1967), 28–31 (31ff), 45.

9. During the first few years, the government asked for volunteers, who were taken whenever available. But the law also provided for conscription if not enough volunteers were obtained. Both volunteers and conscripts typically had two-year tours of duty in Japan. New laborers were generally given three months' training before being assigned to a job. The Japanese government had promised political equality, better working conditions, more pay, and other advantages to all Koreans. It was not until 1942 that the Koreans in Japan became subject to conscription.

process. Thereafter, Koreans and Chinese in Japan were not entitled to vote or to be elected.

Koreans and Chinese in Japan also lost protection against discrimination after the war. Initially, U.S. occupation forces had planned to guarantee equal rights to foreign residents in Japan and to prohibit discrimination on the basis of race and national origin.[10] General Douglas MacArthur and his staff included an article (Article 16) in the draft constitution that explicitly stated: "All foreigners are to receive equal protection by law." However, a translator of the draft constitution, Satō Tatsuo, argued that Article 13 already guaranteed protections for resident aliens because the Japanese word *"kokumin"* implied all people, including foreigners.[11] While the Americans accepted Satō's argument, Japanese conservatives interpreted the word "kokumin" in the 1945 Constitution to mean Japanese nationals alone.[12] Thus, foreign residents were not covered under the basic human rights provisions in the new Constitution.[13]

An additional blow came in May 1947 when the government enacted the Alien Registration Law, which reclassified Koreans and Chinese from imperial subjects (like other Japanese) to foreigners.[14] This law effectively established a system of control over Korean and Chinese residents in Japan, imposing strict surveillance and coercive assimilation policies. On April 28, 1952, Koreans and Chinese officially became "foreigners" in Japan and were obliged to register as resident aliens. The

---

10. See U.S. Office of Strategic Services, "Aliens in Japan" (Washington, D.C.: U.S. Office of Strategic Services, Research and Analysis Branch, June 29, 1945), 29.

11. See Tanaka Hiroshi, "Nihon ni okeru gaikokujin no jinken hoshō to sono keifu" [Human Rights for Foreigners in Japan and Its History], in Tanaka Hiroshi and Ebashi Takashi, eds., *Rainichi gaikokujin jinken hakusho* [White Paper on Human Rights of Newcoming Foreigners in Japan] (Tokyo: Akashi Shoten, 1997), 13–37; Robert Ricketts, "GHQ no zainichi chosenjin seisaku" [GHQ's Policy on Zainichi Koreans] *Ajia Kenkyū* 9 (1994):4–36; John Dower, *Embracing Defeat: Japan in the Wake of World War II* (New York: Norton, 1999), 393–394.

12. Satō conflated the two articles into Article 14 of the postwar Constitution, which states: "All people are equal under the law and there shall be no discrimination in political, economical or social relations because of race, creed, gender, social status or family origin."

13. Foreign residents in Japan did not enjoy equal rights and discriminatory protection until 1995, when Japan became the 146th country to sign the UN Treaty on the Abolition of Racial Discrimination.

14. Although the Alien Registration Law was issued in May 1947, Koreans and Chinese retained Japanese nationality until April 1952 when the San Francisco Peace Treaty was effected.

Alien Registration Law required fingerprinting and the possession at all times of an alien registration card.

Since 1952, roughly 300,000 Koreans have become naturalized Japanese citizens. Those who naturalize must give up their original names and take Japanese ones. Koreans and Chinese who wish to maintain their distinct cultures may also stay in Japan, but as foreigners. The situation for zainichi Koreans improved in 1965 after Japan and South Korea signed a treaty that gave Koreans in Japan with South Korean citizenship a "special permanent resident" status. Koreans in Japan with North Korean citizenship received similar treatment in 1981. This status was later extended to zainichi Chinese.

With this "special" foreigner status, the Japanese government permits zainichi Koreans and Chinese to reside indefinitely in Japan. They are free to live and work in Japan and receive comprehensive social and welfare benefits from the government. Most zainichi Koreans live in Tokyo, Kawasaki, Osaka, Kobe, and Kitakyushū, while most zainichi Chinese reside in Tokyo, Yokohama, Osaka, and Kobe. Zainichi are self-employed, typically in the service sector. Zainichi Koreans frequently run *yakiniku* (barbecued beef) shops, *yakitori* (barbecued chicken) stalls, and many *pachinko* (pinpall) parlors, while zainichi Chinese frequently operate many Chinese restaurants. Since the early 1970s, some zainichi have also joined Japanese corporations, where they are usually offered lifetime employment and bonuses similar to those given to other Japanese employees. The corporate doors began to open in the early 1970s after a zainichi Korean, Park Chong Seok, took the Hitachi Corporation to court for employment-related racial discrimination. As a result of this case, the situation of zainichi Koreans improved considerably; they increasingly found work in worksite (nonoffice type) operations and low-ranking office work in private companies. This also meant that job competition against Japanese workers was beginning to apply to zainichi foreigners.[15] In Japanese corporations, discrimination against zainichi occurs, if at all, during the hiring and promotion process (similar to the discrimination faced by many Japanese women, *burakumin* [descendants of outcast communities] and ethnic minorities). However, zainichi cannot vote in the national election and work in most national civil services, nor do they have the right to

---

15. On job competition between native and foreign workers, see Michael Piore, *Birds of Passage: Migrant Labor and Industrial Societies* (New York: Cambridge University Press, 1979).

membership in district welfare commissions, boards of education, or human rights commissions. Although zainichi Koreans often experience housing discrimination from Japanese landlords, they encounter little discrimination when applying for public-subsidized apartments. Overall, zainichi "special" foreigner status puts them at the top of the racialized hierarchy in terms of immigration status and rights but does not afford them equal rights with Japanese citizens, even though they are born and raised in Japan.

Asian Wives

Approximately 200,000 foreign women, mostly from China, South Korea, the Philippines, and Thailand, are married to Japanese men. Some came to Japan as brides to middle-aged Japanese farmers who could not find a Japanese woman to marry. In the late 1980s, 56 percent of Japan's municipalities reported a shortage of Japanese women willing to marry local farmers. Japanese women increasingly drifted into the cities to escape the harsh farm life, where they would be expected to take care of the husband's family, and often ended up marrying salarymen or choosing to remain unmarried and pursue their own careers. As a result, many male farmers remained single into their late thirties and forties and faced a prospect of having no successor to take over their farms. Municipal governments in affected areas responded by instituting budgetary measures to deal with this situation, hiring marriage counselors and matchmakers, arranging group meetings with prospective brides, sponsoring informal gatherings with women, and providing cash rewards to successful couples. Local governments experimented with arranged meetings (*miai*) with Japanese women, but these were a failure. Then several towns began inviting foreign women to meetings organized through the International Companion/Friendship Association, with the town mayors as the presidents of these associations. These meetings with foreign women turned out to be highly successful because foreign women's expectations were based in romantic and uncorrected assumptions about the role of a Japanese farmer's wife.[16] In other cases, local

---

16. Yamazaki Hiromi, "Japan Imports Brides from the Philippines: Can Isolated Farmers Buy Consolation?" in The Migrant Women Worker's Research and Action Committee, ed., *NGOs' Report on the Situation of Foreign Migrant Women in Japan and Strategies for Improvement* (Tokyo: Mimeograph, 1995), 33–35.

governments actively sponsored *miai* tours to East Asian countries, seeking wives for their local farmers. Local government officials viewed these
interracial marriages as opportunities for international exchanges and
"special events that will help the survival of the towns."[17] Local governments encouraged not only marriage but also procreation because they
needed children for their schools with dwindling student population to
sustain the same level of funding from the central government.

Other Asian women, particularly from the Philippines, came to Japan
to work in the entertainment industry (e.g., as singers, dancers, and bar
hostesses) and overstayed their visas before marrying Japanese men.[18] Foreign spouses are not allowed to be listed in the "family registry" (*koseki tōhon*)
of a Japanese national.[19] This often causes problems for the couple when
they want to buy a condominium, apply for public loans, or find schools
for their children, because the couple must present their residency register. With the foreign spouse's name not listed in the registry, the Japanese
spouse publicly remains unmarried and the couple's children are considered illegitimate, thereby jeopardizing their chances for a successful
application.

Foreign women also face difficult times with their Japanese partners,
who are often twice their age. Lack of familiarity with the Japanese language, culture, religion, and climate is to be expected, but the harsh conditions of farm life and social discipline by Japanese mothers-in-law can
be overwhelming. A high percentage of such interracial marriages have
ended in divorces. In recent years, according to staff of several women's
shelters, Asian women who are victims of domestic abuse have increasingly sought help at these shelters.[20] Overall, the ability of Asian wives to

---

17. Yamazaki Hiromi, "Some Thoughts on Arranged Group Interviews between Southeast
Asian Women and Japanese Farmers," in Asian Women's Association, ed., *Women from across the
Seas: Migrant Workers in Japan* (Tokyo: Asian Women's Association, 1988), 52–58 (esp. 55).

18. See Nobue Suzuki, "Between Two Shores: Transnational Projects and Filipina Wives in/
from Japan," *Women's Studies International Forum* 23, no. 4 (2000): 431–444.

19. In 1967, the Ministry of Home Affairs issued a notice granting the head of a non-Japanese
household the right to be listed in the remark column (*bikōran*) of her or his spouse's family registry. Despite this notice, several local governments still have not allowed foreigners to be listed in
the family registry.

20. Interviews with: Nīkura Hisano of Saalaa in Yokohama, July 20, 2003; Yamagishi Motoko
of Kalakasan in Kawasaki, August 4, 2004; Kikutani Hideko of Mizula in Yokohama, July 16,
2004; Ōtsu Keiko of HELP in Tokyo, July 9, 2003.

produce offspring of Japanese bloodlines give them a higher status and greater rights than most other foreigners, but they are not given equivalent rights to their Japanese husbands or even recognized as being part of legitimate marriages among equal partners.

Nikkeijin

The third group of legal foreign workers includes approximately 302,000 nikkei (Japanese descendant) Brazilians and 58,000 nikkei Peruvians, typically second- and third-generation "Japanese" who were born and raised abroad. As a response to an influx of "illegal" foreign workers and a need to clarify the residency status of foreigners, the MOJ modified the immigration law and eased working visa requirements for nikkeijin in 1990.[21] Nikkeijin were given the legal status of "spouses or children of Japanese" or "long-term residents" in order to counterbalance the "special permanent residents" status that had already been granted to resident Koreans.[22] While government officials determined zainichi to be "special" foreigners, they designated nikkeijin as "almost Japanese"—a reflection of the government's concern with an individual's bloodline in determining "Japaneseness." With a temporary resident status, nikkeijin were below zainichi foreigners but above most other foreigners. Once the MOJ officials established this racial view of nikkeijin, the Ministry of Labor (MOL) then established the Nikkeis Employment Service Center in 1991, with offices in Tokyo, Nagoya, and São Paolo, to create job opportunities and to provide labor counseling services for nikkeijin. In addition, MOL implemented an employment management and improvement program that provides counseling, seminars, and assistance on employment management and working lifestyles to nikkeijin through its Employment and Livelihood Counseling Centers for Nikkeijin in Tochigi, Gunma, Chiba, Shizuoka, and Osaka prefectures. With the 1990 revised Immigration Control and Refugee Recognition Act (Immigration Control Law hereafter) and

21. Interview with an official of the Ministry of Justice Immigration Bureau, January 8, 1999.
22. Kajita Takamichi, Tanno Kiyoto, and Higuchi Naoto, *Kao no mienai teijūka: Nikkei burazirujin to kokka-ichiba-imin nettowaaku* [Invisible Residents: Japanese Brazilians vis-à-vis the State, the Market, and the Immigrant Network] (Nagoya: Nagoya University Press, 2005).

campaigns by government agencies to attract nikkeijin, the number of nikkeijin entering Japan increased from 20,000 in 1990 to over 371,700 in 2006.

Nikkeijin are "ethnic Japanese" by blood, but their foreign birth and upbringing make them "foreigners."[23] Their daily-life activities are Brazilian or Peruvian, and few speak Japanese fluently.[24] Two waves of out-migration of Japanese to South America occurred in 1923–1941 and 1953–1973. Japanese government policies supported these waves of migration, as well as the subsequent acceptance of the South American–born "ethnic Japanese" back to Japan during the 1990s. Japanese first emigrated to South America in large numbers in 1899, working under harsh conditions in Peru's sugarcane plantations. In 1908, Japanese emigration expanded to Brazil. In 1921, the Japanese government subsidized the Overseas Development Company (Kaigai Kōgyō Kaisha) to handle the recruitment of new emigrants who sought better economic opportunities abroad. It also began subsidizing prefectural emigrant associations and private emigrant organizations, and through these organizations propagated the idea of "great ventures abroad." By 1923, 33,000 Japanese, mostly from Kagoshima and Okinawa, had emigrated to Brazil. In 1924, the Japanese government actively supported and promoted Japanese emigration to Brazil in order to solve the problem of its ever-growing population and as a way of providing relief to victims of the 1923 Great Kanto earthquake.[25] Beginning in October 1924, the Ministry of Home Affairs subsidized travel expenses and commissions for Japanese emigrants. As a result, 158,000 Japanese ventured to Brazil between 1923 and 1941. World War II temporarily interrupted Japanese emigration to South America.

---

23. Tsuda Takeyuki, "The Stigma of Ethnic Difference: The Structure of Prejudices and 'Discrimination' toward Japan's New Immigrant Minority," *Journal of Japanese Studies* 24, no. 2 (1998): 317–359 (342ff).

24. Kajita finds that only 11.7 percent can speak Japanese well. See Kajita Takamichi, "Dekasegi 10 nengo no nikkei burajirujin: 1998 nen no nikkeijin rōdōsha ankēto shosa ni kizuka saikensho" [Japanese Brazilians after 10 years' stay in Japan: Reexamination of their reality of life according to a questionnaire to Brazilian workers in 1998] *Kokusai Kankeigaku Kenkyū* [Studies of International Relations] 25 (March 1999): 5–6.

25. Tsuchida Motoko, "A History of Japanese Emigration from the 1860s to the 1990s," in Myron Weiner and Hanami Tadashi, eds., *Temporary Workers or Future Citizens?* (New York: New York University Press, 1998), 77–119 (100ff).

Between 1945 and 1950, Japan experienced another population crisis, as approximately 6.25 million people returned to Japan after the war and another 6.4 million babies were born. Meanwhile, the Japanese economy was foundering. In 1949, the Diet proposed a "resolution concerning the population problem" (*Jinkō mondai ni kan suru ketsugi*) by promoting Japanese emigration. In 1953, the Japanese government reinstated its emigration policy to South America. Two years later, the government established an Emigration Division within the Ministry of Foreign Affairs (MOFA) and set up the Japan Overseas Migration Promotion Corporation to provide loans to Japanese emigrants. In 1956 the government opened a Migration Mediation Office in Yokohama, adding to the office already in operation in Kobe. Bilateral migration agreement contracts were signed with Bolivia (1956), Paraguay (1959), Brazil (1960), and Argentina (1961). Between 1953 and 1973, almost 60,000 Japanese emigrated to Brazil alone.[26] Japanese emigration programs to South America continued until 1973, when Japanese economic prosperity suddenly eliminated the economic advantages of emigration.[27]

Nikkeijin are not considered ethnic immigrants returning to their home country but as migrants coming to work in Japan.[28] They can live and work temporarily in Japan, but cannot vote or work in the civil service. Their family members, including those of non-Japanese descent, are permitted to join them during their stay in Japan. Most nikkeijin, usually between twenty and thirty-five years of age, work for secondary or tertiary subcontractors in production sites with more than twenty employees in manufacturing (particularly automobile and electronic) or transport-related services sector jobs in Aichi, Shizuoka, Gunma, and Kanagawa.[29] They receive good salaries, slightly lower than Japanese workers. In 2003, Nikkei men and women earned an average of 308,000 yen (US$2,825)

26. Keiko Yamanaka, "'I Will Go Home, But When?': Labor Migration and Circular Diaspora Formation by Japanese Brazilians in Japan," in Mike Douglass and Glenda Roberts, eds., *Japan and Global Migration: Foreign Workers and the Advent of a Multicultural Society* (New York: Routledge, 2000), 129.

27. Interview with an official of the Ministry of Foreign Affairs' Consular and Migration Policy Division, May 19, 2000.

28. Kajita et al., *Kao no mienai teijūka.*

29. Yoko Selleck, "Nikkeijin: The Phenomenon of Return Migration," in Michael Weiner, ed., *Japan's Minorities: The Illusion of Homogeneity* (London: Routledge, 1997), 178–210 (esp. 194).

and 204,000 yen (US$1,870) per month, respectively.[30] However, nikkeijin rarely receive bonuses or welfare benefits and are not guaranteed lifetime employment like their Japanese and zainichi counterparts. Nor can they rely on regular pay increases or promotion in accordance with the length of their employment, given their short-term employment contracts. Nikkeijin enjoy full access to medical care and public health services, although few subscribe to them, as most refuse to allow the employers to deduct social insurance premiums from their wages.

Most nikkeijin work for contract companies and are thus indirectly employed.[31] While most contract companies prefer to directly recruit nikkeijin already residing in Japan, they also hire nikkeijin from travel and local recruitment agencies in Brazil. Labor contractors have actually created a mobile labor pool both in Japan and Brazil that can provide a "just-in-time" delivery of Brazilian workers to client companies.[32] Typically, a contract company makes an initial two- to three-month contract with a client company. If the client company is satisfied with the nikkei worker, then the contract company will conclude a six-month or one-year contract with the client company. As contract workers, nikkeijin often work without health, welfare, and employment insurances. When a dispatched nikkeijin suffers a job-related accident, for example, the contract company, as the direct employer, is responsible for reporting the accident to Labor Standards Inspection Office (LSIO) officials and paying a minimum compensation. However, contract companies prefer not to make such reports for fear that their client companies will be unhappy with LSIO's investigations. Client companies, in turn, tend to hide their involvement in accidents and leave the contract company to deal with these cases. Consequently, injured nikkeijin often end up receiving no accident compensation.[33] In 2004, the

---

30. Hiroaki Watanabe, "Human Resource Management for Nikkei Workers and the Increase of Indirect Employment," *Japan Labor Review* 2, no. 4 (2005): 72–106. These figures include overtime pay at about thirty to fifty hours per month.

31. During the 1990s, nikkeijin used brokers, which typically took a dispatching fee from their client companies and a brokering fee from the workers' wages, to immigrate and find work in Japan. In the late 1990s, those brokers transformed themselves into "travel agencies."

32. Naoto Higuchi and Kiyoto Tanno, "What's Driving Brazil-Japan Migration? The Making and Remaking of the Brazilian Niche in Japan," *International Journal of Japanese Sociology* 12 (November 2003): 33–47.

33. See Joshua Roth, *Brokered Homeland: Japanese Brazilian Migrants in Japan* (Ithaca: Cornell University Press, 2002).

government deregulated the Workers Dispatching Law, allowing the dispatching of nikkei workers to be expanded in manufacturing, services, and other industries. Such deregulation has resulted in more corporate abuses against nikkeijin. Overall, nikkeijin's Japanese bloodlines make them eligible for a higher immigration status and greater rights than other migrants, but their "foreigner" status puts them below Asian wives.

Foreign Students and English Language Teachers

Another group of legal foreigners include approximately 117,000 foreign students and 26,000 English language teachers. Almost 80 percent of foreign students come from China and South Korea. Foreign students increasingly chose to come to Japan for study after the Nakasone Yasuhiro government reformed the education system and launched an internationalization campaign in 1983 to attract about 100,000 foreign students by the early twenty-first century. Because foreign students were thought to be "ambassadors from the future," the government hoped to improve international understanding and to deepen friendship with other countries through them. In 1984, the government simplified visa procedures for foreign students, who need only to register in any school, including Japanese language schools, to receive a visa. As a result, the number of foreign students has risen dramatically from 10,000 in 1983 to 132,000 in 2006.

To help pay for their tuition and living expenses, at least two-thirds of foreign students engage in part-time (*arubaito*) work, usually in food-shops and restaurants. As part-time workers, these foreigners typically receive an hourly wage of 800 yen (US$7.30). With a "permit to engage in activity other than that permitted by the status of residence previously granted," foreign students with "college student" and "pre-college student" visas can work up to twenty-eight hours per week. As discussed below, however, many work longer and without a permit. In fact, the number of "bogus" foreign students, who are registered in language schools or remote private colleges but rarely attend classes, is steadily rising. Although local governmental organizations have begun to supply information and consulting services to foreign students, many privately funded students face difficulty in finding housing.

Young college graduates from the United States, United Kingdom, Canada, Australia, and New Zealand come to Japan to teach English in the private sector in urban metropolitan areas on a "specialist in humanities/ international services" visa and in public junior and high schools under the Japan Exchange and Teaching (JET) Program in rural areas on an "instructor" visa. They typically are employed with a fixed contract and earn about 300,000 yen (US$2,750) per month. After persistent pressure from the U.S. government for Japan to internationalize and improve cultural understanding between Japanese and people from other nations, the Japanese government launched the JET Program in 1987.[34] The JET Program, which "aims to promote internationalization in Japan's local communities by helping to improve foreign language education and developing international exchange at the community level," annually brings about 5,800 young graduates from English-speaking countries to Japan as assistant language teachers at about 2,000 contracting public junior and high schools. In general, English language teachers hold a relatively "privileged" position in Japanese society, as they enjoy semi-extraterritorial rights and can call on the credible protection of their home governments in the form of *gaiatsu* (pressure from the outside) if they need it. Overall, although they have limited rights in Japan, their rights outside of Japan ensure that they rarely face the kinds of problems that other foreigners encounter. They work and live in a relatively good environment due to their home governments' concern.

Legal Asian Workers

Legal workers from Asia include about 150,000 trainees and 65,000 entertainers. Most trainees labor at inferior, temporary positions in dying sectors and industrial niches not occupied by Japanese or other foreign "races" of labor (e.g., textile and clothing manufacturing, metal processing, and fishery processing). They are in their twenties, and come from China (70 percent), Indonesia, Vietnam, the Philippines, and Thailand— countries where Japanese multinational corporations have established a

---

34. David McConnell, *Importing Diversity: Inside Japan's JET Program* (Berkeley: University of California Press, 2000). The JET Program is operated by local authorities in cooperation with MOFA, the Ministry of Internal Affairs and Communication (MIC), the Ministry of Education, Culture, Sports, Science, and Technology (MEXT), and the Council of Local Authorities for International Relations (CLAIR).

strong presence.[35] Most entertainers are young female singers and dancers from the Philippines—where the U.S. military has helped to develop this industry. Both trainees and entertainers work demanding jobs and have limited rights.

Trainees.   According to Japanese government stipulations, trainees are allowed to engage only in activities to learn and acquire the technology, skills, or knowledge at public or private organizations in Japan. In reality, trainees rarely receive "training" and work in unskilled or semi-skilled jobs. Trainees' compensation is limited to commuting and living expenses. Moreover, since foreign "trainees" are not considered "workers," they are not protected under Japanese labor laws during the first year. Originally, the trainee system was intended to aid the transfer of technology overseas, by bringing foreign employees of Japanese-owned plants from abroad and teaching them new high-tech skills for one year. Trainees had to be at least eighteen years of age, and the number of trainees in a company could not exceed 5 percent of its workforce. Companies with no capital or trade relations with foreign counterparts and with fewer than twenty full-time employees were not entitled to benefit from this system. In 1990, the MOJ reformed the trainee system, opening new channels for the introduction of trainees through various mediating organizations.[36] Thereafter, smaller companies with no international operations were permitted to invite trainees through mediating organizations, such as the Chamber of Commerce and Industry, the Association of Small Enterprises, the Corporate Vocational Training Organization, and the Agricultural Cooperative Association. Some local governments also created their own training centers, bringing trainees from countries where they had established sister-city or regional relationships.[37]

In 1991, the MOJ, the MOFA, the MOL, the Ministry of International Trade and Industry (MITI), and the Ministry of Construction set up the

---

35. For the impact of multinational corporations on international migration from developing countries to industrialized societies, see Saskia Sassen, *The Mobility of Labor and Capital: A Study in International Investment and Labor Flow* (New York: University of Cambridge Press, 1994).

36. Interview with an official of the Ministry of Justice Immigration Bureau, January 9, 1999.

37. These sister-city or regional training centers are different than those that already exist for technical trainees.

Japan International Training Cooperation Organization (JITCO) to provide "support and services to companies and organizations...that accept foreign trainees." JITCO builds overseas networks with foreign governmental organizations, particularly in Asia, and regularly sends missions overseas to promote the training program in Japan. In 1992, JITCO set a goal of bringing in 100,000 trainees from foreign countries annually. In April 1993, JITCO instituted a technical internship program (TIP) to transform "trainees" into "interns." Trainees who pass JITCO's evaluations are given "designated activities" visa status and are permitted to work legally with labor protection for one year after the technical training period. In 1997, MOJ extended this practical period to two years and expanded the program to other fields. As a result, the number of trainees, mostly from Asia, increased almost fivefold from 17,081 in 1987 to 83,319 in 2005. The number of trainees from China increased dramatically from 2,688 to 55,156 during this period. Another interesting trend is a change in the source of these trainees. Prior to 1990, two-thirds of the trainees came through either local affiliates of Japanese multinational corporations or their business partners in a joint venture.[38] By 1998, more than 80 percent of foreign trainees came through governmental or quasi-governmental organizations (e.g., JITCO, Japan International Cooperation Association, Japan Socioeconomic Productivity Center, and Association for Overseas Technical Scholarship). In 2003, the government designated regions troubled by a lack of workers as "special zones" to allow them to admit workers from abroad through the trainee system.

Most foreign-worker trainees undergo "training" in small firms in Tokyo, Aichi, Shizuoka, Gifu, Osaka, Hyōgo, Ibaraki, Tochigi, and Gunma. Trainees are concentrated in the ready-to-wear clothing, construction, food processing, and marine product–processing industries—industries that do not attract Japanese workers because they are *kitanai* (dirty), *kitsui* (demanding), and *kiken* (dangerous). Trainees are sometimes forced to perform strenuous tasks not connected to training. One Chinese woman complains, "I come to Japan to learn about farming but have been sent to a construction site. I have been forced to work overtime with little time left for learning."[39]

38. Komai Hiroshi, *Migrant Workers in Japan* (London: Kegan Paul International, 1995), 45.
39. *Japan Times,* January 3, 2007.

Some work and live in slavelike conditions: working from 8:30 A.M. until midnight, being fined for bathroom breaks, having half of their pay being put into a bank account that they cannot access, and having their passports taken away.[40] Most trainees receive low pay: In 2004, trainees received a monthly compensation of about 120,000 yen (US$1,100).[41] More than one thousand trainees have gone missing each year. One Indonesian man, who abandoned his training program along with fifteen others, explains,

> The contents of the training were inadequate, for the training was only one month long.... This system pretends to be a training system, though it is in reality a labor system. If I had received enough training, I would have been satisfied with the allowance of 80,000 yen.[42]

Such conditions cause many foreign trainees to abandon their trainee programs and find work as illegal foreign workers, with wages usually twice as high as their trainee allowance.

Entertainers. Another major group of legal Asian workers include female entertainers, mostly singers and dancers from the Philippines (80%). They are usually in their twenties and thirties and work in Tokyo, Kawasaki, Yokohama, and various small towns in the countryside. They typically enter Japan on a six-month "entertainer" visa and earn about 200,000 yen (US$1,830) per month to sing and dance at nightclubs. Many entertainers receive part of their salary while in Japan and the rest after six months before they leave. Without much money to live on (as little as 1,000 yen or US$9 per day), foreign entertainers often rely on commissions and tips from customers. Some clubs and snack bars in the entertainment industry establish a *dōhan* (dating) system, which forces foreign women entertainers to date their clients after business hours (often during the daytime)—or be fined. The dual requirements of the entertaining job in conjunction with the *dōhan* system impact the health of foreign "hostesses." Hostesses

---

40. See *Chūnichi Shimbun,* March 9, 2007.

41. *Asahi Shimbun,* January 12, 2006. During the first year of training, monthly pay is limited to 60,000 yen (US$550).

42. Published interview with an Indonesian trainee in "Many 'Trainees' Face Tough Conditions Here," *Kalabaw Newsletter,* no. 34 (June 1998): 4–6.

typically work their formal entertaining shift between 5 P.M. and 4 A.M. The less formal (but required) work of dating clients is usually during the daytime, which forces them to give up their opportunity to rest.

A visa and residence category of "foreign entertainers" has its origin in the 1950s when the U.S. government requested that the Japanese government allowed English-speaking women, particularly from the Philippines, to come and entertain the U.S. troops who were stationed in Japan. In 1981, the government eased its requirement for the issuance of entertainers' visas, allowing the entry of Filipina women without the minimum two-year work experience as long as they are certified by a government agency or an equivalent public or private organization. By 2004, approximately 80,000 Filipina women per year were arriving in Japan on the entertainer visa. In 2005, after NGOs had reported repeated wide-spread abuses against foreign women to the media and international community, the government imposed a stricter standard for accepting foreign entertainers, requiring two-years' minimum educational training or international work experience outside of Japan.

Overall, legal Asian workers including trainees and entertainers are ranked at the bottom of the racialized hierarchy because they have no Japanese associations (bloodline, birthplace, or marriage) and—unlike foreign students and English teachers—are not well protected by their governments. Their minimal rights and status, however, still ranks them higher than their illegal Asian worker counterparts.

Illegal Asian Workers

The Immigration Bureau estimated that at the end of 2005 about 194,000 foreigners were overstaying their visa, while another 30,000 entered the country illegally with forged passports or by other illegal methods. They come mostly from East Asian countries, particularly Korea, China, the Philippines, and Thailand. Other illegal Asian workers include *men* from Bangladesh and Pakistan. Three quarters of overstayed foreigners enter Japan as "temporary visitors," with fifteen- or sixty-day visas. Others enter as "entertainers," "pre-college students," "college students," and "trainees," with visas that range from three months to one year. Given their visa status, these foreigners, who are mostly in their twenties and thirties, do not have the right to work in Japan as "unskilled workers."

About two-thirds of illegal foreigners find employment around the Tokyo metropolitan area. They tend to occupy low-paying, dirty, difficult, and dangerous jobs. Men work as construction workers, factory workers, cooks, and kitchen helpers. Most women work in bars, but some also work as waitresses and factory workers. About half of illegal foreign workers earn 7,000 to 10,000 yen (US$60–90) per day, while a third makes less than 7,000 yen per day. Their jobs are not guaranteed, and none provide bonuses, paid holidays, or company insurance. Typically, illegal Asian workers tend to work in small companies with fewer than twenty employees. Japanese small businesses prefer to hire illegal foreign workers because they are then not obligated to pay health insurance premiums—a great saving for the company.[43] Illegal Asian workers in Japan are obliged to rely on informal channels to find jobs—through recruiting agents, brokers, or friends. These "middle people" often take advantage of the workers' illegal status by taking dispatching fees from them without securing them a job. A former Thai broker who smuggles Thai workers into Japan asserts that this practice is quite common within the Thai communities in Japan.[44]

Some female entertainers have overstayed their entertainer visas and work in the sex industry, which often overlaps with the "entertainment" industry. In other cases, Filipina and Thai women have been deceived and forced into sex slavery. As forced prostitutes, they receive between 25,000 and 35,000 yen (US$230–320) per customer.[45] Many Thai and Filipina women have told Japanese NGOs that they had no forewarning of the huge debt they would incur and servitude they would be forced into by coming to work in Japan.[46] Brokers in Japan usually pay local brokers in Thailand between 1.5 million to 1.8 million yen (US$13,750–16,500) for each Thai woman bought to Japan, which covers transportation fees and

---

43. Interview with the representative of a business association, whose members hire illegal foreign workers, in Yokohama, November 28, 1998.

44. Interview with a former Thai broker in Tsuchiura-shi, Ibaraki, December 28, 1998.

45. Interviews with Thai entertainers in Iwai-shi, Ibaraki, June 17, 1998. For testimonies and surveys in English, see International Labour Organization (ILO), *Human Trafficking for Sexual Exploitation in Japan* (Geneva: ILO, 2004); Human Rights Watch, *Owed Justice: Thai Women Trafficked into Debt Bondage in Japan* (New York: Human Right Watch, 2000).

46. Given the extensive publicity in Thailand and the Philippines about prostitution in Japan—not to mention widespread prostitution in their own countries—one wonders whether most knew about the job expectations in Japan.

falsified travel documents. After these women arrive in Japan, they are sold to a broker or a *mama-san* (a woman in charge of running a nightclub and looking after the "girls") for around 2 million yen (US$18,350). By then, the women have incurred a debt of 3.5 million to 3.8 million yen (US$32,000–35,000), which they must pay back in order to reclaim their freedom.[47] To make matters worse, these women must pay rent to their brokers or to the mama-san, since they cannot get an apartment on their own. They are also burdened by medical and other miscellaneous expenses. Moreover, Japanese brokers can resell them to other brokers elsewhere as a way to make additional profits. Hence, opportunistic brokers can keep foreign women in a situation of perpetual debt.

Japanese workers, mama-san, and *yakuza* (Japanese organized crime groups) closely monitor foreign women workers. A 1997 survey of one hundred Filipina sex workers in Japan revealed that ninety-four of the women lived in places assigned by their employers so they could be monitored.[48] Some of the women were not allowed to go out shopping or on other errands without an escort. Almost half reported that they did not have adequate food and heating. The brokers and mama-san often threatened them if they entertained any idea of escaping. To intimidate and discipline these women, the brokers and mama-san (themselves or through hired thugs) often beat them.[49] A Thai man, who was brought to Japan illegally during the bubble economy of the late 1980s and whose job was to entertain Thai women, was cornered in his apartment by a yakuza and had one of his arms sliced with a samurai sword. His explanation for this brutality was that he was thought to be involved with a Thai woman who was

---

47. Support Group for Three Thai Women of the Shimodate Incident, ed., *Sono hi, nihon de* [That day in Japan] (Tsukuba-shi, Ibaraki: Support Group for Three Thai Women of the Shimodate Incident, 1994), 26–28.

48. International Organization of Migration (IOM), *Trafficking in Women to Japan for Sexual Exploitation: A Survey on the Case of Filipino Women* (Geneva: IOM, May 1997).

49. See Woman's Rights Kamarado, ed., *Tai kara no tayori: Sunakku "mama" satsukai jiken no sonogo* [Letters from Thailand: After the Killing Incident of a Snack Mama] (Tokyo: Gendai Shokan, 1998); Support Group of the Three Thai Women of the Shimodate Incident, ed., *Baishun shakai nihon e, taijin josei kara no tegami* [To prostitution society Japan, letters from Thai women] (Tokyo: Akashi Shoten, 1995); Saalaa, *Shierutaa riyō jokyō hōkoku* (Report of shelter activities), January 1995.

contemplating escaping.[50] As sex industry workers illustrate, unskilled foreign workers have a high level of personal insecurity because of their illegal status.

Although its aging population and shrinking domestic labor supply mean that Japan benefits in many ways from unskilled foreign workers, Japan does not welcome them and actively prevents their entry. The presence of unskilled foreign workers without working visas is largely a by-product of Japan's failed policy to control their entry and departure. The 1990 revised Immigration Control Law effectively denies these people, mainly Asians, the rights to exist as "unskilled foreign workers" in Japan. It essentially turned Asian unskilled workers into illegal residents. The government clearly wants only "good" foreigners—those with Japanese blood or specialized skills. Therefore, MOFA instructs its embassies abroad to conduct rigorous examinations before issuing visas in order to prevent people from entering Japan to obtain illegal employment. At the same time, MOFA aims to promote international exchanges with different countries by simplifying and accelerating its visa-issuing procedures for certain foreigners.

As part of this approach, the government has engaged in a number of campaigns to restrict illegal workers in Japan. One example is the MOJ's annual one-month Campaign against the Employment of Illegal Foreigners with raids of business establishments that hire illegal foreign workers. These occasional raids prevent illegal Asians from forming permanent communities, as they are constantly hiding or on the run. When a close-knit community of several thousand Thais was formed in Tsuchiura-shi in the Ibaraki Prefecture in the early 1990s, the Immigration Office conducted several raids that effectively dissolved the local Thai community.[51] Thereafter, the Thais were afraid to come together in large numbers, fearing that they would again be an easy target for raids. In 1998, the Immigration Bureau chief of the MOJ, Takenaka Shigeo, called for a joint action with the National Police Agency (NPA) and the Ministry of Health, Labor, and Welfare (MHLW), establishing the Liaison Council of Government

---

50. Interview with a formerly overstayed Thai worker who had returned to Thailand in Bangkok, June 7, 1994.

51. Interview with an official of the Tsuchiura-shi Board of Education International Exchange Section, June 5, 1998.

Agencies on the Affairs of Illegal Foreign Workers to gather information on illegal foreign workers and to prevent illegal employment.[52] These government agencies joined forces nationwide to crack down on illegal foreign workers.

Another example is the 2003 government formulation of an "Action Plan for the Revitalization of a Society Resistant of Crime" with a goal of halving the number of illegal foreign residents, whom they associate with criminality (as will be discussed in chapter 6), by 2008.[53] As a result of the Action Plan, the Tokyo metropolitan police have been conducting random checks on foreigners in areas where illegal foreigners are known to congregate such as Shinjuku, Shin-Okubo, Takadanobaba, and Shibuya. Any Asian can be asked to show her/his immigration document and be placed in custody if s/he fails to produce proper documentation. The Japanese police have also arrested illegal foreign workers in order to investigate other presumptive offenses. When illegal foreigners are arrested as criminal "suspects," they rarely receive visits from their friends and compatriots, who often are also illegal foreigners. Moreover, officials sometimes prohibit the use of non-Japanese languages in prison. As a result, most foreign suspects feel intensely isolated in Japanese detention centers.[54] They are also sometimes tortured in detention centers. A former official at a detention house in Tokyo's Kita Ward reported that illegal foreign detainees who do not follow instructions, particularly Iranians, Chinese, and Koreans, are routinely tortured.[55]

Despite policies restricting illegals in Japan, the Foreign Workers' Affairs Division of the MHLW has maintained that Japan's Labor Standards Law (Article 3) protects all workers in Japan from "discriminatory treatment with respect to wages, working hours or other working conditions," regardless of their nationalities, including overstaying foreign workers. Foreign workers are also entitled to fundamental labor rights such as the

52. Interview with an official of the National Police Agency, December 10, 2000.

53. Interview with an official of the Ministry of Justice Immigration Policy Planner's Office, July 26, 2006.

54. Interviews with Father Nakaya Isao of the Yamasato Consulting Office and a detained Chinese man on death row inside the Tokyo Municipal Prison in Kosuge, Tokyo, December 3, 1998.

55. *Mainichi Shimbun,* December 23, 1994; *Japan Times,* December 24, 1994.

right to organize a trade union and hold collective bargaining negotiations. When these unskilled foreign workers encounter labor rights violations by their employers, the Foreign Workers' Affairs Division steps in if a complaint is made by the employee, making no distinction between overstayed and legal foreign workers in providing labor protection. MHLW officials may enforce article 3 to discourage Japanese employers from developing a two-tiered labor market for Japanese and foreign workers, which could undermine labor standards in Japan.[56]

Although discrimination is prohibited in law, however, illegal foreign workers do not receive full legal protection in practice. As illegals, they sometime encounter irregular Japanese business practices such as uncompensated accident insurance, unpaid wages, and arbitrary dismissal. Because they fear the disclosure of illegal employment, employers sometimes insert Japanese names in employment contracts for illegal foreign workers.[57] This practice leads to serious problems when illegal foreign workers suffer from industrial injuries but cannot claim accident insurance because their names do not match those in the employment contracts. In other cases, employers simply refuse to cooperate with insurance claims for illegal foreign workers.[58] Moreover, employers may stop paying illegal Asian workers or dismiss them for arbitrary reasons, assuming that illegal workers will be too afraid to report irregular labor practices to authorities. One Burmese man was unjustly dismissed from his job at a drinking establishment in Tokyo with the following threat: "You are an overstayer, I am going to report you to the Immigration Office!"[59] Although the employer would also be punished, illegal Asian workers often accept such abuses quietly, for fear of being exposed.

Moreover, the National Health Insurance Division of MHLW has made it difficult for illegal foreigners to maintain a safe and healthy life in Japan.

---

56. Interview with an official of the Ministry of Health, Labor, and Welfare Foreign Workers' Affairs Division, July 20, 2006.

57. For such cases, see *Kanagawa Shimbun* (November 9, 1991, November 10, 1991), *Tokyo Shimbun* (January 26, 1995, June 27, 1997), *Asahi Shimbun* (February 7, 1992).

58. According to a 1992 study, only 19 percent of employers directly compensate injured overstaying foreign workers. Japan Occupational Safety and Health Resource Center, ed., *Gaikokujin rōdōsha no rōsai hakusho* [White papers on industrial accidents among foreign workers] (Tokyo: Kaifū Shobō, 1992).

59. Interview with an overstayed Burmese worker, October 18, 1998.

Faced with Japan's aging population and increased financial constraints, MHLW officials state that their priority is Japanese residents not foreign residents with no legal status.[60] In 1990, MHLW stopped offering illegal foreigners publicly subsidized medical assistance, which has traditionally been a significant resource for those living in poverty or burdened with large unpaid medical expenses. Two years later, the ministry instructed local governments to limit application for National Health Insurance (kokumin kenkō hoken or NHI) to those foreigners who "had registered themselves, and who will be in the country for over one year." As will be discussed in chapter 6, this became an official and written policy in 2004. Consequently, overstayed foreigners cannot be insured under any public insurance scheme and must bear all medical costs themselves.

This creates many problems for illegal foreign workers. For one, many overstayed foreigners compensate for high medical expenses by treating themselves, which can have disastrous results. This was the case for one Malaysian woman who died while trying to treat her acute abdominal pains with over-the-counter medicine (with directions written in Japanese). Due to her tourist visa status, she did not have health insurance, and she thought that it would be too expensive to see a doctor.[61]

A second problem that arises is that lack of medical insurance effectively limits illegals' access to preventive medical care, which increases their need for emergency care. For example, since pregnant foreign women often do not receive necessary prenatal care due to high cost, problems during delivery are not uncommon among illegal foreign women.[62] The infant mortality rate is unusually high among foreign mothers. According to a 1997 report, the number of stillborn babies of Thai mothers in Japan was 2.1 times higher than that of Japanese mothers. The number of babies who died before their first birthday was 3.8 times higher for Filipina mothers, and 2.5 times higher for Thai mothers, than for Japanese mothers.[63] This

---

60. Interviews with an official of the Ministry of Health, Labor, and Welfare National Health Insurance Section, January 7, 1999, and May 18, 2000.

61. Takayama Toshio, "Gaikokujin wo shimedasu iryō—fukushi," [Shutting Foreigners Out of Medical Treatment and Welfare] in Forum on Asian Immigrant Workers, ed., *Okasareru Jinken Gaikokujin Rōdōsha* [No Rights for Foreign Workers], (Tokyo: Dai-san Shokan, 1992), 127–145 (133–135ff).

62. Interview with Sawada Takashi of SHARE, May 26, 1998.

63. *Asahi Shimbun,* October 8, 1999.

is not just a problem for pregnant women. In numerous cases, foreigners without NHI coverage often wait until the illness worsens before going to the hospital because they cannot afford to pay medical bills.[64] High medical fees kept one overstayed Thai hostess, who had been diagnosed with symptoms of ovarian cancer, from checking into the hospital for treatment until it was too late. One month after the initial diagnosis, she arrived in an ambulance with the lower half of her body covered with blood. The doctor asked, "Why haven't you come until now?" She replied, "I don't have money and I couldn't afford to take days off from work."[65] Without NHI, the cost would have been 2 million yen (US$18,350). With NHI, it would have been only 60,000 yen (US$550), an amount that most likely would not have deterred this woman from attending to her illness at an earlier stage.

To make matters worse, some hospitals turn away nonregistered overstayed foreigners, assuming that they cannot pay their medical bills because they are not insured by the public health insurance.[66] For instance, one Southeast Asian woman in her twenties, who fell about thirty feet from the fifth floor of a hotel onto an iron scaffolding, was refused entry by four hospitals because she was a foreigner and had no fixed address. Although she suffered from a fractured spine and broken right arm and was unable to move, hospital officials refused to accept her, saying that they would not treat foreigners without permanent residency. Only after a five-hour search were Yokohama police and firefighters able to find a hospital to admit her.[67]

Overall, overstayed Asian workers are at the bottom of the racialized hierarchy and have no rights and a high level of personal insecurity. Although officially this low position is because of their illegal status, it is facilitated by Japanese government policies that give greater rights and security to certain ethnic groups and that consequently encourage those at

---

64. *Nikkei Shimbun,* May 11, 1991.

65. *Sankei Shimbun,* December 21, 1993.

66. Since 1990, all hospitals in Japan have reported an increase in unpaid medical bills, especially by illegal foreigners. According to a 1991 survey conducted by the AMDA International Medical Information Center in 1991, 33 out of 49 (67 percent) hospitals reported that they had encountered problems with 26,980 foreign patients, more than half of whom were not eligible for any health insurance. These problems typically involved unpaid medical bills or prescription. See *Yomiuri Shimbun,* March 22, 1992.

67. *Asahi Shimbun,* September 11, 1992.

the bottom of the hierarchy to slip into illegal (and even less secure) lines of work (i.e. unauthorized employment and prostitution).

Diverging Life Experiences of Illegals

An intriguing and troubling consequence of Japan's racialized hierarchy of foreign workers is the way in which Japanese laws have divided foreigners from the same ethnic and cultural backgrounds—such as Koreans, Chinese, and Filipinos—into legal and illegal categories. Zainichi foreigners differ from their illegal compatriots in their ability to speak Japanese and in the labor markets in which they participate. More important, legal foreigners do not share the same life experiences with illegal compatriots, even with shared ethnicity, language, and culture. For example, a Korean who overstays her temporary visitor visa is most likely to have a different life experience both at work and at home than a zainichi Korean. This difference in life experiences is determined in large part by their hierarchy in the labor market (or socioeconomic class), legal rights as accorded by their visa status, and gender. Consequently, an overstayed Korean woman is likely to have more immediate public concerns over subsidized medical insurance rather than discrimination in the workplace or housing.[68]

As a result of government policies, overstayed foreigners in Japan encounter problems much more serious than those of legal foreigners. These include not only the labor and health-related issues discussed above, such as unpaid wages, unlawful dismissal, uncompensated accident insurance, and inability to pay medical fees, but also personal and social problems rooted in their vulnerable position as illegals in Japanese society. Such vulnerability promotes criminal gang activity among communities and gambling and alcohol abuse among individuals.

For example, lack of legal protection for Asian workers drives them to turn to the yakuza, contributing to the expansion of underground activities.

---

68. For the linkage and differences between *zainichi* and *rainichi* (newcomers) Chinese, whose population in Japan has risen dramatically in the past two decades, see Junko Tajima, "Chinese Newcomers in the Global City Tokyo: Social Networks and Settlement Tendencies," *International Journal of Japanese Sociology* 12 (November 2003): 68–78; Robert Efird, "Japan's War Orphans and New Overseas Chinese: History, Identification and (Multi)ethnicity" (Ph.D. diss., University of Washington, 2004).

A Thai in Ibaraki reports that snack bar owners pay 20,000 to 30,000 yen (US$180–275) per month to the yakuza. If they do not pay, then "the organization" sends someone to have a few drinks there. He pretends to get drunk and then breaks a table or two—all at the owner's expense. If the owner pays, then "the organization" provides protection services twenty-four hours a day. For example, if a customer gets out of hand (i.e., gets overly drunk and begins to damage property), then the snack bar worker can call the yakuza for help at any time. And they show up within a few minutes. Why? Because they can make *even more* money by threatening the drunken troublemaker. Moreover, the yakuza can protect foreigners from Japanese clients and generate income for snack bar owners when they follow those clients who refuse to pay. As a result, some overstayed foreigners are actually on good terms with the yakuza and even see them as their protectors. They claim that the yakuza do not harm someone physically unless that person has done something "really, really terrible" to them.[69]

Gang strength is also increased because the status of foreigners as illegals puts them into a situation where they must settle ethnic conflicts among themselves. A Japanese police officer at the Kotobuki-chō in Yokohama revealed that much of the crime committed by Korean workers in that area involves other Koreans. Thais in Ibaraki report a similar pattern in their community. Some Thais have been known to hire yakuza to beat up other Thais who possess physical advantages.[70] They hire yakuza to avoid direct criminal activity, since arrest would mean deportation.

A more personal impact of the vulnerability of illegals is gambling and alcoholism. Because their illegal status isolates unskilled Asian workers, morale, social, and economic opportunities can be reduced.[71] Indeed, loneliness and a feeling of exclusion have driven some illegal foreigners into alcoholism and gambling. Many overstayed foreigners live a lonely life; they assuage their loneliness with alcohol and gamble away their hard-earned

---

69. Interview with an overstayed Thai worker in Tsuchiura-shi, Ibaraki, June 17, 1998.

70. Interview with an overstayed Thai worker in Tsuchiura-shi, Ibaraki, December 28, 1998.

71. An Organization for Economic Cooperation and Development (OECD) survey finds that, among the OECD countries, Japan has the highest level of social isolation, or "the lack of contact with other people in normal daily living." See OECD, *Society at a Glance* (Paris: OECD, 2005), 82–83.

money in pachinko parlors. Among illegal foreigners from Thailand, for example, female Thai entertainers, who usually drink with their Japanese clients at work, often spend after-work hours with their Thai friend(s) or Japanese clients in drinking establishments where Thai men readily entertain them. They usually wake up around noon and head directly to a Thai restaurant where they order beer with their first meal of the day. By two in the afternoon, some are already drunk. Many have died in Japan from alcoholism.

In addition, most Thai workers in the Ibaraki Prefecture appear to be addicted to pachinko machines. Customers complain that one Thai hairdresser in Tsuchiura-shi spends most of his time in pachinko parlors. They often have to fetch him there in order to have their hair cut. An entertainer, who grumbled, "I am bored and have nothing to do here," revealed that she loses somewhere between 250,000 to 400,000 yen (US$2,300–3,670) per month to these money-sucking machines.[72] When asked why she did not return to Thailand, she calmly replied, "I live a comfortable life here...much better than in Thailand. I will continue to work until the *nyūkan* [Immigration Office] catches me. Then I will go back." This phenomenon is also common in other foreigner communities. In the Kotobuki-chō district of Yokohama where Korean and Filipino day laborers try their luck at landing a job in the early mornings, many foreign workers escape isolation and boredom inside the pachinko parlors. Once socially isolated, they face greater difficulties in reintegrating into Japanese society as a contributing member and in fulfilling personal aspirations to the family back home.

As in other affluent countries, the legal resident status of certain foreigners in Japan (such as spouses of nationals and foreign students and professionals with the legal right to work) creates a social distance between legal foreign workers and their illegal compatriots. Regardless of education, social background, or occupation, legal foreigners hold a position above that of their illegal compatriots in terms of effective rights and social status. Whereas legally recognized foreigners enjoy extensive public institutional support and can create their own self-help groups to fight for the improvement of their livelihood in Japan, illegal foreigners can form no

---

72. Interview with an overstayed Thai worker in Tsuchiura-shi, Ibaraki, June 17, 1998.

such groups, for fear of arrest and deportation. As we will see in chapter 3, ethnic associations organized by zainichi Koreans and Chinese or legal Filipinos do not support their illegal compatriots. Legal foreigners tend to stay away from their illegal compatriots and refuse to support them in order to maintain their privileged status or for fear of jeopardizing their residency in Japan. A variety of social pressures encourage legal residents to avoid intervening in their plight. In other instances, legal foreigners outright exploit their illegal compatriots by acting as labor brokers and mama-san. As a result, illegal foreigners typically turn to Japanese NGOs for assistance.

Instead of an immigration policy, Japan has a foreign worker policy in the professional and technical fields that targets certain races and nationalities. In its efforts to control foreigners, the government places them into a racialized (and gendered) hierarchy, privileging those with specialized skills or Japanese birth or blood over unskilled Asian workers. This political constructed hierarchy structures the working and living conditions for each type of foreigner with differentiated rights and benefits but without paternalistic accommodation policies. Specifically, government officials have declared zainichi as "special" foreigners and nikkeijin as "almost Japanese," giving these groups the rights to engage in unskilled labor; yet at the same time they have declared unskilled labor done by non-zainichi or non-nikkeijin Asian workers to be "illegal." These policies create and maintain structural divisions in Japanese society among people of different legal status and ethnic identification.

Not only does this hierarchy exist among ethnic groups, but also among members of the same national groups. As evident from the gatherings of Filipinos at church, two foreigners from the same ethnic background but different legal status can coexist in Japan with few shared life experiences and, therefore, little sense of shared identity. Illegal foreigners work in Japan without full legal protection. They live without basic rights and access to public health insurance or publicly subsidized medical assistance. Because most public welfare services are closed to them, illegal foreigners must pay all medical costs themselves. Efforts by illegal foreigners to create their own self-help groups have been stymied by governmental raids of illegal communities. In contrast, legally recognized foreigners have successfully created their own self-help groups. Because Japan lacks an active integration policy and does not promote political participation of its foreign residents into its political system, these groups tend to concentrate their activities on creating emotional ties to their homelands. The way in which they do this and its implication to Japan's multicultural democracy are the focus of the next chapter.

3

LONG-DISTANCE NATIONALISM

Political Activities of Immigrant Ethnic Associations

There are limited opportunities for immigrant ethnic associations to form in Japan because immigration control policies restrict the institutional development of temporary foreigner groups. The groups that do develop tend to consist of foreigners with more permanent status (especially zainichi and Asian wives). Living in a country with no active policies to fully incorporate foreigners into its society, such foreigners in Japan with no political rights inevitably feel vulnerable as outsiders and turn to building closer ties with their co-ethnics and their home countries. As a result, they have created numerous immigrant ethnic associations, groups that provide ethnic identification and various kinds of support for legal foreigners, although generally not for their illegal compatriots. Some of these associations have strong ideological views and are preoccupied with political activities in the home countries. Others are primarily cultural, fostering identification with the culture and customs of the homeland. On the whole, rather than foster immigrant rights, Japan's immigrant ethnic associations focus on creating ties with the homeland—a land that, in some cases, their members have never known.

While legal foreigners in Japan can create their own associations, illegal foreigners can form no such support groups, for fear of arrest or deportation. Nor can newly arrived and illegal foreigners expect to find support from immigrant ethnic associations, even if they share ethnic and cultural backgrounds. Because these associations are focused on the connection with their brethren overseas in the homeland, they understandably have little interest in improving conditions for fellow co-ethnics or co-nationals within Japan. In addition, as discussed in chapter 2, the legal resident status of their members creates a strong social separation from their illegal compatriots. Zainichi Koreans and Chinese do not want to jeopardize their privileged status by assisting newly arrived illegals. Associations of Filipinos and Thais tend to function as elite social clubs, where legal Asians gather for cultural and social activities, build social networks, and work to improve the living conditions for legal foreigners (namely, themselves). Such associations can be expected to make only limited contributions to the development of Japan's multicultural democracy. Although they foster socioeconomic and cultural integration in some ways, they also hinder national unity and deliberative democracy through their preoccupation with their homelands, promotion of ethnic and class exclusivity, and disinterest in a public discourse to improve conditions for fellow co-ethnics or co-nationals.

Immigrant Ethnic Associations

Secular immigrant ethnic associations can be characterized according to whether they are supportive or critical of their home state. Those associations for Koreans, Chinese, and Thais tend to be more supportive, with Korean and Chinese associations (whose homelands were divided during the Cold War) promoting highly political and ideological attachment to their home countries. Associations for Vietnamese, Burmese, and some Filipinos tend to be more critical, with Vietnamese and Burmese newcomers engaging in radical politics that attempt to undermine their undemocratic home governments. Other legal foreigners, and particularly nikkeijin (who are ethnic Japanese, although foreign nationals), have few such secular immigrant ethnic associations. Rather than establishing immigrant associations for ethnic identification and political voice, they create ethnic enclaves that rely on private ethnic businesses for assistance.

Ethnic Associations Supporting Their Home State

Korean Ethnic Associations. Zainichi Koreans are ideologically divided within their ethnic group and have established two ethnic associations with distinct political orientations. Zainichi Koreans who feel politically or ideologically connected to South Korea belong to the Korean Residents Union in Japan (*zainihon daikan minkoku mindan;* Mindan hereafter), which claims 410,000 members. Another 200,000 zainichi Koreans, who feel ideologically connected to North Korea, are members of the General Association of Korean Residents in Japan (*zainihon chōsenjin sōrengokai;* Chōsen Sōren hereafter; the group is also known by its Korean name as Ch'ongryŏn). Both organizations limit their membership to Koreans born in Japan. Both organizations are highly centralized, with several hundreds of branches and offices along with their affiliated financial institutions and Korean schools throughout Japan.[1]

Both Chōsen Sōren and Mindan emerged out of the League of Koreans in Japan (*zainichi chōsenjin renmei;* Chōren hereafter), established by Korean nationalists and activists on October 15, 1945. Chōren gradually fell under the control of Korean communists, and its turn toward the radical left ignited a split within Chōren. On October 3, 1946, a conservative group, including former Chōren members and new members, established Mindan with Pak Yol as its first leader.[2] This organization, which quickly became Chōren's archrival, followed the anti-communist position of South Korea. Chōren itself was forced to dissolve in 1949 after members of the group attacked the Mindan office. On August 15, 1950, former members of Chōren, particularly those who were active in the communist movement, formed the Democratic Front for Unification of Koreans in Japan (*zainichi chōsen tōitsu minshu sensen;* Minsen hereafter) to protest the Korean War and to push for a democratic and communist unification

---

1. Mindan, ed., *Kankoku mindan 50 nen no ayumi* [The 50 Year Path of Mindan] (Tokyo: Gosatsu Shobō, 1997); Chōsen Sōren, *Chōsen sōren* (Tokyo: Chōsen Sōren, 2005).

2. Mindan, ed., *Kankoku mindan 50 nen no ayumi.*

of Korea. Most of Minsen's activities, however, focused on supporting the Japan Communist Party's (JCP) attempt to foment internal revolution in Japan. After Minsen assisted the JCP with several riots in Tokyo and other industrial areas, the government responded in 1953 by increasing security controls over Koreans. By 1954, the North Korean regime had come to view Minsen's preoccupation with revolution in Japan as a mistake and suggested to Minsen members that they loosen their ties with the JCP and concentrate on Korean problems. On May 26, 1955, Minsen was dissolved. One day later, a left-wing labor activist, Han Deok Su, established the Chōsen Sōren under the direct control of North Korea.

From the time of their split in October 1946 until their reconciliation agreement in May 2006, ideological and political opposition to the other group or government has characterized the organizational activities of both associations. When Chōsen Sōren (Minsen then) protested against the Korean War and supported the North Korean effort to unify Korea under communist rule by helping to spread the North Korean propaganda and sending money and letters of encouragement to North Korean troops, Mindan launched its own propaganda campaign to condemn the aggression and "Red Imperialism" of North Korea. When Chōsen Sōren organized a repatriation program to North Korea (*hokusō jigyō*) during the late 1950s and early 1960s, Mindan quickly opposed such programs.[3] Even the name of Mindan's campaign against repatriation, "Committee Opposing Repatriation to North Korea" (*hokusō hantai tōsō iinkai*) reflected its ideological conflict with Chōsen Sōren). During this period, these two groups maintained subunits that engaged in intelligence-gathering activities and political maneuvering against each other.

Chinese Ethnic Associations.   Like zainichi Koreans, overseas Chinese have two types of ethnic associations, which are distinguished by their ideological orientation and/or political ties with different Chinese homelands—mainland China (People's Republic of China [PRC]) and Taiwan. The

---

3. Approximately 50,000 zainichi Koreans repatriated to North Korea between 1959 and 1960 alone. Over 43,000 more repatriated before 1984. Many thought they were returning to a more prosperous and better North Korea, because the North Korean government had regularly sent enormous sums of money to Chōsen Sōren. Moreover, the economy of North Korea, with financial assistance from the communist block, grew faster than that of South Korea after the Korean War.

Taiwanese groups in Japan oppose the PRC's reunification policy and strongly support the Democratic Progressive Party (DPP), which pushes for an independent Taiwan.[4] They support Taiwan's participation as an independent state in international organizations, such as the United Nations and the World Health Organization. The mainland Chinese groups support the PRC and its patriotic cry for a unified China. They also seek to improve Japan's relations with the PRC. Despite their ideological and political divisions, both types of Chinese ethnic associations call themselves "Overseas Chinese Association" (*kakyo sōkai;* OCA hereafter). Unlike ethnic associations for zainichi Koreans, OCAs in Japan are not centralized and do not have a central headquarters. These associations operate with a smaller number of staff members and executives.

Both types of OCAs exist in Tokyo, Yokohama, Kobe, Osaka, and Fukuoka. The two largest associations are located in Tokyo, with membership of 60,000 for the pro-Taiwan group and 20,000 for the pro-PRC group. The larger membership for the pro-Taiwan group reflects the unique feature that the majority of overseas Chinese in Japan have been Taiwanese rather than mainland Chinese for most of the twentieth century. Both associations limit their membership to *kakyo* (overseas Chinese) who have lived in Japan for at least eight years. Therefore, these associations also include those overseas Chinese who were not born in Japan, but came to study and decided to stay in the country after the completion of their studies. These OCAs do not coordinate their activities with each other, even among their own ideologically and politically affiliated groups. The pro-PRC Tokyo OCA, for example, rarely works with the pro-PRC Yokohama OCA.[5]

Unlike Korean ethnic associations, the geographic origins of overseas Chinese contribute substantially to the political orientation and decentralized structure of Chinese ethnic associations. In each Japanese city, the Chinese community came primarily from particular regions of China; in Kanagawa, for example, most old overseas Chinese were from Taiwan

---

4. In contrast, the Koumintang of China (KMT) originally believed that it would one day retake mainland China from the communists. At present, the KMT holds a more ambiguous position on reunification with mainland China.

5. Interviews with: In Chu Yuu of the pro-PRC Tokyo OCA, December 9, 1999; Wen Yao Quan of the pro-PRC Yokohama OCA, May 31, 1999.

and Canton. To assist each other, these Chinese typically formed "native place associations" (*huiguan*), which have traditionally "provided support to members, exploited trading links with their home province, and developed a monopoly within the Chinese community for particular goods and services."[6] Recent overseas Chinese in the Tokyo metropolitan area, in contrast, come from northeastern provinces of China (formerly Manchuria) such as Liaoning and Heilongjiang.[7]

Overseas Chinese Associations were established as self-help groups to assist resident Chinese in adapting to life in Japan. Their activities typically include consultations on marriage and lifestyle in Japan. They also organize social gatherings with members, trips to the PRC or Taiwan, and Chinese festivals in Japan. They publish their own newspapers and operate Chinese schools (with their own parent-teacher associations and alumni associations), youth clubs, women clubs, economic associations (such as chambers of commerce), and public meeting halls. Their goals focus on the promotion of Chinese educational, cultural, and business activities in Japan.[8] The pro-PRC Yokohama OCA has the promotion of Chinese (PRC) patriotism as one of its major goals, while the pro-Taiwan Tokyo OCA encourages its members to participate in Taiwan's elections (and to vote for the DPP) by offering to help pay for their travel costs.[9]

Thai Ethnic Associations.   Thais in Japan have established two ethnic associations, the Thai Student Association in Japan and the Association of Thai Professionals in Japan, to promote cultural activities and socialization among Thai students and professionals. Thai students, many of them from elite families, established the Thai Students Association in Japan as an exclusive social club with "patronage" from the Thai royal family. Members include students who have received scholarships from the Japanese or Thai governments, as well as rich students who come to study

---

6. Andrea Varsishht, "A Model Minority: The Chinese Community in Japan," in Michael Weiner, ed., *Japan's Minorities: The Illusion of Homogeneity* (London: Routledge), 108–139 (120ff).

7. Robert Efird estimates that over 100,000 Chinese, or a quarter of the Chinese in Japan, are family members of Japanese orphans from Manchuria. See his "Japan's War Orphans and New Overseas Chinese: History, Identification and (Multi)ethnicity," (Ph.D. diss., University of Washington, 2004), 171.

8. Interview with Seki Hiroyoshi of the Yokohama OCA (Taiwan), May 28, 1999.

9. Interview with Wen Yao Quan of the Yokohama OCA (PRC), May 31, 1999.

in Japan with their family's financial support. Even among the government scholarship students, most come from affluent families in Bangkok. The Association of Thai Professionals in Japan mostly consists of former Thai students who have completed their studies in Japan and decided to work in Japan for a few years after graduation. Members of this group are mostly former members of the Thai Students Association in Japan.[10]

Both these associations focus their activities on helping people in Thailand. The members of the Association of Thai Professionals in Japan focus on acquiring technological knowledge and professional experience in Japan to bring back to Thailand when they eventually return. During the early 1990s, the Thai Students Association in Japan helped impoverished people in Thailand by collecting used clothing from Thais in Japan and sending it to various slums in Bangkok and impoverished rural areas in Thailand. It also created a scholarship fund to assist poor students in rural Thailand. Both associations organize religious and secular ethnic festivals and celebrations. They also hold cultural activities, sports events, and entertainment activities with Japanese. These activities have united the legal Thai community in Japan and enabled these associations to become providers of social welfare services to the underprivileged people in Thailand. Neither association, however, has become an institutionalized voice for all Thais in Japan.

Ethnic Associations Critical of Their Home State

Vietnamese Ethnic Associations. The Vietnamese community is similarly divided along ideological lines between pro-government Vietnamese (recent students and technical trainees) and anti-government Vietnamese (former "boat people" or refugees who departed communist Vietnam en masse during the late 1970s). The latter group, which is the majority, can be separated further into Catholics, who join the Zainichi Vietnamese Catholic Association (*Giao Doan Cong Giao Viet Nam tai Nhat*), and Buddhists, who join the Vietnamese Buddhist Association in Japan (*Giao Hoi Phat Giao Viet Nam Thong Nhat Hai Ngoai tai Nhat Ban*). Many anti-government

---

10. Interview with Vuthichai Ampornaramveth of the Association of Thai Professionals in Japan, May 19, 2000.

Vietnamese in Japan become members of the Vietnamese Association in Japan (*Hiep Hoi Nguoi Viet tai Nhat*); they adamantly oppose the communist regime in Hanoi and try to mobilize former Vietnamese "boat people" against the home government through the distribution of monthly news magazines. This group also offers Vietnamese language classes to Vietnamese children and sponsors various cultural activities such as the celebrations of the New Year, the Vietnamese New Year (*Tet*), and the anniversary of the founding of Vietnam (by King Hung Voung 2,800 years ago and not by Ho Chi Minh).

In 2000, six Vietnamese ethnic associations joined to form the Network of Vietnamese People in Japan (*Zainichi betonamujin renraku kyōgikai*) with Father Pham Dinh Son, a naturalized Japanese and Catholic priest, as its leader. Members of the group maintain that they are "lucky people" who were able to successfully leave Vietnam and assert that they should do something for those unfortunate people in Vietnam who could not.[11] Therefore, the group occasionally holds bazaars to raise money for street children and orphans in Vietnam as part of its Children Rights Campaign. More important, this group is the only immigrant ethnic association that was established for the purpose of helping foreigners in need, including all overstayed foreigners. About half of their consulting services on legal, immigration, medical, and family matters are provided to non-Vietnamese foreigners.

Burmese Ethnic Associations.   Burmese in Japan have formed several groups, including the Burmese Office Japan (with funding from Rengo), the Federation Trade Union of Burma (FTUB)—Japan, the League for Democracy in Burma (LDB), the People's Forum on Burma (PFB), the National Democratic Front (NDF), and the National League for Democracy—Liberated Area (NLD-LA). However, none of these groups assists Burmese in Japan. They concentrate their activities on the democratization process in Burma, lobbying the Japanese government (through Rengo and the Democratic Party of Japan [DPJ]) and promoting awareness and publicity about the abuses of the Burmese military government.

---

11. Interview with Father Pham Dinh Son of the Network of Vietnamese People in Japan in Kawasaki, November 1, 2005.

On July 17, 2003, for example, they organized a demonstration in downtown Tokyo, which was attended by about 300 people, to call for the release of Aung San Suu Kyi.[12] In 2004, the FTUB-Japan called for the release of two labor activists who received death sentences on November 28, 2003, for their labor organizing activities in Burma. Members of the FTUB-Japan argue that the two labor activists were unjustly arrested and sentenced without proper legal representation.[13]

The Burmese refugee community is organized into various ethnic minority groups, including Shan, Mon, Karen, Arakan, Kachin, Chin, Naga, Palaung, and Rakhine. In 2003, representatives from these highly political, non-Burmese ethnic groups joined together to form the Association of United Nationalities in Japan (AUN) with the aim of publicizing the ongoing government abuses against its peoples and working to eventually overthrow the military dictatorship in Burma. At its monthly meetings, a representative from each ethnic minority group gives a report (in Burmese!) on the situation of its ethnic group in Burma and makes an appeal seeking cooperation from members of other ethnic minority groups. Members of the AUN regularly campaign in front of the Burmese embassy in Tokyo to criticize the Burmese government, such as the national military and the People's Assembly. As one AUN member stated: "The military regime is forcing the People's Assembly onto its people in order to legitimize military rule, although the National League for Democracy, which was led by Suu Kyi, overwhelmingly won the 1990 election. Therefore, the People's Assembly cannot be considered as valid."[14] Some groups also raise money in their ethnic communities in Japan and send it to their political ethnic organizations in Burma to support the military struggles against the repressive Burmese regime.[15] Burmese workers in Japan who encounter labor or immigration problems, however, typically turn to Japanese NGOs or community workers unions.

---

12. Interview with Muang Min Nyo of the Burma Office Japan in Tokyo, October 7, 2005; also see *Burma Journal* 3, no. 7 (2003): esp. 8–9.

13. "Biruma rōdōsha no jōkyō," [Situation of Burmese Workers], *Burma Journal* 4, no. 3 (2004): 5.

14. Interview with Mai Kyaw Oo of the Association of United Nationalities in Japan in Tokyo, October 30, 2005.

15. Interview with Sai Nyunt Maung of the Shan National for Democracy in Tokyo, October 30, 2005.

Filipino Ethnic Associations.   Filipino women married to Japanese men organize informal meetings in their neighborhoods and have created numerous Filipina wives clubs throughout Japan to promote cultural exchange and introduce the Philippines' culture and traditions to Japanese.[16] Some of these groups try to empower their members by focusing on providing support to one another, particularly on issues relating to the education and upbringing of their children. One unusual Filipina wives group, the Philippine Women's League of Japan, was organized in 1986 to "counter-attack the media blitz on the plight of Filipino women working in Japan as bar hostesses that was wreaking havoc on the Philippine image in Japan."[17] The League has a national chapter and six provincial chapters. Its activities include searching for lost relatives, counseling on marriage problems and immigration procedure, and providing shelter for battered Filipino wives. During the late 1990s, the group blasted the Philippine government for its "failure to address properly the unemployment problem" by not creating jobs. In 2007, some of the Women's League group leaders helped Amnesty International launch a campaign against political killings in the Philippines.

The Politics of Long-Distance Nationalism

On August 15, 1974, a second-generation, *zainichi* (Japan-born) Korean, Moon Se Kwang, assassinated South Korea's first lady on behalf of North Korea. The South Korean government claimed that Moon had been trained by special agents of North Korea and its ethnic association in Japan and that his intended target was President Park Chung Hee, whose regime he considered the main impediment to the unification of North and South Korea. This is an extreme example of a striking characteristic of many overseas Asians in Japan and their ethnic associations: identification with the culture, ideology, and, in many cases, the politics of an experienced

---

16. Interview with Rose Kawashima of Kapatiran in Tokyo, November 16, 2005. Also see Nobue Suzuki, "Between Two Shores: Transnational Projects and Filipina Wives in/from Japan," *Women's Studies International Forum* 23, no. 4 (2002): 431–444.

17. Philippine Women's League of Japan, http://japan.co.jp/~ystakei/pwll.html (accessed October 23, 1998).

or imagined homeland. In general, foreigners typically build a strong relationship with the homeland when they are not well integrated into the host society.[18]

Foreigners are prevented from participating in Japan's political life both by the lack of a policy to actively integrate foreigners into Japanese society and by institutional impediments created by the Japanese. Resident foreigners and permanent residents cannot vote or run for public office; they cannot hold membership in district welfare commissions, boards of education, or human rights commissions. Many are active in their immigrant ethnic associations, but until the mid-1990s, no institutional arrangement allowed these associations to participate in governmental bodies. As a result, the political focus of most immigrants and their associations has been on the politics of long-distance nationalism, either advancing or protesting the politics of their homelands. For example, the organizational goals for Mindan and Chōsen Sōren focus on: "strict defense of national [South Korea] policy" for Mindan and "peaceful [communist] unification of Korea" for Chōsen Sōren. In addition to fierce political activities against their ideological counterparts, these associations actively promote ethnic attachment to either South Korea or North Korea.[19] For most Vietnamese and Burmese groups, the central goal is to protest the ruling undemocratic regimes and to help promote democratization in their home countries. The Philippine Women's League of Japan also calls for Philippine government officials not to "burden other countries like Japan to provide jobs for Filipino workers. The government should now endeavor to create jobs and call fathers and mothers to come home and take direct supervision and care of their children."[20] The Japanese government, in turn, encourages legal foreigners to channel their energy in such efforts to promote long-distance nationalism through official recognition of their

---

18. Gabriel Sheffer, *Diaspora Politics: At Home Abroad* (Cambridge: Cambridge University Press, 2003).

19. The official goals of Mindan are (1) strict defense of the national (South Korean) policy; (2) protection of Korean rights and interests; (3) economic development; (4) cultural advancement; and (5) world peace and international friendship. Interview with Chung Mong-Joo of Mindan, December 8, 1999: The official goals for Chōsen Sōren include (1) peaceful unification of Korea; (2) protection of Korean racial rights; (3) promotion of racial education; and (4) normalization of relations between North Korea and Japan. Interview with So Chung-on of Chōsen Sōren, December 8, 1999.

20. Ibid.

associations and provision of public funds. This is because these efforts are premised on a kind of essentialism the Japanese endorse, as they further feed into a "we-Japanese" versus "they-Korean" or "they-Chinese" multiculturalism.

Benedict Anderson conceptualizes imagined communities abroad in terms of "long-distance nationalism."[21] For Anderson, being abroad allows some to express greater nationalism than being at home. Specifically, living abroad allows long-distance nationalists to engage in radical politics with no accountability. Well and safely positioned in industrialized and free societies, they can circulate propaganda *against* a home government that is seen as undemocratic or corrupt. Living legally in democratic societies, they need not fear reprisal—such as prison, torture, or even death—by the home government. Yet, they rarely pay taxes in their home country, they are not answerable to its judicial system, and they probably do not cast absentee ballots in its elections. This characterization aptly describes the activities of many small, secular Vietnamese and Burmese associations in Japan, which engage in radical politics to bring liberal democracy to their home countries. However, it is less apt in describing the activities of other groups.

While Anderson's long-distance nationalists speak mostly *against* their states, his concept can be extended to many legal foreigners in Japan who selflessly express love for their homelands and actively support the politics and ideology of their home states through their ethnic associations. Large ethnic associations of zainichi Koreans and Chinese, for example, focus on nationalistic activities relating to North or South Korea, mainland China, or Taiwan, despite the fact that some, especially North Korean members, have little, if any, experience with their "home" lands. For them, "home" is more *imagined* through their ethnic associations than *experienced* by them or even their ancestors. Most of the ancestors of members of the North Korean ethnic association, for example, come from South Korea, and yet they proclaim in a lesson to first graders that North Korea is a "paradise on earth" or "the most beautiful country in the world," where "people live…very happily."[22]

21. Benedict Anderson, "Exodus," *Critical Inquiry* 20 (Winter 1994): 314–327.
22. Sonia Ryang, *North Koreans in Japan: Language, Ideology, and Identity* (Boulder: Westview Press, 1997), 127.

As such, the concept of long-distance nationalism includes supportive as well as critical forms of political activities with implications for the
host country as well as the homeland. As Anderson suggests, critical long-
distance nationalists can disrupt authoritarian practices of their home
governments. However, *long-distance nationalism* as a concept can be interpreted more richly. This analysis develops this concept by demonstrating that (1) *supportive* long-distance nationalists can *help* their home
governments, and (2) both *critical* and *supportive* long-distance nationalists
make only limited contributions to multicultural democracy in their *host*
countries.

Immigrant Ethnic Associations and Home Governments

While critical long-distance nationalists undermine their home governments, supportive long-distance nationalists can help their home governments in a variety of ways. Chōsen Sōren and Mindan promote ethnic
attachment to North Korea and South Korea, respectively, through
(1) political participation of elite associative members in the home country's politics; (2) official exchange of gifts, letters, and financial assistance
with their "home" governments; and (3) the administration of their respective Korean Schools.[23]

First, certain prominent members of Chōsen Sōren and Mindan pos-
sess high-level political influence in the government of North Korea and
South Korea, respectively. Members of the People's Congress of North
Korea have included seven of Chōsen Sōren's high-ranking administrators, the president, and three vice presidents of Chōsen Sōren, the rector
of the Korean University (*Chōsen daigaku*), the president of the Dong-Hai
(Eastern Sea) Association, and the director of the Women's Association.
Jang Chul, the former president of Chōsen Sōren, has been a member of
the North Korean Politburo since the 1970s and currently holds a senior
position within the government. Similarly, members of Mindan have been
elected in the South Korean National Congress. Yeonja Choi is the most
recent congressman with a Mindan background.

---

23. On the promotion of ethnic attachment of Koreans in Japan to North and South Korea,
see Hai Kyung Jun, "The Role of the Home Country in Shaping Assimilation and Attachment:
The Case of Koreans in Japan" (master's thesis, Massachusetts Institute of Technology, 1996).

Second, Korean ethnic associations also promote ethnic attachment with their home governments through official exchanges of gifts, letters, and financial assistance. For example, the South Korean Central Intelligence Agency (KCIA) claimed that Chōsen Sōren regularly sends about 40 billion yen (US$367 million) to North Korea every year for the celebration of Kim Il Sung's birthday.[24] Chōsen Sōren has sent automobiles, medical instruments, electronic devices, and other manufacturing products to North Korea. For Kim Jong Il's 1999 inauguration as the head of North Korea, Chōsen Sōren sent 800 million yen (US$7.3 million) as a congratulatory gift. Similarly, Mindan has sent monetary gifts to South Korea, albeit at far smaller sums than Chōsen Sōren to North Korea. Between 1963 and 1995, Mindan sent over 52 million U.S. dollars to South Korea.[25] When the financial crisis hit South Korea in late 1997, Mindan launched a campaign to send remittances into the country; between December 1997 and May 1999, Mindan sent 78 billion yen (US$715 million) to South Korea. In the past decade, most of the money that Mindan has sent to South Korea has gone into relief funds for victims of natural disasters such as flood and fire.

In response, North and South Korean governments maintain close relations with Chōsen Sōren and Mindan respectively. North Korean leaders customarily send telegrams and personal letters to Chōsen Sōren during every New Year celebration, anniversary of the organization, and other festivities. The North Korean government sent over 45 billion yen (US$413 million) to support Korean education in Japan between 1957 and 2005.[26]

---

24. For Kim Il Sung's sixtieth birthday (1972), Chōsen Sōren built and donated a glassworks and a textile factory to North Korea. For his sixty-fifth birthday (1977), it built and donated an instant noodle manufacturing facility. For his seventieth birthday (1982), Chōsen Sōren sent 400 delegates (who each paid 200 million yen) and 350 zainichi Koreans (who each paid 250,000 yen plus 30,000 to 50,000 yen for Kim Il Sung's birthday present). The monetary gift from Chōsen Sōren totaled more than 321 million U.S. dollars (calculated at the 1981 exchange rate). For his eightieth birthday (1992), Chōsen Sōren donated 4 billion yen (US$32 million) to the construction of a one-ton ship, *Man-Kyung-Ho 92,* and sent 650 zainichi Koreans with over 627 million U.S. dollars. Ibid.

25. About 45 million U.S. dollars went for support of the 1988 Seoul Olympics. Over 2.5 million U.S. dollars went to various construction projects such as the Independence Memorial Hall, the Peace Dam, and the Foreign Students Abroad Hall. The rest was sent as relief for national disasters in South Korea. Mindan also sent over 420,000 U.S. dollars to support the National Defense of South Korea between 1972 and 1983. Mindan, ed., *Kankoku mindan 50 nen no ayumi,* 27.

26. Chōsen Sōren, *Chōsen sōren,* 55.

Interestingly, in 1999, Kim Jong Il sent 100 of the 800 million yen that he received from Chōsen Sōren as a congratulatory gift for his inauguration back to the group for its scholarship fund. Similarly, South Korea has provided financial support for Mindan, sending 100 million yen (US$917,000) for education during the period of 1945 through 1960. To help Korean victims of the Hanshin Earthquake in 1995, the South Korean government sent Mindan 11 billion yen (US$100 million).[27] The financial support from the South Korean government to Mindan goes primarily to the maintenance and administration of Mindan headquarters and branches.[28] In 1977, the Park administration paid for the construction of a new Mindan headquarters in Tokyo, which now shares the same building as some offices of the South Korean embassy in Japan.

Third, to promote ethnic attachment of the zainichi Koreans to North Korea and South Korea, Chōsen Sōren and Mindan have built several Korean schools and urge their members to send their children to these schools. Chōsen Sōren sponsors 45 kindergartens, 62 elementary schools, 38 middle schools, 11 high schools, and 1 university.[29] And its Central Education Institute works closely with the North Korean government to oversee the direction of Korean education in Japan. Portraits of Kim Il Sung and Kim Jong Il hang in most classrooms and inside all university dormitories. The North Korean government encourages Chōsen Sōren members to study the Korean language and history at Korean schools in Japan as part of its "loyalty education subjects." A 1983 fourth grade textbook, for example, contains a lesson that begins by thanking Kim Il Sung for "endless happiness and joy" and urges the fourth graders "to safeguard our Respected and Beloved Leader Marshal Kim Il Sung with our own lives and to become your faithful soldiers. . . . We would walk through fire and jump into water if it were demanded to fulfill your precious teachings!"[30] The majority of the lessons stress patriotism to North Korea and loyalty to Kim Il Sung. The North Korean government has historically supplied

---

27. Interview with Chung Mong-Joo of Mindan, December 8, 1999.

28. Mindan, ed., *Kankoku mindan 50 nen no ayumi.*

29. Chōsen Sōren, *Chōsen sōren,* 57. The number of these Korean ethnic schools has steadily decreased since 1990, from 68 kindergartens, 81 elementary schools, 56 middle schools, 12 high schools, and 1 university. Chōsen Sōren, *Chōsen sōren* (Tokyo: Chōsen Sōren, 1991), 78–81.

30. Quoted in Ryang, *North Koreans in Japan,* 30.

these schools with textbooks from North Korea designed specifically for Korean children living in Japan. Chōsen Sōren reformed the curriculum in 1993, but it continues to stress patriotism and loyalty to the fatherland. Students at these schools wear uniforms that distinguish them from Japanese and Mindan-sponsored Korean students, with female students wearing traditional Korean clothing called *chima jeogori* (a white shirt with an ankle-length black or blue dress). Students at Chōsen Sōren schools typically befriend their Korean schoolmates and isolate themselves from the larger Japanese society. The North Korean government advocates for this isolation to promote the loyalty of zainichi Koreans to North Korea. However, most zainichi North Koreans (86 percent) attend Japanese high schools because graduates of Chōsen Sōren–sponsored high schools cannot take entrance examination for Japanese national universities. For those Koreans who graduate from Korean high schools, Chōsen Sōren established the Korea University in Tokyo on April 10, 1956, to give them an opportunity to receive a communist education (e.g., the revolutionary history of Kim Il Sung) at the university level and administrative training at Chōsen Sōren offices. Professors at Korea University are appointed by the North Korean government. Graduates typically take a graduation trip to North Korea and often find employment at Chōsen Sōren schools, headquarters, branches, and local offices.[31]

In 1957, having noticed the propaganda disseminated by the North Korean regime through Chōsen Sōren, the South Korean government began to send money to Mindan to fund educational programs at Mindan-sponsored Korean schools. In 1963, after Park Chung Hee took over as president, he became concerned with the ethnic education of South Koreans in Japan. To counter the "communist" Korea University, the Park administration initiated the Mo-Kook-Soo-Hak program, an educational program for overseas Koreans who were interested in studying in South Korea. Mindan operates four Korean schools in Japan. The Tokyo Korean School, which uses the same textbooks as those used in South Korea, is the largest of the four, with 868 students in 1996. However, many students at this school are children of Korean diplomats and businessmen who are temporarily living in Japan. In 1996, only 13.2 percent of the students were

---

31. Ryang, *North Koreans in Japan,* 37.

children of zainichi Koreans. Most children of Mindan members attend Japanese schools and therefore have many Japanese friends.[32]

Mindan and Chōsen Sōren have been changing as a result of the passage of generations—with less activity toward homeland politics. Their memberships have suffered as newer generations of Koreans view that these organizations remain attached to Korea. The reconciliation agreement between the two associations in May 2006 signaled a change to concentrate their institutional activities on improving the lives of zainichi Koreans in Japan. This shift will likely generate a more unified demand from zainichi Koreans for more rights and services in Japan, which potentially could improve Japan's multicultural democracy.

In the case of Chinese ethnic associations, financial links between the home country and the ethnic association foster ethnic attachment to their homelands. A large proportion of the operation funds for these groups comes from the Taiwanese and PRC governments. At the same time, both OCAs in Japan regularly donate money to their homelands for support during natural disasters. Most important, they have established close business ties between their members and homeland governments. Business and political networking is the central concern for these Chinese associations. The fact that four Chinese companies occupy four floors of the eight-story Tokyo Overseas Chinese Hall illustrates the importance of the pro-PRC group for business networking, ironic as it may seem. The representative of the pro-Taiwan group, Jan Dershun, who is also the president of Fuji Coin Company, boasts extensive business and political ties with both Taiwanese and Japanese companies and high-level government officials. His Fuji Coin office in Kanda, Tokyo, displays several pictures of him with former and current presidents of Taiwan. Dershun avers that the association needs to have good political ties with government officials of Taiwan "in order to ease business operation for overseas Chinese and Japanese investors in Taiwan."[33] Not surprisingly, the president of Taiwan appointed Dershun to head Taiwan's Overseas Chinese Affairs Commission soon after the DPP was voted into office in 2000.[34]

---

32. Mindan, ed., *Kankoku mindan 50 nen no ayumi*, 77.

33. Interview with Jan Dershun of the Tokyo OCA (Taiwan), May 24, 2000.

34. The president also appointed another prominent Tokyo OCA member, Chin Meilin, as his political consultant.

Similar to Korean ethnic associations, each OCA operates its own Chinese schools. Taiwanese (Formosa) schools follow the ideological position of an independent Taiwan and have close political ties to the DPP. Taiwanese schools in Tokyo, Yokohama, and Osaka teach their students about Taiwan prior to the arrival of the Koumintang of China (KMT) to the island and hope to build a Taiwanese identity that is disconnected with mainland China.

Vietnamese ethnic associations offer Vietnamese language education to members' children at their offices. They also organize educational trips for Vietnamese children in Japan to visit Vietnam in an effort to help these children, who are without nationality, establish a sense of identity.

For Thai ethnic associations, an ethnic attachment to Thailand is reinforced through "patronage" from the royal family, as in the case of the Thai Student Association. Members are invited to attend the annual New Year party at the Thai embassy in Tokyo. The ambassador and Thai bureaucrats regularly participate in the activities of the Association of Thai Professionals. Moreover, these associations provide members with opportunities to maintain ties with Thailand and to meet their fellow-Thais with similar social class backgrounds. Since both associations keep and regularly update directories of their current and former members, members in both of these Thai associations maintain their networks for business or professional purposes even after they have returned to Thailand.

Finally, many immigrant ethnic associations publish, support, or distribute ethnic media. The media of the ideological pro-home government ethnic associations often contain articles that attack the governments associated with their archrival ethnic associations and others that build national pride and solidarity.among members. Articles in the ethnic media of the political anti-government ethnic associations are usually critical of the political situation in their home countries. In the case of the pro-government ethnic associations, their ethnic media typically provide political news of their homelands and the latest gossip about the most popular stars back home. These publications also contain advertisements for cheap international phone cards, international cargo delivery services, international money transfers, and grocery stores that sell food products from home. All this information helps foreigners stay emotionally connected to their home country while assisting them in adapting to life in Japan.

Immigrant Ethnic Associations and Democracy

What impact do legal foreigners and their immigrant ethnic associations have on Japan's multicultural democracy? In general, although these immigrant associations make less of a contribution to multicultural democracy than immigrant rights NGOs, they do have a limited positive role. For example, immigration ethnic associations help promote cultural citizenship (or cultural attributes necessary for acceptance as members of the national community).[35] They function to preserve immigrants' cultures and to reproduce distinctive identities while achieving socioeconomic and cultural integration.[36] These associations organize religious and secular ethnic festivals and celebrations. They also hold cultural activities, sport events, and entertainment activities. Often, these "self-help groups" offer home-country language classes and some provide social welfare services. Large ethnic associations, particularly those for Koreans and Chinese, provide employment and social capital to their members through the offering of loans from their affiliated financial institutions and mediating interactions with Japanese-run businesses. Since the mid-1990s, these associations have become an institutionalized voice for legal immigrants as they advance demands and set political agendas to further their claims in local deliberative institutions. As such, they can ensure interest representation and policy formulation with the goal of promoting the rights and status of their legal ethnic constituencies.

Although immigrant ethnic associations provide ethnic identification, social welfare services, employment opportunities, and representation to legal immigrants, their contribution to the development of Japan's multicultural democracy is limited. Legal foreigners often choose to involve themselves mostly with their own ethnic associations, which serve either as institutional and cultural extensions of their "imagined" homelands (as in the case of Korean, Chinese, and Thai ethnic associations) or as an

---

35. Aihwa Ong, *Flexible Citizenship: The Cultural Logics of Transnationality* (Durham: Duke University Press, 1999).

36. See inter alia John Rex, Daniele Joly, and Czarina Wilpert, eds., *Immigrant Associations in Europe* (Aldershot: Gower, 1987); Shirley Jenkins, ed., *Ethnic Associations and the Welfare State: Services to Immigrants in Five Countries* (New York: Columbia University Press, 1988); Yasemin Nuhoglu Soysal, *Limits of Citizenship: Migrants and Postnational Membership in Europe* (Chicago: University of Chicago Press, 1994), esp. chap. 6.

arena for radical politics either for or against their home governments. In promoting their members' attachment to the "home" lands, ethnic associations also foster psychological and political detachment from Japanese society, thereby weakening national identity.[37] Such immigrant ethnic associations can further undermine multicultural democracy because of the inequality they foster within their own ethnic groups. Immigrant ethnic associations do not foster immigrant loyalty to the host country, engagement in public discourse, or exposure of host exclusionary policies.

Some immigrant ethnic associations serve as a force for disunity rather than cultivating national unity in the face of Japan's increasing social diversity. For instance, Chōsen Sōren's opposition to suffrage in local elections for permanent residents aims to further distance its members from Japanese society. Historically, as discussed above, both Mindan and Chōsen Sōren opposed all policies or actions that might lead to assimilation, with some members even rejecting proposals to reduce barriers to citizenship. Although Mindan now supports local voting rights for permanent residents, members of Chōsen Sōren oppose suffrage and insist that their members, who are North Korean citizens residing in Japan, stay out of Japan's internal affairs.[38] They fear that voting rights will promote the assimilation of zainichi Koreans into Japanese society and weaken their political ties to North Korea.[39]

Immigrant ethnic associations rarely participate in Japan's local politics, a situation problematic for the development of multicultural democracy and justice. Although Mindan and Chōsen Sōren participated in several local political movements, independent, smaller civic groups led the effort.[40] Mindan and Chōsen Sōren, indeed, played an important role in the opposition to the closure of Korean schools (1948), the opposition to

37. On the importance of national identity to a deliberative democratic setting, see David Miller, *On Nationality* (Oxford: Oxford University Press, 1995), 132.

38. Korean in Japan Human Rights Committee, ed., *Zainichi chōsenjin jinken hakusho* [White Paper on Human Rights of Zainichi Koreans] (Tokyo: Chōsen Seinensha, 1996), 191–198.

39. Meanwhile, the government of North Korea tries to push Chōsen Sōren to pursue a Chōsenization policy, a policy to promote ethnic attachment of the zainichi Koreans to North Korea.

40. Higuchi Naoto, "Taikō to kyōryoku," [Confrontation and Cooperation], in Miyajima Takashi, ed., *Gaikokujin shimin to seiji sanka* [Foreign Residents and Political Participation] (Tokyo: Yushindo, 2000), 20–38 (3ff).

the Japan–South Korea agreement on the legal status of resident Koreans (1965), the opposition to the Alien School Act (1968), and the opposition to the revision of the Immigration Control Law between 1968 and 1975.[41] But most major gains in civil and social rights for resident Koreans resulted from the efforts of smaller, independent civic groups, who organized the protest against employment discrimination of the Hitachi Corporation (1970–1974), the campaign for the elimination of nationality requirements for professors of national and municipal universities (1975–1979), the campaign for the elimination of fingerprinting imposed on foreign residents (1980s), the campaign for the elimination of nationality requirements for public housing and child allowance (1970s), the campaign to revamp Japan's education policy for foreigners, and the campaign to provide financial aid for the aged excluded from the national pension system (1990s). For example, a group of resident Koreans organized the Council for Combating Discrimination against Ethnic People in Japan (*minzoku sabetsu to tatakau renraku kyōgikai,* or Mintōren) to protest employment discrimination in the Hitachi Corporation. In 1970, Hitachi offered a position to a zainichi Korean, Park Chong Seok, but later withdrew the offer after Park could not produce a copy of his family register. Because only Japanese are allowed to possess family registries in Japan, Park took Hitachi to court, accusing the corporation of racial discrimination in employment practices. The court decided in 1974 in his favor. Since then, situations for zainichi Koreans improved considerably; they have increasingly found work in work-site operations and low-rank office work in private companies.[42] Neither Mindan nor Chōsen Sōren supported Mintōren's campaign, which they viewed as fostering assimilation.

---

41. The movement to revamp Japan's educational policy for foreigners is an exception because Chōsen Sōren (then known as Chōren) launched this political campaign for the Freedom of Ethnic Education (*minzoku kyōiku no jiyūsei*) since 1948 when the Japanese government began to regulate Korean schools. The movement gained momentum in 1968, three years after the establishment of the Korea University. By 1994, the organization had successfully fought for the school children at Chōsen Sōren–sponsored high schools to be able to take the entrance examination in about 40 percent of Japan's private universities. During the same year, the Japan Railway began granting the same train discount for Korean schools' students as it does for Japanese schools' students. Korean in Japan Human Rights Protection Committee, ed., *Zainichi chōsenjin jinken hakusho,* 97–99.

42. Mintōren, *Zainichi kankokujin/chōsenjin no hosho jinkenhō* [A Law for Compensating and Respecting the Rights of Zainichi Koreans] (Tokyo: Shinkansha Mintōren, 1989), 136–138.

Independent civic groups also led the 1970s' and 1980s' effort to abolish nationality requirements for public service employees, such as municipal administrative personnel, teachers, and professors. The "movement to abolish governmental discrimination" (*gyōsei sabetsu teppai undō*) began when zainichi Koreans in Kawasaki City pressed city officials to abolish discrimination on public housing.[43] The movement spread to Osaka, where zainichi Koreans further demanded nondiscriminatory treatment toward their children at schools and that the application of national pension be extended to them. By 1978, the movement had expanded nationwide without the support of Mindan and Chōsen Sōren. Although the antidiscrimination campaigns gained support throughout Japan, "many of the changes toward Koreans made in the early 1980s are attributable to newly ratified international covenants."[44] Japan abolished state discrimination in public housing and extended its home loans to foreigners in 1980 after it signed the United Nations Treaty on Human Rights. After Japan ratified the United Nations Refugee Treaty in 1982, it improved treatment toward foreign children and extended the national pension to permanent foreign residents.

A multicultural democratic civil society demands some level of loyalty to the host country and empathy for citizens, compatriots, and other foreign residents.[45] An absence of loyalty to the host country can lead to a lack of willingness of foreigners to engage in public discourse, to demand greater public goods, and to expose and criticize exclusionary policies of the host society. With the exception of the Network of Vietnamese People in Japan, immigrant ethnic associations in Japan, however, tend to develop private, narrower concerns for their own ethnic groups. Korean ethnic associations, for instance, display social and political concerns for the improvement of Korean permanent residents in Japan while ignoring the plight of the newly arrived Asian workers, including South Koreans. When the Japanese government was revising the Immigration

---

43. Interview with an official of the Kawasaki City Government's Citizens Bureau, December 25, 1998.

44. Amy Gurowitz, "Mobilizing International Norms: Domestic Actors, Immigrants, and the Japanese State," *World Politics* 51 (1999): 413–445 (412ff).

45. On this point, see Iris Marion Young, *Inclusion and Democracy* (New York: Oxford University Press, 2000).

Control Law in 1990, Mindan submitted a request that the revision should not cause any disadvantage to permanent Korean residents in Japan.[46] Perhaps the only political activity conducted by Korean ethnic associations that made an impact on *all* foreigners was their campaign to abolish fingerprinting of foreigners for the alien registration process. During the 1980s, several Korean and Chinese ethnic associations organized demonstrations at the National Diet and various political party headquarters. In 1985, the Kawasaki City government became Japan's first city not to fingerprint its permanent foreign residents. In 1991, the central government officially exempted permanent residents from being fingerprinted. By 2000, the Japanese government abolished the practice of fingerprinting for registration purposes altogether. Note that Korean and Chinese ethnic associations asked only for permanent residents (zainichi foreigners) to be exempted. It was the *Japanese government* that decided in 2000 to exempt *all foreigners.*

Moreover, these ethnic associations offer little respect and support for their co-ethnics or co-nationals, despite their loyalty to the homeland. For example, the recent influx of Korean newcomers into Japan may pose a challenge for the Korean ethnic associations because both Chōsen Sōren and Mindan set exclusionary conditions for their membership.[47] Since Korean newcomers are not *zainichi* but *rainichi* (which literally means "coming to Japan"), they do not meet the criteria for membership in these groups. Chōsen Sōren ignores recent Korean newcomers in part because they come from South Korea. Mindan also pays little attention to newly arrived compatriots, many of whom have overstayed their visas. A Mindan official claims with little compassion that "*rainichi* Korean workers usually go to the South Korean embassy for assistance. Mindan has little experience in helping Korean workers, since most *zainichi,* until recently, did not work in Japanese corporations. Instead, they have been working in their own businesses, particularly running *yakiniku* restaurants and *yakitori*

46. Kajita Takamichi, "The Challenge of Incorporating Foreigners in Japan: 'Ethnic Japanese' and 'Sociological Japanese,'" in Myron Weiner and Tadashi Hanami, eds., *Temporary Workers or Future Citizens? Japanese and U.S. Migration Policies* (New York: New York University Press, 1998), 120–147 (140ff).

47. Kou Hyonmi, "Yureru zainichi korian shakai," [Rocking Zainichi Korean Society] *AWC Tsushin* 9 (June 1999): 10.

stalls."[48] Overall, zainichi Koreans have done little to assist recently arrived and overstayed Koreans.

Although the number of overstayed Chinese has steadily increased in recent years, Chinese ethnic associations also try to distance themselves from illegal foreign workers and offer no services to Chinese newcomers. They do not want the Japanese police to suspect their legitimate organizations of conducting illegal activities, particularly during a time of numerous illegal entries of Chinese workers and media hype on crimes committed by Chinese. The pro-Taiwan Tokyo OCA, in fact, stays completely out of providing employment-related services.[49] Like the Korean ethnic associations, Chinese ethnic associations had little experience in assisting Chinese workers, for most zainichi Chinese worked in their own restaurants and other service-related businesses. In addition, neither OCA in Yokohama assists Chinese newcomers on labor or immigration problems because many owners of the two hundred Chinese restaurants in Yokohama's Chinatown, who are OCA members, employ (and probably exploit) newcomers in their restaurants.

The same can be said for the Thai ethnic associations. In 1993, a Japanese man approached the chair of the Social Service Committee of the Thai Student Association in Japan and asked for help with translations for detained Thai women in prisons. People in the Association advised the chair not to get involved because of what had happened to another Thai student who had volunteered for similar services. According to their story, *yakuza* disapproved of this young student's involvement and decided to teach him a lesson by sending illegal drugs from Thailand (through their gang connections in Thailand) to his apartment. Consequently, he was arrested and charged for drug trafficking. Up to this day, the Thai ethnic associations do nothing to help their illegal compatriots in Japan; their activities are concentrated on helping people in Thailand.[50]

Similarly, members of the Philippines Women's League of Japan, who are mostly women with Japanese spouses and thus "legal" aliens, feel that

48. Interview with Chung Mong-Joo of Mindan, December 8, 1999.

49. Interview with Jan Dershun of the Tokyo OCA (Taiwan), May 24, 2000.

50. Some Thai students and professionals volunteer to help illegal Thai workers in Japan, but they do it on an individual basis or through the Japanese NGOs. This was the case of Romdej through SHARE, Busaya through Women's Shelter HELP, and Purapaporn through AMDA International Medical Center.

illegal Filipino workers sully the reputation of all Filipinos. In their own words, "we are fed up with being identified as domestic helpers,...mail-order brides, and worst, as prostitutes." For them, "to tolerate, grant recognition and support to illegal Filipino migrant workers, most of whom do not even have proper identities and passports, is like saying that there is nothing wrong with Filipinos stealing in foreign lands as long as they remit their loots to the Philippines. We cannot allow ourselves to be part of such racket and a farce!"[51] Due to their work or personal ties with the Japanese police, League leaders often encounter Filipinos locked up in prisons and may have developed a biased view of their illegal compatriots. Two executive members of the League have close ties with the Japanese police. Takei Yoko works as an interpreter/translator for the police, court, and prosecutor's office in the Kanto area. The auditor, Ester Iinaga, is married to a former policeman from Kyoto. They are also "opposed to the deployment of Filipino workers overseas, particularly women being sent to Japan as bar hostesses. We have reasons to believe that the deployment of Filipino workers abroad had caused more social problems and economic woes."[52] Yuko Takei, the chairperson of the League, insists that "contrary to claims by supporters of illegal foreign migrant workers in Japan, a majority of the illegal Filipino migrants are not innocent but willing victims of exploitation by both Filipino and Japanese recruiters."[53]

In short, ethnic associations occasionally make self-interested political demands of the Japanese government while demonstrating an unwillingness to communicate or cooperate with others from the same ethnic background. Ethnic difference then becomes more and more exclusive with immigrant ethnic associations. As these associations make private demands, they destroy public commitment to a common good. In addition to a lack of unity within each ethnic group, dialogue among different groups is rare. Although ethnic media flourish in Japan, they are printed almost exclusively in their native languages, with the exception of some articles published in English by Filipino groups. As a result, since most foreigners and Japanese cannot read print media from other ethnic groups, these media rarely engage the general public in critical discussion. This

---

51. Philippine Women's League of Japan, http://japan.co.jp/~ystakei/pwl1.html (accessed October 23, 1998).

52. Ibid.

53. Ibid.

retribalization of foreigners into exclusive immigrant ethnic associations makes dialogue difficult both within and among different ethnic groups, impeding the development of deliberative democracy.

Some immigrant ethnic associations further undermine multicultural democracy because they foster inequality within their ethnic group. The Thai ethnic associations, for example, often function as social institutions for reproducing social and class hierarchy that exists in Thailand among their co-nationals. They not only refuse to help overstayed Thai workers but also look down on overstayed Thais who perform dirty and socially degrading work. This attitude is most obvious during the annual *Songkran* (Thai New Year) festival on April 13th when Thai students, professionals, and illegal workers come together to celebrate, purchase Thai food, and watch various Thai performing arts. The Thai Student Association in Japan typically organizes this celebration in a Buddhist temple in Tokyo, and several thousand Thai workers attend. Upperclass students and professionals usually gather to watch performing arts such as performances of Thai traditional court instruments, while workers who hold dirty, dangerous, and difficult jobs gather to see *muay thai* (Thai kick boxing), a martial art popular and associated with people from the rural regions. These two social groups rarely mingle. In general, immigrant ethnic associations do not appear to undermine class solidarity as some Marxian theorists have expressed concern.[54] On the contrary, these institutions maintain their group exclusivity and fail to unite foreigners with the same ethnic background behind the common dream of a society that meets everyone's basic needs.

Finally, as a consequence of being closely attached to their "home" lands and less loyal to Japan, these ethnic associations can be targets of attack by natives who may see them as representative institutions of foreign governments, rather than organizations that help immigrants. For example, because North Korea does not have diplomatic relations with Japan, Chōsen Sōren functions as the "unofficial embassy" of the North Korean government in Japan. Kim Il Sung negotiated with the Japanese government through Chōsen Sōren on repatriation of Koreans to North Korea

---

54. On this concern, see David Harvey, *Justice, Nature, and the Geography of Difference* (Oxford: Blackwell, 1996), esp. chap. 12.

(*hokusō jigyō*) during the late 1950s and early 1960s. Similarly, the pro-PRC Tokyo OCA functioned as the "unofficial embassy" for the PRC before Japan normalized relations with the PRC in 1972. While these associations served as unofficial embassies of communist regimes, they received countless threats and demonstrations by Japan's right-wing, anti-communist groups.[55]

Public opinion and the government attitude toward Chōsen Sōren have turned increasingly hostile since North Korea launched a ballistic missile test over Japan in 1998, Japan had two encounters with North Korean spy boats in the Sea of Japan in 1999 and 2001, and it was confirmed in 2001 that North Korea had abducted Japanese citizens. Korean children attending Chōsen Sōren's schools have faced harassment, and regional offices of Chōsen Sōren have received many hundreds of threatening phone calls. Local citizens in those communities where the abductions took place have suspected members of the Chōsen Sōren's branch in the area of providing intelligence, particularly educational backgrounds, to the North Korean abductors.[56] Moreover, two conservative groups, the National Association for the Rescue of Japanese Kidnapped by North Korea (NARKIN) and the Association of Families of Victims Kidnapped by North Korea (AFVKN), have emerged to protest against North Korea and Chōsen Sōren. In early 2005, NARKIN filed a lawsuit against Kumamoto public officials for granting tax benefits to Chōsen Sōren for running its Kumamoto Korean Hall. Although the Kumamoto District Court ruled in Chōsen Sōren's favor, the group appealed to the Fukuoka High Court, which ruled in February 2006 that Chōsen Sōren's work does not benefit the general public. The presiding judge, Nakayama Hiroyuki, stated that Chōsen Sōren "conducts activities to benefit Korean residents of Japan under the leadership of North Korea and in unity with North Korea and is not an organization that in general benefits the society of our country."[57] Clearly, many Japanese do not view Chōsen Sōren as a civic group that

---

55. Interviews with So Chung-on of Chōsen Sōren, December 8, 1999; and In Chu Yuu of the Tokyo OCA (PRC), December 9, 1999.

56. Interview with a local resident in the Sado Island of the Niigata Prefecture, March 13, 2006.

57. *Japan Times,* February 3, 2006.

promotes trust and multicultural understanding among its members and Japanese citizens.

Because of this kind of perception, some government officials have tried to undermine Chōsen Sōren and force it into dissolution. In November 2001, the Public Security Investigation Agency raided Chōsen Sōren's central headquarters in the investigation of a controversial bond issue by a Chōsen Sōren–affiliated financial institution.[58] The Financial Services Ministry also required four Chōsen Sōren–affiliated financial institutions that were authorized to take over the failed *chōgin* (credit unions) to sever ties with Chōsen Sōren as a condition of receiving financial assistance from the Japanese government. In 2003, Tokyo Governor Ishihara Shintarō decided to end the group's tax-exempt status in Tokyo, and other local governments (with additional pressure from NARKIN and AFVKN) followed suit. In March 2006, the police raided another Osaka business group affiliated with Chōsen Sōren, ostensibly to investigate the 1980 abduction of Hara Tadaaki to North Korea.[59] A representative of Chōsen Sōren maintains that the group had nothing to do with the abductions and claims the raid to have been "a vicious manipulation of public sentiment...to deliberately link the abduction to Korean residents in Japan or [Chōsen Sōren]-affiliated groups."[60] In mid-2007, when the Resolution and Collection Corporation prepared to seize the headquarters of Chōsen Sōren as part of the government's debt-recovery efforts, Chōsen Sōren sought a buyer for the building. Ogata Shigetake, a former chief of the Public Security Intelligence Agency, teamed up with Mitsui Tadao, a realtor, to defraud Chōsen Sōren in purchasing its property without any intention of making a payment. They further swindled 484 million yen (US$4 million) from Chōsen Sōren by deceiving the organization that they needed money to cover penalties for pulling money out of investments in China to purchase the headquarters building.[61] Although Ogata admitted to these frauds, the Tokyo Metropolitan Government still imposed a real estate acquisition tax of 75 million yen (US$615,000) on Chōsen Sōren for its return of ownership.

---

58. For details of this incident, see *Shūkan Bunshun,* December 13, 2001.
59. *Asahi Shimbun,* March 24, 2006.
60. Ibid.
61. *Mainichi Shimbun,* August 8, 2007.

Metro authorities impounded the headquarters in August 2007 when Chōsen Sōren failed to pay this tax.

In sum, the contribution of immigrant ethnic associations to multicultural representative democracy in Japan is limited. These institutions do provide ethnic identification, social welfare services, employment opportunities, and representation to legal immigrants. However, they do not represent all members of their ethnic groups. The legal position of their members divides them from their illegal compatriots despite their shared ethnicity, their education, social background, and occupation. Preoccupied with ideological conflict within their own community, their home country's politics, and their own struggle to improve conditions for legal foreigners, Korean and Chinese associations close their doors on newly arrived foreign workers—many of whom come from mainland China and South Korea. These ethnic associations typically make public demands for their own private goods. Groups established by co-ethnics, such as the Association of Thai Professionals in Japan, struggle to improve conditions only for legal foreigners. Illegal foreign workers sometimes seek help from their legal compatriots, but at a personal level. Most interesting, some organizations, such as the Philippine Women's League of Japan, which was established by Filipinos themselves, are outspoken against illegal members of their own ethnic groups in Japan. Legal Asians fear that institutionalizing assistance to their illegal compatriots would jeopardize their own existence in Japan. Thus, existing ethnic associations tend to turn *away from* or *against* their illegal compatriots. Illegal foreign workers, in turn, do not go to these institutions for assistance.

Given this reality, where can immigrants turn to for help with their problems? Do immigrant ethnic associations provide the best institutional form to promote democratic multiculturalism in advanced industrialized countries?

4

Democracy of Illegals

Organizing Support for Illegal Foreigners

For illegal foreigners in Japan, who are unable to form their own support groups for fear of arrest and deportation and who lack significant support from their legal counterparts, assistance and advocacy have come largely from Japanese activists. Since 1983, immigrant rights activists have established approximately two hundred immigrant rights nongovernmental organizations (NGOs) to assist illegal foreigners, fighting for protection of their basic rights and provision of welfare services. Foreigner support groups formed by Japanese citizens provide a range of medical and legal services and work to increase public awareness of the conditions faced by overstayed foreigners. In some cases these associations play an active role in forcing local governments to be more responsive to the exploitation of unskilled foreign workers and more flexible in their treatment of them. Foreigners with problems seek activists out (not the other way around), because they are experienced problem solvers who have been involved in similar problem-solving activities and/or oppositional politics even though their primary focus may not have been immigrant issues.

Established political actors are unlikely to perceive the work of individual groups as a significant threat to the status quo. For example, a small group of doctors providing informal medical services to illegal workers is likely, if noticed at all at the regional or national level, to be seen as a harmless humanitarian effort. Such efforts may conflict with prevailing immigration requirements, but they do not pose a serious threat to existing laws or to the credibility of officials charged with their enforcement.

Some Japanese citizens, however, view these activists as accomplices in "illegal" activities. Indeed, a vast majority of pro-democracy movements have utilized activities that are considered illegal, including nonviolent forms of protests such as demonstrations, marches, and sit-ins. Such perceptions are bolstered by such instances as when *yakuza* seek legal consultations or medical assistance for their foreign "girlfriends." Furthermore, even established political actors become threatened when a number of local, task-specific associations begin to exchange information and publicize their work, which sets the stage for transformation of the social meanings associated with these groups and their activities. In so doing, associative activists advance a grassroots democracy in Japan by creating civic groups to actively support illegal foreigners and push for incremental social and political change.

Japanese activists promote more fully democratic ideals and institutions. These actors advocate for increased justice in the face of laws that are not always just. They make demands on powerful economic political institutions with public reasonableness. They evaluate and question the actions of those in authority. They foster public concern with the greater good by educating the public about the democratic principles of social justice and tolerance. Moreover, they cultivate unity in the face of increasing social diversity because some of their activities build trust between Japanese citizens and foreign residents. Although some members of society may view them as accomplices in a criminal act through their assistance to illegal foreigners, these Japanese activists advance social democracy.

Typology of Support Groups for Overstayed Foreigners

Foreigner support groups established by Japanese citizens include the following categories: faith-based groups, community workers' unions, women's support groups, lawyers' association NGOs, medical NGOs, and concerned citizens' groups.[1] Christians were the pioneers in establishing support groups to help foreign workers (Figure 4.1). In 1983, they began to provide counseling and shelters, mainly to Filipina women. By 1987, there were three Christian groups (Society in Solidarity with Foreigners in Japan, Yokosuka Citizens Group to Think about the Philippines and Japan, and Kapatiran), whose assistance had extended to various ethnic groups, with several concerned citizens' NGOs and a women's group evolving out of the Christian groups. At the end of the 1980s, as foreign men entered the construction and small manufacturing industries, some labor unions and lawyers' association NGOs began assisting foreign workers. After the 1990 revision of the Immigration Control Law and the oral directive to exclude overstayed foreign workers from the national health insurance (NHI) program, numerous medical and occupational safety centers formed foreign worker support groups. By the end of 1992, fifty-seven support groups existed in Tokyo and Kanagawa alone; since 1998, only four new groups have been created.

Faith-based Organizations

Most faith-based organizations that support overstayed foreigners are Christian groups. Although Christians compose only about 1 percent of the population in Japan, it was Christian organizations that first opened their doors to overstayed foreign migrants in distress during the early 1980s. On April 13, 1982, the Catholic Bishops' Conference of Japan (CBCJ) received a desperate call for help from a bishop in the Philippines to assist Filipina entertainers who had been forced into prostitution in Japan.[2] One year later, the CBCJ established the Asian Women in Japan Support Group, which later expanded to become the Society in Solidarity with Foreigners in Japan, to provide various services to both female and male foreigners. During the same year, the Yokosuka Citizens Group to Think about the

---

1. Some groups fall into two or more categories: For example, the women's shelter, House in Emergency of Love and Peace (HELP) can be categorized as either a Christian group or a women's support group. On such cases, I focus on the group's activities for my categorization.
2. Interview with Sister Ishii Yoshiko of the Society in Solidarity with Foreigners in Japan, August 27, 1998.

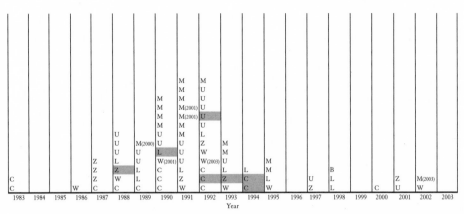

Figure 4.1. Year of Establishment for Foreigner Support Groups in Tokyo and Kanagawa.

C = Christian NGO
W = Women's shelter/NGO
Z = Concerned citizens' NGO
L = Lawyers' association NGO
U = Community workers' union
M = Medical support group
B = Buddhist support group
( ) = year incorporated as nonprofit organization (NPO)
Shaded area represents NGOs that no longer exist

Philippines and Japan was established to help suffering Filipina women in Japan. Since then, nine other Christian NGOs have emerged to help overstayed foreigners in Tokyo and Kanagawa. They include the Catholic Tokyo International Center (CTIC), the CTIC-Meguro, the Christian Coalitions on Refugees and Foreign Migrant Workers (Nankiren), the Yamasato Consulting Office, the Society to Struggle Together with Asian Workers in Japan, the Kapatiran, the Makoto Kaibigan, the Philippines Center, and the Pastoral Center for Migrants (PACEM; formerly the Yokohama Diocese: Solidarity Center for Migrants [SOL]). Many of their names summarily describe the goals or activities of these Christian groups. Typically, they help foreign workers with problems related to working conditions, such as unpaid salaries and occupational injuries, and with family and marriage problems. The Yamasato Consulting Office and the Philippines Desk of PACEM provide prison visits to foreign inmates. Each of these organizations was created as a branch of a certain Christian church or diocese, and many provide church services. These Christian groups typically do not have a membership system, as their staff and volunteers are generally church people. Most are subgroups of a religious corporation (*shūkyō hōjin*). Accordingly, Christian groups receive most of their funding from their churches.

The Christian influence on foreign migrant workers and foreigners support groups is tremendous.[3] Christian organizations support foreign migrant workers for two reasons. First, a large population of foreign workers in Japan, especially from Brazil, the Philippines, Peru, and Korea, are Christians. In 2000, the CBCJ estimated that 407,000 foreigners in Japan were Catholics.[4] Another 300,000 or so Koreans in Japan are Protestants. Second, Christians help foreigners because they hold an ethical view that all people—natives and foreigners—are equal as children of God.[5] According to the CBCJ, "these immigrants are brothers and sisters in Christ. This means that we do not merely welcome them, but strive to build up a community that respects differences."[6]

Faith-based support groups also include Buddhist groups, which are far fewer in number and emerged later. Āyus (Network of Buddhist Volunteers on International Cooperation) was formed in 1993, but did not begin to assist illegal foreigners in Japan until 1998. Āyus, which acquired nonprofit organization (NPO) status in 1999, offers HIV/AIDS consultation and referral services to foreign women in addition to providing financial support to numerous immigrant rights NGOs. As a result of Japanese mistrust engendered by the historical link between Buddhism and authoritarian power, Buddhists in Japan have hesitated to reach out beyond the typical social activities of religious organizations. In the early 1980s, however, after witnessing the outpouring of relief support by numerous Christian groups during the Cambodian refugee crisis, their embarrassment led Buddhist groups to begin supporting social welfare activities abroad, mostly in South and Southeast Asia.[7]

---

3. Interview with Father Akimoto Haruo of the Nagano's Society in Solidarity with Foreigners in Japan, June 27, 1998.

4. Catholic Bishop's Conference of Japan, http://www.cbcj.catholic.jp/jpn/data/00data.htm (accessed October 25, 2005).

5. On the Christian concept of equality and a history of Christian activism, see Irwin Scheiner, *Christian Converts and Social Protest in Meiji Japan* (Berkeley: University of California Press, 1970), esp. 147.

6. Catholic Bishops' Conference of Japan, "Seeking the Kingdom of God Which Transcends Differences in Nationality" (Tokyo: Mimeograph, 1993), 5.

7. Interview with Mika Edaki of Āyus in Tokyo, October 20, 2005.

Community Workers' Unions

The second and most confrontational type of foreign workers' support group is the community workers' union. Of these unions, about one third— particularly the Fureai Koto Union, the Foreign Workers' Branch of Zentōitsu (FWBZ), the Foreign Laborers' Union (FLU), and the Kanagawa City Union—were active during the 1990s in assisting overstayed foreign workers. Many unions subsequently divided their activities according to their respective strengths. On June 28, 1997, for example, the Yokohama Workers' Union, the Kanagawa City Union, and the Women Union-Kanagawa established a regional network called the Conference of Kana-gawa Unions (*Kanagawa Yunion Kyōgikai*). According to the Conference agreement, each union is to direct new members to the union that specializes in a specific field of labor disputes. For example, foreign workers are directed to the Kanagawa City Union, women workers to the Women Union-Kanagawa, and Japanese part-time workers to the Yokohama Workers' Union.[8] The Fureai Koto Union, the Sumida Union, and the Edogawa Union established a similar pact, creating the Shitamachi Union on September 15, 1998.[9] The Fureai Koto Union, 90 percent of whose members were foreign workers in 1998, concentrated on labor disputes involving foreign workers.[10] Membership in these groups ranges from 33 to 6,000 workers, and the membership fees provide all their operating funds.

Although enterprise unions are prominent in postwar Japan, not every worker can belong to one of these unions.[11] Strict rules govern who can and cannot join, and many companies do not allow part-time workers to join their enterprise unions. Furthermore, small companies often do not have unions. Hence, part-time workers and workers at small businesses turn to *community workers' unions;* that is, "a union where anyone, even a single

---

8. Interview with Yoshida Yukio of the Yokohama Workers' Union in Yokohama, September 30, 1998.

9. The official name of the Shitamachi Union is the Tokyo Eastern Region Union Conference (*Tōkyō Tōbu Chiiki Yunion Kyōgikai*).

10. Interviews with: Kase Junji of the Fureai Koto Union, May 18, 1998; Okamoto Testufumi of the Sumida Union, May 18, 1998; Udagawa Masahiro of the Edogawa Union, May 23, 1998; also see *Asahi Shimbun,* September 15, 1998.

11. See inter alia Andrew Gordon, *The Wages of Affluence: Labor and Management in Postwar Japan* (Cambridge: Harvard University Press, 1998); Ikuo Kume, *Disparaged Success: Labor Politics in Postwar Japan* (Ithaca: Cornell University Press, 1998).

individual, can join at any time" (*hitori demo itsu demo daremo haireru rōdō kumiai*). In other words, community workers' unions pick up those marginal workers who are not members of the enterprise unions. Because these organizations are open to anyone, foreign workers naturally benefit from this institutional arrangement. To mark their distinction from the mainstream workers' unions, most community workers' unions use the English word *union,* written in katakana (*yunion*), in their names rather than the traditional "*rōdō kumiai.*"

Community workers' unions provide labor consultation and dispute resolution. Foreign workers usually come to them to seek dispute settlement over nonpayment of wages, unjust dismissal, or compensation for work injuries. Once their disputes are resolved, they typically leave the workers' unions. In other words, foreign workers in Japan join these labor unions not to strengthen worker solidarity and the labor movement but to seek resolution of specific labor disputes with employers.

Women's Support Groups

Women's support groups offer temporary shelter and provide legal advice and women's advocacy, primarily to Filipina, Thai, and (increasingly) Chinese women. Only one (Saalaa) was established exclusively for foreign women. Because most of these groups provide welfare services to all women, local governments often turn to them for assistance, and two groups, Mizula and Saalaa, have acquired NPO status. Membership in these groups ranges from 12 to 2,500 people. They are funded through membership fees, lodging fees, church donations, and subsidies from local governments.

Ōshima Shizuko and her associates at the Japan Women's Christian Temperance Union (WCTU) were pioneers in assisting foreign women. The WCTU, which opposes extramarital sex and thus prostitution, founded Women's Shelter House in Emergency of Love and Peace (HELP), a support group, with prestigious foundation status (*zaidan hōjin*) in April 1986 to commemorate its centennial anniversary in Tokyo and to reaffirm its commitment to the needs of all women. HELP's first undertaking was the rescue of two Filipina women who had been forced to work in a snack bar in Nagoya without pay. In addition to HELP, women's support groups include the Asia-Japan Women's Resource Center, the Friends of Thai

Women Association, the Group Akakabu, the International Movement against All Forms of Discriminations and Racism (IMADR), the Kanagawa Women's Space (Mizula), the Women's Shelter (Saalaa), the Japan Network against Trafficking in Persons (JNATIP), and Kalakasan.

These names are creative and revealing. For example, *saalaa* is a Thai word for "resting place," while *kalakasan* is Tagalog for "strong." Mizula is taken from the English word, Ms., and adds the Japanese plural "la" to it. Akakabu has a particularly interesting background. *Akakabu* means "red turnip" in Japanese. This name is derived from a Russian folktale and children's story by Alexei Tolstoi entitled "The Big Turnip," which conveys a message of cooperation: to pull up the big, sweet turnip from the ground, a group of people (even long-time foes) must work together. The founder of Akakabu, Sakai Kazuko, wanted to name her cooperative *Okīkabu* (Big Turnip), but discovered that someone had already registered that name. She then chose *akakabu* (red turnip) because the turnip is red on the outside and white (symbolizing purity) on the inside. This was soon interpreted to mean "red" (i.e., communist). Posting a large portrait of Che Guevera in the window of its building strengthened that image.

Women's shelters provide assistance to women who have been abused and need temporary shelter.[12] While women are residing at the shelters, these groups arrange for the arrest of their abusive employers/partners, custody for their children, payment of medical compensation, and issuance of visas. For many abused, overstayed foreign women, turning to the government for assistance means little more than a ticket out of Japan, so these shelters offer a compassionate alternative, providing both help and confidentiality. Because the shelters have contact with the Thai and Philippine embassies, many Thai and Filipina women hear of them through their embassies. These shelters also have rescue teams to help foreign prostitutes and housewives escape from their captivity or residence. Members

---

12. The period of stay is typically two weeks and usually limited to one month. These shelters charge small fees for lodging and meals. HELP's fees are based on the individual's ability to pay. Saalaa asks 1,000 yen (US $9) per night for board and food, but allows exceptions. Mizula charges 1,500 yen (US $13.75) per night. There is no age limit for women, but accompanying male children are accepted only up to ten years of age. Foreign victims of domestic violence are often advised by activists to bring their children along to the shelter because there are legal advantages (i.e., in maintaining a legal residence status after a divorce) to foreign women when children are involved.

of foreign women's support groups also accompany foreign women to the police station to ensure that male officers do not ask intrusive and embarrassing questions that are not connected to the case.

Japanese women assist foreign women for two reasons. First, many members of these groups hold Christian values on fidelity and social justice. They hope to sway other Japanese people's views on prostitution by pointing to various abuses that foreign women face due to their disadvantaged position. Activists can do so all the more persuasively because the people they represent cannot "talk back" at their oppressors or communicate effectively with Japanese authorities. Furthermore, illegal foreign women are much clearer victims of an oppressive system than are poor or otherwise vulnerable Japanese, like women working in the sex industry. This is because Japanese sex workers are themselves implicated in this unfair system due to their Japanese citizenship and access to social welfare. Second, they believe in gender equality and women's rights that transcend national boundaries. Through their service and activities, these groups aim to help exploited foreign women recover their self-esteem and empower them to launch a new life.

Medical NGOs

Medical service providers, including the Occupational Safety and Health Centers (OSHC), account for nineteen organizations, the most numerous among the six types of support groups. Some medical NGOs are megagroups that encompass smaller groups. For example, the Minatomachi Clinic, the Jujo-dori Clinic, the Yokosuka Chuo Clinic, the Isezaki Women's Clinic, and the Imai International Clinic are part of the Minatomachi Foreign Migrant Workers' Mutual Aid Scheme for Health (MF-MASH) network. Similarly, the Kobayashi International Clinic is part of the Association of Medical Doctors of Asia (AMDA) network.

Medical doctors, such as Temmyō Yoshiomi of MF-MASH and Hirano Toshio of the Kameido Himawari Clinic, both of whom are affiliated with their local OSHC, often treat patients who suffer from industrial illness and job injuries—many of whom are overstayed foreign workers who work in dangerous jobs and are not covered by the NHI. In the early 1990s, they observed that overstayed foreign workers were increasingly seeking assistance with accident claims at their affiliated local OSHC and medical services at their clinics. They then mobilized their medical friends and members of these OSHC to support overstayed foreign workers.

Medical NGOs provide medical treatment and insurance schemes, offer medical translation, and make accident claims for all foreigners. Like women's support groups, medical NGOs offer medical welfare services, which attract the support of many local governments. Moreover, OSHC often coordinate activities with local labor offices, and four medical NGOs have thus acquired NPO status. Their membership ranges from 650 to 6,000 people. They operate, usually at a loss, with funds from membership fees and subsidies from local governments.

Medical doctors assist overstayed foreigners because they believe that medical care should be available to all, particularly to those at higher risk of getting ill and with no means to pay for medical treatment. They have found that some foreigners cannot receive appropriate medical treatment due to language barriers, while others are rejected by medical centers due to their illegal status. As discussed earlier, hospitals and clinics turn away overstayed foreigners for fear that these foreign patients will not be able to pay their medical fees because they are not covered by the NHI. Meanwhile, the staff at OSHC believe it is their duty to protect "all" workers from industrial accidents and job injuries.

Lawyers' Association NGOs

Lawyers' association NGOs provide legal assistance to illegal foreigners. In 1988, the Japan Civil Liberties Union (JCLU) became the first legal institution to assist illegal foreigners when it established the Foreigners' Rights Subcommittee.[13] JCLU began helping foreign newcomers when NGO activists seeking legal protection for foreign workers consulted with one of its lawyers. Other lawyers' NGOs emerged in the early 1990s after several regional bar associations recognized the need to form subcommittees

---

13. JCLU, which consists of mostly lawyers and academics, was established in 1947 during the Occupation Period as an affiliation of the American Civil Liberties Union (ACLU). It "aims to protect human rights for all persons regardless of belief, religion, or political opinion [and] to issue advice, memoranda, and opinions on specific human rights cases relating to activities of the national and local government, the Diet, and the courts of Japan." See http://village.infoweb.ne.jp/jclu/index.htm.

specializing in foreigner issues due to the increased number of foreigners visiting their members' offices. This was the case with the Center for Human Rights of Foreigners, the Japan Legal Aid Association, the International Rights Section of the Dai-ichi Tokyo Bar Association, the Human Rights Protection Committee of the Dai-ni Tokyo Bar Association, the Yokohama Bar Association—Legal Consultation for Foreigners, and the Kanagawa Administrative Lawyer Association—Foreign Negotiation Administrative Research Group. Since all lawyers are required to be members of a local bar association to practice, most organizations providing legal services are subgroups of regional lawyers' associations (*bengoshikai*). The Lawyers' Association for Foreign Criminal Cases (LAFOCC), the Lawyers' Association for Foreign Laborers Rights (LAFLR), and the Immigration Review Task Force, which were founded by Onitsuka Tadanori, are the only exceptions. For a small fee, these NGOs provide foreigners with legal consultation and dispute settlement on issues relating to labor, marriage/divorce, and immigration. Membership in these groups ranges from 19 to 540 people.

The lawyers' associations help overstayed foreigners because they believe that this clientele is subject to injustices, particularly those caused by Japanese government policies. Overstayed foreign suspects typically do not receive legal counsel because they lack the financial resources and personal connections to arrange for legal counsel. Public defenders reject cases involving overstayed foreign suspects because they are troublesome, involve difficulties of language (interpretation), and offer little financial reward. If foreigners are arrested, the institutional regulations of the Japanese legal system are often not explained to them comprehensively. Furthermore, the authorities are known to have verbally and, at times, physically abused foreign suspects even in cases of petty infringements. Lawyers from these foreigners support groups object to such practices as contradicting their beliefs about justice.

Some lawyers also help overstayed foreigners due to their traditional opposition to the central government as a *zaiyahōsō*, an institution that exists apart from authority.[14] Besides handling cases involving foreigners on labor disputes, illegal confinement, and violent acts, they also push for

---

14. Interview with Oshii Tetsuo of the Japan Legal Aid Association, April 28, 1998.

changes in the culture of authority, including better treatment of suspects in detention centers, prisons, and immigration offices, and the professionalization of translators in legal cases involving foreigners who speak Japanese poorly. Some members of these groups have organized an ongoing campaign against incidents of physical abuse of illegal foreigners by Immigration Bureau officials and police. They urge foreign victims to come forward and contact lawyers to file damage suits against the government.

Concerned Citizens' Groups

Concerned citizens' groups are civil rights activist organizations that seek legal rights and protection for marginalized people. Concerned citizens were quick to follow Christian NGOs in establishing support groups to help foreign workers during the late 1980s. These groups include the Solidarity Network with Migrants in Japan (SMJ), the Ōta Citizen's Network for Peoples' Togetherness (OC-Net), the Shibuya-Harajuku Group to Gain Life and Rights (Inoken), the Call Network, the Asian Peoples Friendship Society (APFS), the Forum on Kanagawa's Foreign Workers' Problems, the Kalabaw-no-kai, and the Sagamihara Solidarity with Foreign Workers. Concerned citizens' groups provide lifestyle and labor consultations, as well as dispute settlement services, primarily to South Asians and Iranians. Like women's support groups, some of these groups have close connection with Christian groups. For example, the representative of the Kalabaw-no-kai is Rev. Watanabe Hidetoshi. The SMJ, which functions as the central network organization for all NGOs that support foreign migrants, has office space in a church. Former labor unionists or radical activists started many of these groups. OC-Net, for example, was founded by Kawamata Koshin, who was kicked out of the Japan Communist Party (JCP) in the 1960s due to his "radical" views on China, founded the OC-Net.[15] Similarly, Yoshinari Katsuo—who thinks no political party, including the JCP, can bring "real" changes to Japanese society—helped found the APFS.[16] These groups have 40 to 1,700 members, on whom they rely for membership fees. Some of them also receive additional funds from local governments.

---

15. Interview with Kawamata Koshin of the OC-Net, April 7, 1998.
16. Interview with Yoshinari Katsuo of the APFS, December 17, 1998.

Concerned citizens' groups assist overstayed foreigners due to their beliefs in racial equality and civil rights. Many groups help not only foreign
workers but also the *burakumin* (descendants of outcast communities), the
elderly, the handicapped, and homeless people. As a product of the civil
rights movement, concerned citizens' groups assist foreign workers because of their humanitarianism and their progressive belief in racial justice
that ensures civil rights protection to all.

Many NGO members look to the Kalabaw-no-kai and the APFS as
the fathers of support groups for overstayed foreigners because both were
formed in 1987 when few such NGOs existed. The Kalabaw-no-kai was set
up "to help and establish solidarity with foreigners working in Japan." Members "help foreign workers in trouble, protest when their human rights are
infringed, and try to ensure that they are always treated fairly in [Japan]."
They conduct free telephone and direct consultation on labor problems.[17]
The APFS provides similar services in Tokyo's Ōyama Higashi-machi area.
After the successes of these two groups, other groups such as the OC-Net
emerged to provide services to foreign residents in their areas.

Improvisation in Activism: Activist Strategies
and Institutional Development

The activities and institutional development of Japan's foreigner support
groups might well be characterized by the sociological concept of pragmatism.[18] Activists in these groups engage in problem-solving activities that
lack a formalized theoretical or prescribed way of doing things and often
require a creative approach outside the formal, accepted channels of political and social institutions. Improvisation also occurs in the way these institutions develop, with group decisions—involving collective intelligence
and participation from members—continually taking place.

The activists who form these groups are problem solvers with experience
in helping underprivileged Japanese. Christian activists are accustomed to

---

17. Interview with Imaizumi Megumi of the Kalabaw-no-kai, March 8, 1998.
18. On pragmatism and creativity of action, see Hans Joas, *Pragmatism and Social Theory*
(Chicago: University of Chicago Press, 1993); Joas, *The Creativity of Action* (Chicago: University
of Chicago Press, 1996).

helping the poor. Community workers' unions have a history of representing workers that Japanese enterprise unions have abandoned. Women's groups have struggled to improve the social and legal position of Japanese women. Activist doctors have extensive experience in serving the poor, the homeless, and others prone to sickness or injury. Lawyers, progressive or not, have traditionally assisted victims of injustice. And a small group of concerned citizens have historically sought civil rights of marginalized Japanese. Having little or no experience in helping illegal foreigners, these activists often improvise their actions by applying their experience to the problems of illegal foreigners.

Only when they have grave problems—problems that they or their friends cannot resolve themselves due to language barriers, ignorance of Japanese law, or weak bargaining/financial positions—do foreign workers seek assistance from the Japanese NGOs. When they do, they often seek out particular activists or institutions due to their reputation for helping the underprivileged. For example, many Filipinos are practicing Catholics. They turn to the church for assistance in the forms of legal, medical, financial, shelter, psychological counseling, networking, and other emergency relief and support. Overstayed Filipinos who wish to surrender to immigration authorities and return to the Philippines, as well as women who have escaped from the mama-san or yakuza, often seek shelter in the church facilities and from the Christian NGOs.

In terms of ethnic background, Filipinos, Koreans, and nikkeijin, who tend to be Christian, generally go to Christian NGOs. South Asians and Iranians, who usually suffer from labor-related problems, turn to community workers' unions and concerned citizens' groups. Filipino and Thai women generally seek help and shelter from women's support groups. Desperate overstayed foreigners of all backgrounds use the services of medical and lawyers' NGOs. Consequently, some of these support groups have developed a specialization in helping certain ethnic groups. For instance, the FLU, the Koto Fureai Union, the Santama Joint Labor Union, and the Hachioji Union serve mostly Bangladeshis and Iranians. The Zentōitsu Workers' Union concentrates on Bangladeshi, Pakistani, and Indian workers. The Kanagawa City Union specializes in Korean and nikkei Peruvian workers who have overstayed their visas. Concerned citizens' groups such as the Kalabaw-no-kai, the APFS, and the OC-Net help Bangladeshis (and Pakistanis). Before its dissolution, Inoken specifically concentrated on Iranians. Volunteers at women's shelter Saalaa became experts on Thai women's issues. The Yokohama Bar Association—Subcommittee on Human Rights for Foreigners has developed a specialized understanding of the problems of illegal Chinese. As they deal with individual problems brought to these support groups, Japanese activists become privy to the difficulties, concerns, and life experiences of illegal foreigners, arguably coming to better understand and empathize with the circumstances of illegal foreigners than do legal foreigners of their own ethnic group.

In many cases, immigrant rights groups came into existence in response to individual encounters with foreigners seeking assistance. One example is the concerned citizens' group Kalabaw-no-kai. During the cold weeks of December and January, known as *ettō tōsō* ("struggle to pass the winter"), when jobs are scarce and laborers find it difficult to survive, local volunteers set up temporary tents in Kotobuki Park to feed and house those in need of help. These volunteers were initially surprised when a Filipino man came to their tents, but the encounter led them to recognize the plight of foreign workers. Soon after, they established the Kalabaw-no-kai. Similarly, the women's group Mizula began in 1990 when a group of concerned Japanese women came across a few desperate Thai women and tried to trace the snack bars where they had been forced to work as prostitutes and obtain the help of the police in retrieving their Thai passports and other documents. Since that beginning, Mizula has substantially expanded its support activities for foreign women, responding to requests for assistance that have included finding an inexpensive apartment in Tokyo for a Thai woman and her Japanese boyfriend, helping a Filipino woman escape from her violent yakuza husband, and sending a dying AIDS patient back to Thailand to reunite with her family. By 1997, Mizula was handling almost 400 such cases per year.[19]

The shifting focus and activities of many immigrant rights groups reflect their flexibility and creativity in responding to the problems illegal foreigners bring to their institutions. The concerned citizens' group APFS, for example, originally grew out of Yoshinari's friendship with his

---

19. Interviews with: Yoshida Kyoko of Mizula, March 24, 1998; Abe Hiroko of Mizula, May 28, 1998. Also see Yokohama-shi Women's Association, *Yokohama-shi josei sōdan nīzu chōsa hōgokusho I* [Report I of Women's Consultation Needs in the Yokohama City] (Yokohama: Mimeograph, 1996), 91–183.

public bath buddies from Bangladesh. At first, the APFS concentrated its activities on resolving its foreign members' problems with Japanese language schools and introducing guarantors to foreign members. As foreign workers increasingly encountered labor problems, its activities expanded to more practical issues, such as providing consultations to foreign migrant workers on problems related to their jobs and daily lives. It then began to make appeals to the government and Japanese companies to protect foreign workers' fundamental human rights. It started to hold a May Day meeting in Tokyo every year and to submit requests to the government to expand more legal rights and social benefits to foreign workers.

In recent years, as foreign workers began to settle in Japan, the APFS launched an ambitious campaign to get the government to grant "special residence permission" to certain overstayed foreigners. In September 1999, the APFS organized twenty-one overstayed foreigners to make a collective request for "special residence permission" at the Tokyo Regional Immigration Bureau, a permission that traditionally was granted only to those with Japanese spouses. The group sought the assistance of Professor Komai Hiroshi, who then formed a committee to mobilize academic circles (inside and outside of Japan) through e-mail to sign a petition in support of the APFS Campaign. The committee obtained 593 signatures of Japanese and foreign scholars and submitted the list to the Ministry of Justice in November 1999. These academicians contended that since the overstayed foreigners had lived in Japan for about ten years and their children were born and raised in Japan, they had sufficiently demonstrated that they had established their living bases in Japan and should be granted "special permission" to live permanently in Japan. Komai informed the Immigration Bureau that a refusal to grant "special permission" would draw extended criticism from both domestic and international academic circles. He also threatened to file an administrative suit against the Ministry. As a result, the Ministry eventually granted special permission to these twenty-one overstayed foreigners.[20] By doing so, the Ministry recognized the efforts of the APFS and its academic allies in redefining Japan's membership rules. The APFS hopes to push Japan's membership rules further and has been

---

20. Interview with Yoshinari Katsuo of the APFS, May 16, 2001.

working on cases involving overstayed foreigners without any children since 2004.[21]

In a similar way, the faith-based group CTIC has adapted its focus and activities in response to newly identified problems of illegal foreigners. CTIC originally provided counseling to help Catholic migrants with family and marriage problems. When illegal foreigners started bringing problems related to working conditions, such as unpaid salaries and job accidents, to CTIC, Father Ohara, the group's representative at the time, recruited a 54-year-old, non-Christian, Watanabe Tetsuro, who had more than twenty years' experience at the now defunct General Council of Trade Unions of Japan (Sōhyō), out of his early retirement.[22] CTIC's ability to adapt to the changing problems faced by illegal foreigners enabled the group to expand its offices to other parts of Tokyo.[23]

The Zentōitsu Workers' Union and the Services for Health in Asia and African Regions (SHARE) medical group also transformed to adapt to new problems. After helping illegal foreign workers at the union, Zentōitsu increasingly realized that many of these foreigners did not have regular medical check-ups. Zentōitsu then teamed with SHARE to provide free medical check-ups to foreign workers at its office. SHARE, in turn, realizing that many overstayed foreigners without proper medical check-ups lived in the countryside, started to work with local NGOs in nearby prefectures to mobilize foreign workers for medical check-ups at a Christian church. In sum, the response of activists to new problems brought to them by illegal foreigners has been characterized by ongoing institutional improvisation and creative adaptation.

Examples of creative, pragmatic activism also abound in the strategies employed by community support group activists in dealing with specific problems. For example, because members of community workers' unions come from various occupations and national backgrounds, these unions' most powerful tactic is not strikes but all-day offensives called *ichinichi kōdō* (all-day action). The *ichinichi kōdō* use shame to persuade employers to comply with the unions' demands. Typically, union organizers first try to settle labor disputes through collective bargaining with the employer.

---

21. Interview with Yoshinari Katsuo of the APFS, July 7, 2004.
22. Interviews with Arikawa Kenji and Watanabe Tetsuro of CTIC, May 7, 1998.
23. Interview with Watanabe Tetsuro of CTIC, June 12, 2003.

If they can reach an agreement in this fashion, the dispute is resolved. If complications arise that require extra legal assistance, the union organizers call on labor lawyers for help and further negotiations. If the dispute remains unresolved and union organizers feel that the employer is in the wrong (employers are usually wrong in the eyes of union organizers), the unions mobilize their current members to stage a demonstration outside the employer's central office. The Kanagawa City Union, for example, organizes daylong demonstrations four times a month.[24] In each of demonstrations, the members visit between four and six companies, with each visit usually lasting about one hour. Murayama Satoshi, who organizes these *ichinichi kōdō,* requires union members to participate in at least one of these events before he accepts their cases. This contributes to a high turnout of about fifty foreign workers attending each demonstration.

A typical Kanagawa City Union *ichinichi kōdō* begins at 7:30 A.M. at Kawasaki Station and ends around 8:00 P.M. after dinner. The event is highly organized. The coordinators smoothly direct people from one place to another through subways and train stations and along sidewalks—not unlike Japanese tour groups overseas. Participants wear union armbands so that they can be recognized by the union organizers (and others). The organizers buy and distribute train tickets, decide on a place for lunch and pay for the meal, and skillfully move people through crowded trains and stations, even during rush hours. On the sidewalk, a union organizer stands on each corner where participants need to turn, to point them in the right direction. Once the group has assembled in front of a company building, Murayama screams into a megaphone, denouncing the company's foul play. His messages are not only directed at the accused company but also meant to be heard by other companies in the area as well as by passersby. While Murayama is condemning the illegal practices of the targeted employer, other union members are distributing to pedestrians leaflets that explain the injustice caused by the employer. Occasionally, at Murayama's signal, the participants throw their fists high in the air to demonstrate their solidarity and intention to fight the management to the end. At times, Murayama has the wronged employees come to the megaphone and explain the situation firsthand, although this is difficult when they are foreigners.

---

24. Such tactics are emulated by other community workers' unions, albeit less frequently.

The goal of these activities is to shame employers as a means of pressing for workers' demands. The orderly disruption of the *ichinichi kōdō* is an important tool of critical communication for members of community workers unions, aimed at calling attention to the unreasonableness of company managements—their exploitation of the status of illegal foreigners, their domination over the terms of negotiation, their use of their economic power to cut off negotiation, and their employment of intimidation and/or violence in negotiation. Through these disruptive, annoying, or distracting demonstrations, the community workers' unions effectively engage citizens, including passersby, in communication with one another on issues concerning foreign workers.

Another example of creative activism can be seen in the efforts of medical NGOs to deliver medical services to illegal foreigners at a more affordable rate. Because access to the Japanese Social Insurance and NHI system is closed to most migrant workers who have overstayed their visas, some private medical institutions and NGOs have been established to provide medical treatment to those who are not covered by the national insurance system. In 1991, for example, founders of the MF-MASH established an alternative mutual aid scheme to provide medical treatment to illegal foreigners. Members who pay a monthly fee of 2,000 yen are entitled to receive medical treatment at any of five participating clinics for only 30 percent of the total cost (the same reduction that is given to people who are members of the Japanese NHI program). More than 12,000 overstayed foreigners from dozens of countries are insured under the MF-MASH system. Some doctors have found other creative ways to accommodate illegal foreigners with affordable medical services. Dr. Hirano of the Kameido Himawari Clinic, for instance, provides medical care to foreign workers at half the normal cost.[25] At the Kobayashi International Clinic, Dr. Kobayashi charges normal medical fees to foreigners, but less for medication. He reduces the cost of medications by using older medicines, which he claims to be safe and equally effective.[26]

A final example of creative activism comes from women's groups, who devised safe ways to rescue Southeast Asian women forced to work

---

25. Interview with Hirano Toshio of the Kameido Himawari Clinic, April 30, 1998.

26. Interview with Kobayashi Yoneyuki of the Kobayashi International Clinic, May 15, 1998.

as prostitutes at snack bars, particularly during the late 1980s. Upon receiving an SOS call, women's groups send out a rescue team that typically includes respectable and trustworthy male members, such as a college professor or Christian priest, to visit the snack bar or other place where the foreign woman is working. Pretending to be normal customers, these men request service from the distressed Southeast Asian woman and quietly inform her that they are part of the rescue team. They stay until the place of business closes and leave with the woman as if they were planning to spend the night together. Instead, they discreetly take her to a women's shelter, a secret place sufficiently far away that her former boss cannot easily find her.[27]

Responding to the problems brought to them, activists have generally formed foreigner support groups as extensions of, but separate organizations from, their original institutions. Thus, faith-based NGOs evolved out of Catholic dioceses, the National Christian Council in Japan (NCC/J), or Buddhist sects. Specific support groups for women emerged from a larger movement, and also out of Christian churches. Regional bar associations established most of the lawyers' associations groups. Community workers' unions and medical NGOs are exceptions, for they have served foreigners since they were established. Nevertheless, some community workers' unions, such as the Foreign Workers Branch of Zentōitsu (FWBZ) and the Foreign Laborers' Union (FLU) of the National General Workers Union, have created foreigner sections within their unions. AMDA, SHARE, and Āyus extended their international voluntary relief activities to include foreigners in Japan.

There are three clear benefits of establishing a separate organizational entity to help foreigners. First, it allows the group to accumulate knowledge about how best to improve its assistance to illegal foreigners. Although many Japanese activists have extensive experience in helping the poor and the distressed, they lack experience and know-how in helping newly arrived Asian foreigners. Forming support groups allows them to acquire and share information specific to the problems of foreign workers. For instance, after six years of solving problems for illegal foreign workers, the Kalabaw-no-kai found that "there has been an accumulation of

---

27. Interview with a member of the rescue team in the Ibaraki Prefecture, June 5, 1998.

knowledge and experience in negotiating with employers" and as a result, "there has been an increase in our ability to solve problems [for foreign workers]."[28]

Second, creating a dedicated support group strengthens activists' bargaining power by increasing the number of foreigners they represent and consequently giving them greater moral authority. In the words of staff people at the concerned citizens' group Inoken, "to resolve [problems for illegal foreigners], we need a lot of people."[29] This is particularly true for community workers' unions that support illegal foreign workers. As Abe Fumiko of the Kanagawa City Union was taking attendance at the beginning of an *ichinichi kōdō* she remarked, "numbers are everything in order to have an effective bargaining."[30] Undoubtedly, bringing twenty-one overstayed foreigners to the Immigration Office in Tokyo to petition for their amnesty, together with five APFS lawyers, provides more leverage than would a sole petitioner. Having a separate group with a focused goal guarantees effective mobilization and legal representation of foreign workers during the bargaining process.

Third, by creating a separate entity, Japanese activists can raise needed funds for their activities. Institutionalization requires members, which then begets membership fees. In certain groups, such as the Kalabaw-no-kai, it is the policy to "refrain from asking for expenses or any other financial payment" from their foreign clients, instead relying on various fund-raising activities for financial support.[31] Even Christian groups, which do not rely on membership fees, must institutionalize in order to receive funding from their headquarters—either in Tokyo, Geneva, or Rome. Of course NGOs may stand a better chance of receiving funding from local governments if they are well-established, stable institutions with relatively long histories, and many of the groups considered here are not durable in this sense. But the *issues* addressed by these institutions do tend to be relatively durable, so activists may reap some benefits with respect to local government support by organizing toward clearly defined and longstanding goals.

---

28. Kalabaw-no-kai, "Six Years of *Kalabaw-no-kai:* Evaluation and Future Prospects" (Yokohama: Mimeograph), 3.

29. Inoken internal document.

30. Interview with Abe Fumiko of the Kanagawa City Union, April 7, 1998.

31. Kalabaw-no-kai, "Six Years of *Kalabaw-no-kai,*" 9.

While foreigner support groups such as APFS and CTIC, which have adapted to the changing problems foreigners encounter, have thrived for a long time, many of these groups are relatively impermanent. In some cases, the associated organization dissolves once specific problems are resolved; the "Support Group of Three Thai Women" in the Shimodate City, for example, dissolved in 1996 (five years after it was established) upon the termination of the court case of the three women in question. Similarly, · Inoken dissolved in 1998 after Iranians no longer gathered at the Yoyogi Park. Some groups, such as LAFLR and SOL, have dissolved due to financial difficulties; others, such as FLU, folded as a result of internal struggle within their organizations.[32] Obviously, there are potential gains from permanence for an institution, but short-lived and narrowly focused organizations in contemporary Japanese society enjoy some benefits: No entrenched bureaucracy has time to develop, and thus few interests become vested in the organization itself, as opposed to its specific task. In a political culture characterized by strong deference to institutional status, a short-lived organization also avoids easy capture by existing political interests working through established institutions.[33]

Realizing Motivations through Activism: Problem Solving in Deliberative Networks

Members of immigrant rights NGOs concentrate their activities on solving specific problems that illegal foreign workers bring with them to their institutions. Once their specific problems are resolved, foreigners usually leave these groups, and the organization generally dissolves. But for these

---

32. Interviews with: Yamagishi Motoko of SOL and Kalakasan, August 4, 2004; Yano Manami of the SMJ, July 18, 2003; Watanabe Midori of LAFOCC, June 16, 2003.

33. We would expect some attempt at cooptation by the Japanese state: outright suppression, incorporation of these groups into the government's policy-making process, preferential treatment in terms of financial and logistical support to those groups whose agendas and activities are consonant with government interests, or redirecting some activities of certain groups toward national causes. Indeed, institutional capture can have benefits in terms of improved access to powerful actors, a point I do not deny. But it is an open question whether the promise of improved access is worth the cost of diminished independence in the case of Japanese activists seeking to transform public attitudes about, and official treatment of, illegal foreign workers. Such a trade-off would likely be unattractive to the activists discussed here.

Japanese activists, the resolution of a problem and dissolution of a specific organization are not the end of the matter: rather, their associative activities help them focus their more abstract and inchoate political ideas. Activists' work with foreigners leads them to become more critical of their own society and more engaged in civil and political life. People who join these support groups generally accept the belief of the group as stated in their charters, and members soon find themselves united by a common ideology of social equality in one form or another. This abstract commitment to equality generally includes civil equality, class equality, sexual equality, medical equality ("good health to all"), equality based on the concept of social justice, and equality based on the belief that all humans are children of God. In addition to these general moral commitments, some activists have engaged in opposition politics and have experienced frustrated resistance from the political and business elite prior to their associative activism for foreigners. Through specific problem-solving activities for illegal foreigners and critical reflection on their own society with others who share their abstract moral commitments, their generalized dissatisfaction with the political status quo becomes clarified and refined. They then see opportunities (i.e., motivations) to vent their own objections to Japanese society in a way that they cannot with legal aliens and with Japanese themselves.

These activists were mature adults, most in their thirties, forties, and fifties (the median age for the 107 activists I interviewed in 1998 was forty-one years old). As figure 4.2 demonstrates, half the activists interviewed started their associative activities for illegal foreign workers between the ages of thirty-one and fifty-one. The youngest starting activist was a nineteen-year-old woman and the oldest a seventy-five-year-old woman. The number of starting activists in paid and nonpaid positions was relatively equal. Men (n = 60), particularly those with professional careers such as doctors, lawyers, and labor unionists, outnumbered women (n = 47), who mostly belonged to faith-based organizations, concerned citizens' NGOs, and women's support groups.

As one might expect, these activists included Christians, radical unionists, citizens' rights activists, progressive lawyers, and activist doctors. Except for staff of community workers' union, most were highly educated: sixty-seven had college degrees, and thirteen held master's degrees. Medical doctors graduated from top medical schools, and lawyers tended to come out of prestigious universities before passing the difficult bar exam.

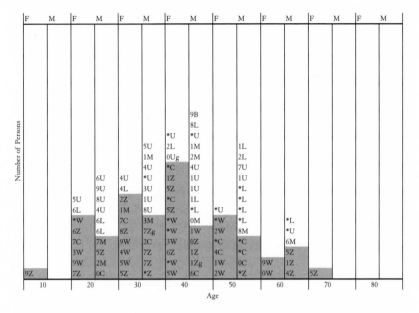

Figure 4.2. Starting Age of Male (M) and Female (F) Support Group Staff and Volunteers.

C = Christian NGO
W = Women's shelter/NGO
Z = Concerned citizens' NGO
L = Lawyers' association NGO
U = Community workers' union
M = Medical support group
B = Buddhist support group
Shaded area represents volunteer work
* = estimated age in their 10s, 20s, 30s, 40s, 50s, 60s, 70s, etc.
g = Local government officials

Note: 9Z in column 10F means a nineteen-year-old woman volunteer from the concerned citizens NGO; 6U in the 20M column means a twenty-six-year-old paid male staff member of a community workers' union.

Kawamoto Hiroyuki of the Kanagawa Occupational Safety and Health Center (KOSHC) graduated from the economics department of the University of Kyoto, and one volunteer at the Kalabaw-no-kai had a master's degree in engineering from the University of Tokyo. Most women activists also received university education from elite schools. The late Matsui Yayori of the Asian-Japanese Women's Resource Center was a University of California, Berkeley graduate, while Yoshida Kyoko of Mizula was working on her Ph.D. at Sophia University. This elite educational background is highly useful in leveling the playing field, not only during negotiation with more powerful organizations but also during the deliberative process with local government officials (as will be discussed in chapter 5). In addition to being able to speak fluent Japanese, these activists understand Japanese expectations about norms of articulateness, which, as in other societies, tend to privilege the modes of expression more typical of highly educated people.[34] In most negotiations and deliberations, participants usually value expression that proceeds from premises to conclusion in an orderly and logical fashion. For these advocates, this entails formulating general ethical/normative principles and applying them to particular cases involving illegal foreigners they are helping.

Unlike those elites who find employment in the government and subsequently are molded to accept and espouse nationalist views, most of these activists hold internationalist views. They are dissatisfied with the social environment in which they live and share an alternative vision for its improvement. For example, Miki Emiko, a lawyer at the Yokohama Law Office and a representative of Saalaa, was raised by a single mother who ran a *ryokan* (Japanese inn) frequented by American GIs and their Japanese girlfriends. Dissatisfied with Japan's political environment, she was active in radical left-wing activities at the University of Tokyo's prestigious Law Department. Rather than joining the bureaucracy after graduation like most of her classmates, she spent two years in communist China, where she eventually became disillusioned with communism as well. She then decided to become a lawyer to confront the establishment and bring about change through legal means. Ōshima Shizuko of the women's shelter HELP grew up in a Christian family that helped Japanese prostitutes escape from their captivity and had been active in the antiprostitution movement since the 1950s before she became HELP's first representative. Onitsuka Tadanori, a founder of LAFLR, LAFOCC, and the Immigration Review Task Force, became interested in fighting discrimination against minorities while studying at Waseda University. Onitsuka took his first case involving a foreigner in 1985 when a zainichi Korean refused to be fingerprinted. Although he lost that case, he went on to take more cases involving foreigners, including illegals, beginning in 1988. Reverend Watanabe Hidetoshi, who regretted his father's role during World War II as a

---

34. On norms of articulateness in deliberation, see Iris Marion Young, *Inclusion and Democracy* (New York: Oxford University Press, 2000), 37–40.

member of the security police in Korea, started helping Koreans in Japan before he left for a two-year study trip in the United States and a year in the Philippines. Two months after his return to Japan, he was recruited to join the Kalabaw-no-kai.[35] Similarly, Dr. Temmyō Yoshiomi of MF-MASH, who deplored governmental neglect and societal prejudice against Japan's marginalized workers from impoverished Tōhoku and Hokkaido, had extensive experience in helping these workers prior to supporting foreign workers. It is Temmyō's conviction that "doctors must not refuse to examine sick people,"[36] and he observes that it is the impoverished and neglected who are prone to get sick.[37] Like Temmyō, Dr. Hirano Toshio of Kameido Himawari Clinic has progressive views and works closely with the local OSHC. After graduating from the University of Tokyo Medical School and before starting his own clinic, Dr. Hirano founded a medical labor union in one of the community hospitals in Tokyo. In terms of their political views, 103 out of 107 Japanese staff members and volunteers interviewed had never voted for the politically conservative Liberal Democratic Party, and the few exceptions had done so only on unusual electoral occasions.

Unlike legal foreigners, who show little empathy for their illegal compatriots, Japanese activists express sincere respect and compassion for illegal foreign workers and do not consider their illegal visa status to lessen their humanity. Instead, these activists accept the presence, albeit illegal, of these foreigners as legitimate because Japanese society needs them. Dr. Temmyō Yoshiomi of MF-MASH, for example, remarks,

> I have always been against using the word "illegal." ... Certainly these working people violate the Immigration Control Law, but is it alright, in terms of medical consultations, to leave this remarkably harsh situation as it is? They take up the 3D jobs [dirty, dangerous, and difficult] that Japanese dislike; they pay income and consumption taxes. As far as illegal acts, they have done nothing.[38]

---

35. Interview with Rev. Watanabe Hidetoshi of Kalabaw-no-kai, June 27, 1998, June 5, 1999; also see *Yomiuri Shimbun,* May 18, 1988.

36. *Mainichi Shimbun,* June 28, 1993.

37. Interview with Temmyō Yoshiomi of MF-MASH, April 3, 1998.

38. *Yomiuri Shimbun,* October 3, 1995.

Reverend Watanabe Hideyoshi of the Kalabaw-no-kai similarly argues that illegal foreign workers help Japanese society because they pay taxes and shop at Japanese stores to maintain their livelihood.[39] He warns that due to Japan's labor shortage, companies could well go bankrupt without foreign workers. Many activists see the government's classification of these people as illegal as jeopardizing their basic human rights, since employers take advantage of their illegal status.[40] They insist that the services and benefits provided to Japanese residents should be provided equally to foreign residents regardless of their visa status. These activists admire illegal foreigners, who encounter numerous problems while living in Japan, for having the "guts" to stand and face their troubles with courage.[41]

Japanese activists commonly express deep compassion for illegal foreigners during their problem-solving activities. A mutually warm and caring relationship is displayed, for example, in the following international phone conversation between Kawamoto Hiroyuki of KOSHC and Iqbal, a former overstayed Pakistani whose right arm was amputated as a result of a work injury in a Kawasaki factory and has returned to Pakistan.

Kawamoto:	Is that Iqbal-san?
Iqbal:	Is that Kawamoto-san? How are you?
Kawamoto:	I am well. Are you receiving the money? [Due to a discrepancy between the Labor Ministry and the bank, his pension did not arrive for the first six months.]
Iqbal:	It's alright. It's coming.
Kawamoto:	Are you working now?
Iqbal:	Yes. I am helping my cousin's business. There is no work here like in Japan.
Kawamoto:	Are your wife and children well?
Iqbal:	Yes, thank you.
Kawamoto:	Your Japanese is still good. You can speak better than me!
Iqbal:	It would be awful if I forgot it.

39. *Yomiuri Shimbun,* September 27, 1991.

40. Interview with Furuya Sugio of JOSHRC, July 1, 1998; also see http://www.jca.apc.org/joshrc/index_e.html (accessed October 15, 2005); APFS, "Annual Report of APFS Activity for 1996" (Tokyo: Internal document, 1997), 25.

41. Published interview in Yano Keiko, "Karera ni wa Ikiru Gattsu ga Aru no yo!" [They Have the Guts to Live!], in Shonan Horitsuka Kyōkai, ed., *Bengoshi ni Naritai Anata e II* [To You Who Want to Become a Lawyer II] (Tokyo: Shonansha, 1997), 7–27.

Kawamoto:	It looks as if the court case will continue for a while.
Iqbal:	It would be good if I could go to Japan once more. Kawamoto-san, please come to Pakistan.
Kawamoto:	Yea. It would be good if we could all go.
Iqbal:	Are Miki-san, Hono-san, Orimoto-san all well? [The members of Iqbal's team of lawyers.]
Kawamoto:	Yes, they're doing their best.
Iqbal:	And the people at Minatomachi and the Union?
Kawamoto:	They are all busy working.[42]

A similar expression of warmth and compassion can be seen in another conversation at the Tokyo Municipal Prison in Kosuge between Father Nakaya Isao of the Yamasato Consulting Office and a Chinese inmate sentenced to death for the murder of a fellow countryman. Noticing the Chinese inmate's red face, Father Nakaya was concerned whether he had been beaten up in prison. "Are you alright?" he asked. "Yes, why?" the Chinese man answered in puzzlement. "Your face is red," explained the concerned priest. "Ah, I just came out of the shower," he answered. It appeared that Japanese prisons have running hot water and this Chinese man, who was wearing an oxford shirt underneath his flashy Nike jacket, seemed satisfied with the prison conditions. Before leaving, Father Nakaya asked, "Do you need anything?" The Chinese inmate answered with little concern for his death sentence, "Maybe a long overcoat. An old, used one is fine. Oh! And an apple."

Perhaps even more than conversations, spontaneous and silent tears offer a powerful display of compassion and empathy for illegal foreigners. During a visit to Saalaa, I encountered a Thai woman who was excited to see a fellow countryman and to hear the Thai language after eight miserable years in Japan. She asked countless questions and addressed me with the honorific *phi,* or big brother, despite my younger age. She then took me inside the shelter, forgetting that the place was off-limits to outsiders, to say nothing of men. When I was preparing to leave, we chatted for a while about her situation in Japan. Apparently, she had married a Japanese man, who often beat her even when she was pregnant. No longer able to bear her husband's violence, she fled to Saalaa with her two children. As she

---

42. *MF-MASH News* 6 (October 1993): 7(English in original).

told her sad story, she kept breaking into tears, and at the end, she pleaded with streams of tears flowing down her cheeks: "Why are these terrible things happening to me? I have never done anything [bad] to anyone. *Phi,* help me a little, *phi . . .*" A Thai-speaking staff member was listening to our conversation and crying quietly. When I asked her if she had not gotten used to hearing such stories, she replied that she had listened to dozens of them, but each one still moved her to tears. In fact, she had stayed up late the night before listening to this Thai woman's story and crying with her.

Although Japanese NGO workers often express compassion and empathy for illegal foreigners, they sometime are disappointed with them. For example, an activist in Gunma said she became frustrated with illegal foreigners who kept saying "yes, yes, I understand" when they actually did not for fear of appearing stupid in front of Japanese. She maintained that this causes greater problems, especially when the situation involves legal matters.[43] Medical doctors at MF-MASH have also expressed disappointment with illegal foreigners who joined their private health insurance scheme when they required medical attention and stopped paying their membership dues after they recovered. They became even more frustrated when the same people returned and, again, stopped paying their dues after they fully recovered.[44] Despite these frustrations, they placed the blame on Japanese predatory society and not on illegal foreigners.

Some activists have made extraordinary sacrifices to assist illegal foreign workers. Murayama Satoshi of the Kanagawa City Union, for example, was ambushed and beaten by a group of *yakuza* in retaliation for his tenacious efforts to help a Korean worker.[45] Similarly, during a negotiation by Zentōistu Workers' Union on behalf of a foreign worker, someone from management threw gasoline on Torii Ippei and lit a match. The incident left a permanent scar on one side of his body.[46] Despite their injuries, these union organizers went on to win their cases for their foreign clients. Murayama and Torii's physical sacrifices earned them enormous respect among several foreign workers as well as fellow activists. Activists at women's support groups often receive threatening phone calls at their

---

43. Interview with Harada Momoyo of Friends, June 9, 1998.
44. Interview with Hayakawa Hiroshi of the MF-MASH, July 23, 2004.
45. Interview with Murayama Satoshi of the Kanagawa City Union, April 3, 1998.
46. Interview with Torii Ippei of Zentōitsu, March 12, 1998.

offices, which they respond to courageously. When Father Nakaya Isao of the Yamasato Consulting Office was threatened by a yakuza for helping a run-away foreign woman, he politely pointed to his forehead and told the yakuza, "if you want to hit me, go right ahead." Fortunately, the yakuza turned away without further incident.[47]

In affirming the legitimacy of illegal foreigners' presence in Japan and offering them respect and compassion, these activists advance a more holistic understanding of Japan's multicultural democracy. Japanese activists' empathy allows them to have an open mind and to absorb detailed information about the conditions of illegal foreigners. As a result, many understand the situation of these illegal foreigners more than their legal compatriots. As will be discussed in chapter 5, this tolerance and empathy for illegal foreigners can expand the concept of democratic citizenship and further enrich democratic deliberation, which attempts to incorporate as many voices as possible from affected residents, with Japanese activists representing the voices of illegal foreigners.

Transformative Force of Social Democracy

Because the staff and volunteers of immigrant rights NGOs tend to be individuals who are dissatisfied with the status quo, express deep compassion for all foreigners, and are willing to make personal sacrifices to bring about change, these groups play an important role in advancing Japan's social democracy. Through their networks of socially minded activists, they advocate for public policies to protect foreign migrants' rights and welfare, including reforms in immigration law, labor laws that give foreign workers benefits equal to those of Japanese workers, and amnesty for overstayed migrants. In effect, they restore rights that have been denied to illegal foreigners while monitoring government actions and abuses. They educate the public and force Japanese society to reflect critically on its

---

47. Interview with Nakaya Isao of the Yamasato Consulting Office, December 3, 1998. Incidents involving the yakuza have not always been confrontational, as they are known to have come to these foreigner support groups asking for help. Staff at LAFLR have received phone calls from yakuza seeking legal consultations for their foreign "girlfriends." A yakuza in the Ibaraki prefecture brought a drug overdosed foreign woman to the office of a Christian group.

national identity. Most significant, they hold cosmopolitan views and push for structural change in Japan as demonstrated by their protests against sex tours, trafficking in women, and criminalization of prostitution. In so doing, they advance democracy by encouraging civic engagement of Japanese nationals, creating other civic groups, and promoting multicultural understanding.

When activists help illegal foreigners with medical and legal problems, they work to restore rights that have been denied. And in dealing with specific issues, they lay the groundwork for realizing a society that guarantees those rights.[48] On July 8, 1998, for example, the APFS protested against a private hospital in Tokyo to demand the removal of a sign, posted above the emergency room reception desk that read in English: "This hospital is obligated to report to the Immigration Office." In Chinese characters, this sign referred to a "Japan Immigration Control Office," although no such office existed. The sign had been put up a decade earlier to scare away "illegal" foreign patients because there had been many cases of overstayed foreigners who had refused to pay after receiving emergency room treatment. APFS criticized hospital officials for putting up such a sign to turn away foreigners who might well need medical treatment for life-threatening problems.[49] Yoshinari Katsuo was successful in obtaining the hospital's admission that it was not "obligated" to report illegal foreigners to the authorities and that the "Japan Immigration Control Office" was a bogus name, and the sign was removed as a result of the APFS protest.

Assisting illegal foreigners also helps activists realize the need for Japan to extend certain rights that have been denied even to Japanese nationals, such as the protection of women from domestic violence. The women's shelter Mizula played an important role in the passage of the Domestic Violence Prevention Law in 2001. Specifically, Mizula participated in a *shingikai* (consultative committee) of the prime minister's office in February 2000 and called for an increase in the number of shelters for victims of domestic violence and a bill to prevent domestic violence.[50] In April, a

---

48. Kalabaw-no-kai, "Six Years of *Kalabaw-no-kai*," 8–9.

49. *Japan Times,* July 9, 1998.

50. The idea, however, originated after the UN Declaration on the Protection of Women Rights in 1993. Kanagawa-Women's Space "Mizula", ed., *Shierutā—Onnatachi no kigi* [Women's Crisis—Shelter] (Tokyo: Akashi Shoten, 2002), 239.

Study Group of the Upper House invited Abe Hiroko of Mizula to a hearing on domestic violence counseling. Mizula and its representative, Fukuhara Keiko, participated in the drafting of the law, supplying the Diet with data on violence against spouses or partners.[51]

Similarly, in assisting illegal foreigners, activists monitor abuses of government power, with lawyers' groups in particular pushing for changes in the culture and abuse of authority. These changes include better treatment of suspects held in detention centers, prisons, and immigration offices, and the professionalization of translators in legal cases involving foreigners who speak Japanese poorly. In 1996, for example, the JCLU assisted an overstayed Bangladeshi who was allegedly assaulted by Japanese policemen during a labor dispute. Members of the JCLU, who regarded the police actions as unjustly coercive and violating the Bangladeshi's civil rights, sent letters to the chief of the police station to request an explanation and demand that appropriate measures be taken to prevent recurrences of such events. This ability to question authority or to evaluate the performance of those with authority is an important element for the development of social democracy.

Immigrant rights NGOs advance grassroots democracy by promoting civic engagement between Japanese and foreigners. Community workers' unions, in particular, have helped to revitalize Japan's declining labor movement by actively organizing part-time and foreign workers, whose numbers have increased steadily since the late 1980s. In recent years, the large centralized labor federations, such as Rengō (Japanese Trade Union Confederation) and Zenrōren (National Confederation of Trade Unions), have been courting the Kanagawa City Union and the Labor Union of Migrant Workers, respectively.[52] On March 8, 1993, a group of community workers' unions organized a "Day for Foreign Workers' Rights," the first organized action by Japanese labor unions on this issue. On that day, the group negotiated directly with the Ministry of Labor and with companies employing foreign workers, submitted petitions to the Tokyo Metropolitan Government and District Court, and held a rally for migrant workers, the largest that had been held in Japan up to that time. These organizers,

---

51. Interview with Kikutani Hideko of Mizula, July 16, 2004.
52. Interviews with: Nakajima Shigeru of Rengō, July 14, 2004; Kawasaki Shunji of Zenrōren, August 17, 2007.

who viewed "migrant workers' rights as an integral task for Japanese labor unions," held a symposium on foreign workers' rights in December 1993 and have organized a "Day for Foreign Workers' Rights" every March since then. They explained: "We think that labor unions should be at the front of the struggle to strengthening the rights of migrant workers and only labor unions have the ability of doing so. We also believe that by doing so, Japanese labor unions will start to mark a new era."[53]

Community workers' unions began assisting foreign workers during the early 1990s and were most active during the late 1990s, when the number of illegal foreigners peaked. Clearly, foreign workers contributed significantly to their added strength. For example, during the Zenrōkyō's (National Trade Unions Council) 1998 *Shuntō* (Spring Offensive), staff at its foreign workers' branch, FLU, brought about sixty foreign workers to demonstrate in front of various companies where Japanese clients of the Zenrōkyō were having disputes with management. The involvement of foreign workers increased the number of participants and thereby helped exert more effective pressure against management. The Shuntō ended at a conference room in the Hibiya Park, where about five thousand members gathered to listen to 1997–1998 activity reports given by ten division leaders, one of them a foreign worker who represented FLU.

Immigrant rights groups also enhance civic activities and promote multicultural understanding in their neighborhoods. The Kalabaw-no-kai maintains excellent relations with all of the volunteer associations and people in the Kotobuki-chō area. It nurtures good relations with officials of the Yokohama Welfare Center, which is located in the community center, and avoids direct conflict with the yakuza, who control the streets of Kotobuki-chō. It helps organize the annual Kotobuki Summer Festival at the Labor and Welfare Center with various volunteer groups from the area. During this three-day event, staff members of the Kalabaw-no-kai contribute both food and labor to the "Mukō Patorō" (Thursday Patrol), who distributes food stamps to the *ot'chan* and *oba-chan* (uncles and aunts) who live in the area. In this way, the Kalabaw-no-kai is an important institution that helps to enhance not only social justice for foreigners but

---

53. Gaikokujin Rōdōsha Kenri Hakusho Henshū Iinkai, *Gaikokujin rōdōsha kenri hakusho* [White Paper on Foreign Workers' Rights] (Tokyo: Executive Committee to Edit the White Paper on Foreign Workers Rights, 1995), 4.

also peaceful coexistence and interracial understanding in Kotobuki-chō. Similarly, staff and volunteers of the Yamasato Consulting Office help the Yama-nichi-rō Labor Union organize the San'ya annual summer festival and engage in similar activities for local residents. CTIC organizes the annual International Day in April at St. Mary's Cathedral in Tokyo, where it brings Japanese and foreigners together for social gatherings. The road is not always smooth. The Kobayashi International Clinic, which has its office inside an apartment complex, initially encountered resentment from Japanese building residents, even receiving two letters from residents expressing concerns that foreigners visiting the clinic might rape female residents. Relations improved after group members began to participate in activities with building residents and to promote multicultural understanding.[54] These activities by immigrant rights NGOs help foster trust between illegal foreigners and Japanese. As has been shown elsewhere, greater trust among residents allows the state to function more effectively as a democracy.[55]

Despite the positive impact of most immigrant rights groups, not all such NGOs promote multicultural understanding in their neighborhoods or in foreigner communities. For example, the Society to Struggle Together with Asian Workers in Japan (hereafter Zai-a-kyō from its Japanese acronym) encounters resentment from its Japanese community in San'ya, particularly from Gya-san (Mr. Loudmouth) of the Yama-nichi-rō Labor Union. Gya-san resents that "although its office is in San'ya, no one from this Christian group comes to San'ya or care about San'ya people; it is just an empty office with nobody there."[56] He contrasts the Zai-a-kyō to the Yamasato Consulting Office, which distributes *onigiri* (rice balls wrapped in seaweed) to San'ya day laborers every Thursday evening. More surprisingly, the aid of NGOs can be limited to individual cases, as immigrant rights NGOs have not yet made a positive impression in broader illegal foreigner communities. Most overstayed foreigners do not even know about

---

54. Interview with Kobayashi Yoneyuki of the Kobayashi International Clinic, May 15, 1998.

55. Robert Putnam, *Making Democracy Work: Civic Traditions in Modern Italy* (Princeton: Princeton University Press, 1993).

56. Interview with Mr. Gya (not his real name) of the Yama-nichi-rō Labor Union in Tokyo, July 3, 1998. Gya is Japanese for "loud-mouth." Japanese called him this because he goes around the neighborhood shouting into the loudspeaker while trying to organize day-laborers.

the existence of these groups. And many remain suspicious after they were informed about the existence of these NGOs. They were afraid that the NGO people would inform the Immigration Office. In an interview with a Thai entertainer in Ibaraki, I asked her what she usually does when she becomes sick. She replied,

"I will do as all the Thais here do: treat myself."

"Isn't that a little dangerous? Do you know that there are medical NGOs in Tokyo and Yokohama that will treat you?" I asked her.

"Nonsense... If I go there, they will report me to the *nyūkan* [Immigration Office] and send me back to Thailand," she answered with a laugh.[57] Although I assured her and other Thais that Japanese NGOs would not do such things, they remained suspicious. They maintained that it was ridiculous that anyone would help them for free.[58] One Thai man asked me,

"If these NGOs are really sincere about helping us, why aren't they here in the community talking to us like you?"[59]

He raised an important point: Most of these NGOs do not enter the foreigner communities but wait for foreigners to come to them with their problems. As a result, these Thais do not trust Japanese NGOs. My experience with overstayed foreigners was that one could earn their trust simply by entering their communities and talking with them. Even the first meeting, many have asked me to eat or drink or sleep with them. Yet Japanese NGOs appear not to make this effort.

Despite their limitations, immigrant rights groups have had a significant positive impact in creating new civic groups and coordinating activities with other groups in their network. Some immigrant rights NGOs have also created other civic groups. PACEM, for example, established the Filipino Desk and Latin Desk. The Kalabaw-no-kai, Mizula, and SOL helped found Saalaa. Āyus created the HIV/AIDS: Network on Supporting Migrant Labors and the Buddhist NGO Network, among others. This cross-institutional breeding allows these support groups to interact more

---

57. Interview with an overstayed Thai women, June 17, 1998. Interestingly, the Thais in Japan appear to have adopted the Japanese word *nyūkan* (Immigration Office) into their everyday Thai vocabulary.

58. This is the reason why some support groups began charging these foreigners, albeit at a minimum cost. They hope that this would lessen the foreigners' suspicion. This is a major concern of lawyer NGOs.

59. Interview with an overstayed Thai man, June 17, 1998.

easily within a network for problem solving. In trying to solve problems for illegal foreigners, community workers' unions build networks with medical and lawyers' NGOs, Christian groups with women's and concerned citizens' NGOs, and women's NGOs with all types of support groups with the exception of labor unions. The concerned citizens' NGOs use the most extensive network.

Japanese activists meet together regularly for staff meetings, seminars, study groups, and conventions. They also hold an annual nationwide meeting of NGO activists, where they share information about their activities, raise pressing issues, and work together to resolve shared problems. During these meetings, activists eat, bathe, and play together, and they sometimes sleep in shared quarters. Such networking and regular interactions among Japanese activists from various groups create a warm atmosphere and a sense of shared purpose—specifically, a sense that there are others who share similar visions and act to fulfill those visions through their day-to-day activities. In this critical sense, they create shared meanings associated with their respective activities. This emergent solidarity is not bound up with the institutional structure of specific associations, which again tend to be relatively ephemeral, dissolving after their tasks are complete. Rather, it arises out of a shared commitment to egalitarian ideals that are in tension with existing Japanese law and policy.

Out of activists' shared experiences in helping illegal foreigners has emerged a critical reflection about Japan's national identity and ultimately a larger social and political movement for structural change in Japan, as well as in the capitalist world more generally. For instance, Japanese activists at SOL feel that "Japanese society has put too much stress on homogeneity. This indicates that we should take up the challenge of living with migrants."[60] SMJ members explain that Japan's people are not only Japanese but also Koreans, migrant workers, and ethnic minorities. Therefore, they "pledge to struggle together to destroy the seeds of assimilation and xenophobia planted by Japanese society and the state, and to resist all forms of discrimination against non-Japanese residents."[61] Christian groups, particularly the NCC/J, locate the foundation of Japanese ideas of racial

---

60. Interview with Yamagishi Motoko of SOL, April 1, 1998.
61. *Migrant Network News* 13 (April 1999): 3.

superiority and discrimination in the imperial system and call for its abolition to create a society that is based on racial equality. Assisting foreigners
also strengthens the NCC/J's longstanding campaign against the popular
deification of the Japanese emperor, which provided the foundation for Japanese racial superiority.[62] Thus, the NCC/J pursues this struggle through
its Foreign Workers Issues Committee, challenging the traditional concept
of racial superiority of the Japanese people and introducing the idea that all
humans are equal (as children of God).[63]

The devoted Christian and woman activist, Matsui Yayori, and her
Asia-Japan Women's Resource Center set up the Migrant Women Worker's Research and Action Committee to prepare for the 1995 Fourth World
Conference on Women in Beijing. Its report states: "We are trying to change
Japanese society, with the goal that someday women will be treated equally
with men. This goal directly links our work with migrant women. We
desperately need a society where migrant women can live with dignity."[64]
Generally, women's groups try to educate the Japanese public on the idea
that prostitution is a severe form of human rights violation against women.
Many Japanese men do not consider buying sex from a woman to be an
immoral or shameful transaction.[65] Information on buying prostitutes,
such as advertisements for massage parlors or "soaplands," often appear
in Japanese weekly magazines and evening newspapers, which are widely
read by businessmen on commuter trains.[66] To challenge this dominant
male attitude, the Friends of Thai Women Association took legal action
against the Japanese publishing company Data House for its 1994 publication of the *Thai Prostitution Handbook* [*Tai Baishun Dokuhon*] written by
four male freelance writers. The title, "Thailand Nightzone" in English,
markets the publication as a handbook on buying women in Thailand.

62. National Christian Council in Japan, "The Salt of the Earth," (Tokyo: Internal Document
of the NCC/J, 1993).

63. Interview with Rev. Ōtsu Kenichi of the NCC/J, April 10, 1998.

64. Migrant Women Worker's Research and Action Committee, ed., "NGO's Report on the
Situation of Foreign Migrant Women in Japan and Strategies for Improvement" (Tokyo: Forum
on Asian Immigrant Workers, 1995).

65. Group to Think with Men About Prostitutes, *Baishun ni tai suru dansei ishiki chosa*
[Survey Study of Men Attitudes Toward Prostitution] (Tokyo: Asia-Japan Women's Resource
Center, 1998).

66. Yoko Yoshida, "Why Do Men Buy Women?" *Women Asia* 21, no. 3 (1997): 26–28.

It provides names and locations of local massage parlors and brothels in Bangkok and Chiangmai—accompanied by pictures of women on almost every page. It also gives instructions on how to take a taxi or bicycle rickshaw to these places. It sold more than ten thousand copies during the first year following its publication. Viewing the publication of such a book as not only promoting buying prostitutes in Thailand but also violating and humiliating all women, the group launched a protest against the publisher and the four authors. After Data House published a revised edition in 1995 that contained degrading remarks about the group and women's rights in general, they took the publisher to court and won. For the Saalaa women's shelter, its ultimate goal is "to build a society in which no one needs shelter."[67] These activists realize that solving problems for illegal foreign workers involves working to change and improve Japanese society.

Some foreigner support groups possess more global and ambitious goals. Members at the Kalabaw-no-kai, for example, have stated,

> Along with taking up individual infringements of the human rights of foreign workers, we have also endeavored to appeal to society as a whole, and to promote movements which highlights related issues inherent in the structural exploitation of our world by capital. Though not intended, those endeavors have made up the special character of our organization.[68]

The women's shelter HELP also expresses a more general commitment to "strive against the problems associated with the internationalization of prostitution and to eliminate the underlying structure of violence."[69] Similarly, JNATIP views human trafficking as "a transnational organized crime that knows no boundaries... Underlying the issue of trafficking are problems such as the economic disparities between sending and receiving countries, migrant labor, and globalization."[70] The group believes that the human trafficking business is built and thrives on the exploitation of the aspirations of people who seek a better life in a different land. Most women's groups acknowledge that these global problems may have been

---

67. Interview with Fukushima Yuriko of Saalaa, March 17, 1998.
68. Kalabaw-no-kai, "Six Years of *Kalabaw-no-kai*," 2.
69. Interview with Ōshima Shizuko of HELP, December 2, 1998.
70. See http://www.jnatip.org/aboutthejnatip.html (accessed May 14, 2006).

exacerbated by Japan, a major destination country for prostitution and the trafficking of persons. In 2004, the JNATIP appealed to Diet members to address the human trafficking problem and aggressively lobbied Diet members for an action plan on counter-trafficking measures. Soon after, special committees on human trafficking were created within the Liberal Democratic Party (LDP), the Democratic Party of Japan (DPJ), the Kōmeitō (Clean Government Party), the Japan Communist Party (JCP), and the Social Democratic Party (SDP). JNATIP members were invited to study groups of these parties, where they provided data on victims of trafficking in persons, particularly from Thailand and Colombia, and exchanged ideas. In December 2004, the government of Japan adopted an action plan to combat human trafficking and implemented legal changes such as amending the Penal Code to make human trafficking a crime. In October 2005, it agreed to set up a joint task force to combat human trafficking with the government of Thailand.[71] Here, the JNATIP holds a globally ambitious goal of eradicating human trafficking and aiding such victims from all over the world.

Japanese activists engage in pragmatic or problem-solving activities, which entail creativity and improvisation in action. They tend to be highly educated, holding internationalist views and generalized ideologies of social justice and equality. They often come into these groups with prior experience of oppositional politics. In the process of assisting illegal foreigners, these activists come to know well and empathize with the problems and life experiences of illegal foreigners and discover the ways in which these problems intersect with and illuminate broader societal issues. Through promotion of greater civic engagement between Japanese and foreigners and advocacy for social change, these activists advance grassroots democracy in Japan. At the same time, associative activism leads activists to clarify and refine their political concerns with others who share their abstract moral commitments. Out of their shared experiences in helping illegal foreigners emerges a critical reflection about Japan's national identity and ultimately a larger social and political movement for structural change in Japan, as well as in the capitalist world more generally.

---

71. Interview with Ōtsu Keiko of JNATIP, June 29, 2006.

The existence of immigrant rights NGOs that advocate for the protection of illegal foreigners poses a paradox for democratic theory. On the one hand, activists of these institutions are Japanese who represent the interest of a particular foreigner or non-Japanese group. Moreover, they represent a group of foreigners whose existence in Japan is illegal under Japanese law. As such, these NGOs appear undemocratic in terms of both democratic representation and the upholding of membership rules. On the other hand, they better represent the interests of illegal foreigners and advance public concerns about greater good than do immigrant ethnic associations. The next two chapters will show how these Japanese activists participate in greater politics and engage the governmental elite in public discourse. In this sense, these groups are critical forces for advancing social democracy in Japan.

5

LOCAL PARTNERS

Local Governments and Immigrant Rights NGOs

In recent years, a growing partnership has developed between Japanese immigrant rights NGOs and local governments. As increasing numbers of foreigners come into their areas, local governments have felt compelled by their own sense of responsibility to offer emergency public relief to those in immediate need. In the process of delivering social welfare services to foreign residents, these local authorities, particularly in progressive areas, have come to recognize and appreciate the work and expertise of the NGOs. They have established a dialogue with associative activists by inviting activists to give talks, arranging discussion meetings and citizens' assemblies, volunteering at their organizations, and even setting up NGO advisory councils in an effort to incorporate them into the process of setting policy priorities for foreign residents in their areas.[1] Local authorities

---

1. Although the Ministry of Internal Affairs and Communications (MIC) governs local government bodies, many local policy initiatives have long come from local officials at the prefecture,

seek institutional ideas and innovation from these NGO activists and work closely with them in implementation.

Through this partnership with local officials, Japanese activists engage in greater politics of paternalism. They effect transformation at the local level as they push certain local governments to assume broader responsibilities for caring for all their residents and help them to formulate local policy initiatives that incorporate foreign residents. In this way, immigrant rights' groups and local governments are local partners in redefining state responsibilities (and membership rules) in their areas. At the same time, this partnership demonstrates the political influence and independence of these small, foreigner support groups.

Local Governments and Foreign Residents

Local governments, whose officials must interact directly with residents in their areas, typically function as intermediary institutions between the central government and residents in delivering social welfare services and collecting information on the welfare needs of their residents. The Local Government Law requires that local governments ensure the safety, health, and welfare of all their residents, including the rapidly growing foreign populations in their areas. Therefore, local governments have created various support organizations for foreigners, including international exchange associations, labor consultation offices, and consultation centers for foreigners, to protect them as both residents and workers. These public institutions offer to foreigners information and consultation in various languages regarding labor, social security, education, family protection, housing, and cultural exchanges. Local governments then collect information on the welfare needs of their foreign residents and make recommendations to the central government.

During the 1980s, when Japanese cities were increasingly invited to participate in sister-city relationships, the Ministry of Internal Affairs and Communications (MIC) authorized local authorities to establish and fund International Affairs Divisions within their local government offices

---

city, town, village, and ward levels. See Richard J. Samuels, *The Politics of Regional Policy in Japan: Localities Incorporated?* (Princeton: Princeton University Press, 1983), esp. chap. 3.

and international exchange associations (*kokusai kōryū kyōkai*) in newly constructed buildings to promote local internationalization projects.[2] International Exchange Associations offer foreigners consultation services on family issues, immigration status, health insurance and pension, and labor-related issues. Meanwhile, local authorities, which tried to promote civic activities of their residents, also actively developed their own international exchange associations at the city, town, village, and ward levels inside City Halls, Town Halls, or Ward Offices. The activities of these smaller regional associations typically involve international cultural exchanges and information services, providing publications of foreign language materials.

Many local governments have also established special consultation centers for foreigners to answer inquiries in various foreign languages on family life, schools, housing, emergency contacts, social welfare system, insurance procedures, traffic accidents compensation, and Japanese customs.[3] These institutions, which are usually located inside public buildings, clearly benefit legal foreign residents such as *zainichi* and *nikkeijin*. As mentioned earlier in chapter 2, local governments in areas where *nikkeijin* are prevalent have provided various services such as translators at government offices and free Japanese language classes.[4] Only when a center teams up with an NGO are other languages such as Thai and Tagalog included in their services.[5]

2. Purnendra Jain, *Japan's Subnational Governments in International Affairs* (New York: Routledge, 2005); Katherine Tegtmeyer Pak, "Foreigners Are Local Citizens, Too: Local Governments Respond to International Migration in Japan," in Mike Douglass and Glenda Roberts, eds., *Japan and Global Migration: Foreign Workers and the Advent of a Multicultural Society* (Honolulu: University of Hawai'i Press, 2003), 244–274.

3. Interview with an official of the Tokyo Metropolitan Government Foreign Residents' Advisory Center, May 12, 1998. See Kanagawa Prefecture Government, *Gaikokuseki kenmin shien jissen no tame ni* [For the Practice of Assisting Foreign Residents in the Prefecture] (Yokohama: Kanagawa Prefecture Government, Foreign Affairs Division, 1994), 53. Some city halls, town halls, and ward offices also offer their own consultation services to foreigners. Foreigners in the Kanagawa Prefecture can also receive advisory service on human rights issues at the Human Rights Consultation Window. Interview with an official of the Kanagawa Prefecture Government Foreign Affairs Division, December 1, 1998.

4. Tsuda Takeyuki, "The Stigma of Ethnic Difference: The Structure of Prejudices and 'Discrimination' toward Japan's New Immigrant Minority," *Journal of Japanese Studies* 24, no. 2 (1998): 317–359 (349ff).

5. Interview with an official of the Tokyo Metropolitan Government Bureau of Citizens and Cultural Affairs, May 12, 1998. Tokyo Metropolitan Government, *Kokusai ni kan suru kakukyoku no torikumi jōkyō* [Situation of Each Bureau Concerning Internationalization] (Tokyo: Tokyo

Local governments with large populations of foreigners have set up labor consultation systems, through which they and their foreign interpreters offer free advisory services to foreign workers on working conditions and other general labor problems as part of their administrative services.[6] Labor consultation offices give advice on Japanese labor laws and on domestic employment practices in English and sometimes in additional languages, such as Chinese, Korean, Portuguese, and Spanish. Dispatched interpreters for other languages can also be arranged. These offices specialize in labor dispute settlement in the areas of labor contracts, work conditions, paid holidays and working hours, dismissal and nonpayment of wages, compensation for workplace injury and medical expenses, and labor union law. Officials at these offices also mediate labor disputes between foreign workers and their Japanese employers, acting as third-party conciliators at the consent of both the foreign worker and the employer and assisting them in reaching an acceptable solution to the problem or matter in question.[7] They do not represent either party, but try to bring the parties to a reasonable conclusion by taking both parties' views into consideration.[8] As neutral mediators, government officials at these offices

---

Metropolitan Government, Bureau of Citizens and Cultural Affairs, 1998), 68; Kanagawa Prefecture Government, *Shin-kanagawa kokusai seisaku suishin puran shinchoku daichō* [Proposed Plan of the New Kanagawa on International Policy: Progress Registry] (Yokohama: Kanagawa Prefecture Government, Foreign Affairs Division, 1998), 43.

6. Labor offices in Tokyo, which has a high population of foreign workers, appeared to be most active. Over half of the cases involved nonpayment of wages, unlawful dismissal, and labor contract infringement. Tokyo Metropolitan Government, *Rōdō sōdan oyobi assen no gaiyō (Heisei 9 nendo)* [1997 Outline of Labor Consultation and Mediation] (Tokyo: Tokyo Metropolitan Government, Labor and Economic Bureau, 1998), 27–33. Although labor offices in Tokyo handled 2,875 cases in 1997, only about 400 of them involved illegal foreign workers. The Zentōitsu Workers' Union alone worked on approximately 1,500 cases involving illegal foreign workers the same year. And this number did not include consultations. Interview with an official of the Tokyo Metropolitan Government Labor Administration Division, December 21, 1998.

7. Interview with an official of the Tokyo Labor Administration Office (Kameido), October 9, 1998.

8. For instance, a part-time Chinese worker at a restaurant sought advice at the Tokyo Labor Administrative Office after the employer refused to pay him fifteen days' worth of owed wages. The Chinese worker explained that he had quit working because the manager complained he took time off without giving any notice. The advisor approached the manager and discovered that the manager tried to tell the Chinese worker that he did not want to pay the wages except in the presence of the person who had introduced the employee to him. But in the presence of the advisor, he would pay the wages and deduct 30 percent as a fine for the loss the employee incurred to the restaurant due to his unexpected absences. The advisor then explained to the manager

try to listen to both sides and do not make demands on any concerned party. If the dispute concerns nonpayment of wages, the mediator simply asks the employer why s/he did not pay. This differs from activists at community workers' unions, who *always* take the position of the foreign worker. When the case appears complicated, advisors at some labor offices usually refer the foreign worker to a Japanese NGO that supports foreign workers.[9] Where a conciliation effort fails, the foreign employee may then want to seek further consultation with a lawyer and bring the matter to court.

In solving problems and conflicts involving foreign residents and ensuring their security and livelihood, local governments cannot always treat foreigners strictly in terms of legal residence; in some cases they must break with the central government on issues concerning foreigners' social, civil, and political rights.[10] Certain local governments, for instance, have split with the national government in their decision to extend medical services to all foreign residents, regardless of their visa or residential status.[11] Local governments in Tokyo, Osaka, Utsunomiya, Kawasaki, Yokohama, Kanagawa, and Saitama have done this by reviving the 1899 Sick or Dead Travelers Treatment Law (*ryokō byōnin oyobi shibōnin toriatsukai hō*), originally aimed at providing medical care to foreign travelers who were taken ill while traveling in Japan and had no caretaker. Illegal foreigners have benefited from this law, as it applies to any foreigner who temporarily visits Japan and does not have to register as a foreign resident. Many illegal foreigners who have not registered with their local authorities meet these

---

that Japanese Labor Laws stipulate that sanctions must be explicitly stated as a part of the rules of employment and fines cannot exceed half the wages for one day's work or 10 percent of the total wages over one payment period. When the Chinese worker met the employer, he apologized for taking absence without notice and the manager paid fifteen days' wages and transportation expenses. Interview with an official of the Tokyo Metropolitan Government's Economic and Labor Division, May 12, 1998.

9. The advisor gives a list of all Japanese NGOs to foreign workers and does not support any particular NGO. Interview with an official of the Kanagawa Foreign Workers Consulting Office, August 27, 1998.

10. These three dimensions of membership, as espoused by local authorities in progressive areas, are similar to T. H. Marshall's conceptualization of citizenship. See his *Citizenship and Social Class and Other Essays* (Cambridge: Cambridge University Press, 1950).

11. Yasuo Takao, "Foreigners' Rights in Japan: Beneficiaries to Participants," *Asian Survey* 43, no. 3 (2003): 527–552.

criteria. Some prefecture governments also have set up an "Emergency Medical Fee Subsidiary System" (*gaikokujin miharai iryō seido*) to cover unpaid medical expenses for emergency medical care. According to this system, the prefecture government covers 70 percent of the unpaid medical bill; the city, town, and village 20 percent; and the employer 10 percent. The Gunma Prefecture Government introduced this system in 1993 and was subsequently followed by Kanagawa, Hyōgo, Chiba, Saitama, Tokyo, and Yamanashi. In 1993, the Tsukuba government in the Ibaraki Prefecture initiated a free AIDS consultation service in English and Thai at the Tsukuba Health Center. Some progressive local governments have even requested that the central government expand its medical system to financially assist foreigners who cannot pay medical bills and reinstate the Livelihood Protection Law for overstayed foreigners. In sum, despite the actions of the central government to limit national health insurance (NHI) to certain foreigners, local governments in many areas have found alternative ways to offer direct relief to all foreign residents in immediate need.

In protecting the civil rights of their foreign residents, local governments, particularly in Kawasaki City where many zainichi Koreans live, have directly challenged conservative national policies. In 1985, Kawasaki officials acted against the national government and sided with the Koreans when they decided not to take legal action against Koreans who refused to be fingerprinted for their alien registration cards.[12] After other local governments began to follow Kawasaki's example, the central government eventually eliminated the fingerprinting requirement for foreigners in 2000. In 1996, Kawasaki officials also played a leading role in the movement to eliminate the requirement of Japanese nationality for city civil service positions (except firefighters), an initiative subsequently replicated by other cities and prefectures.

Local officials have also been active in the movement to obtain voting rights for foreigners in local elections. In 1990, eleven Koreans in Osaka sued for foreigners' suffrage. In 1995, the Supreme Court held that granting suffrage to foreign residents at local levels was "not unconstitutional" and should be left to the National Diet to legislate. By 2001, more than 1,400

---

12. Interview with an official of the Kawasaki City Government Citizens Bureau, December 25, 1998.

local governments (representing about 73 percent of Japan's total population) had adopted resolutions urging voting rights for non-Japanese residents in local elections. They believe that foreigners, especially permanent residents, who have close relationships with local communities in their daily lives, should be granted local suffrage. Since 1995, all political parties except the LDP have begun to support local suffrage for foreign residents in an effort to enhance their support bases. Each year since 1998, the Kōmeitō (Clean Government Party) has submitted a bill for consideration by the National Diet on local voting rights for foreign residents, but all have been shut down by conservative LDP politicians.[13] Meanwhile, some municipalities have passed ordinances to allow permanent foreign residents to vote in plebiscites that seek residents' opinions on local issues, and the Kanagawa Prefecture government, in particular, has pressed for MIC to examine ways for foreigners to be able to participate in local policy-making in the regional Committee for the Protection of Human Rights.[14]

In the absence of local suffrage for foreigners, some local authorities have created foreigner advisory councils to elicit foreign residents' opinions on public services and welfare needs. In 1994, local government officials in Kawasaki City set up Japan's first foreign resident advisory council, the Kawasaki City Representative Assembly for Foreign Residents (*Kawasaki-shi gaikokujin shimin daihyōsha kaigi*), which brings selected

---

13. Interview with Tōyama Kiyohiko of the Kōmeitō and the House of Councilors, August 4, 2007. The Kōmeitō's proposal "would extend permanent foreign residents the rights to vote in local assembly and mayoral elections if they have lived in the same municipality for a minimum of three months." See http://www.komei.or.jp/en/policy/08.html (accessed December 13, 2005). In an effort to reach a compromise with the LDP, the Kōmeitō proposed in 2000 that local suffrage be limited to permanent residents from countries with which Japan had diplomatic ties (i.e., not to North Korean nationals). Conservative LDP politicians invoked Article 15 of the Constitution, which states that political suffrage is a right for citizens of the country, and argued that giving this right to foreign residents would violate the supreme law. Some (including Koizumi Junichirō) argued that foreigners who desire suffrage should naturalize, while others proposed that conditional local suffrage be reciprocated by home countries. As a result, a network was formed in South Korea to mobilize the government to grant its permanent foreign residents, mostly Chinese, local suffrage for the 2006 local elections. This new development in Korea has taken by surprise the LDP politicians who had proposed the idea. Some (e.g., Etō Takami) argue that granting local suffrage to foreign residents would undermine national security and education. See Takao, "Foreigners' Rights in Japan," 548–550.

14. Kanagawa Prefecture Government, *Heisei 11 nendo kuni no shisaku-seido-yosan ni kansuru yōbō* [Demands Concerning the Country's Measure-System-Budget for 1999] (Yokohama: Kanagawa Prefecture Government Department of Planning, 1998).

foreign residents together to discuss issues concerning their livelihood.[15] The Citizens' Bureau of the Kawasaki City Government formed a six-person team to develop an institutional design for political participation of foreign residents. Professor Shimohara Hajime, who had taught European politics at the University of Tokyo's prestigious Law Department, headed the research committee. Believing that something had to be done to combat discrimination against foreigners and that Japan was not ready to grant foreigners voting rights, Shimohara concluded that the most appropriate action would be the establishment of an institution where foreign residents could express their opinions.[16] After another scholar-member, Nakai Takeshi, visited various European cities and studied several institutional designs for political participation of their foreign residents, the team decided to borrow the German institutional design from Frankfurt's Representative Assembly for Foreign Residents.[17]

Kawasaki's Representative Assembly meets four times a year to discuss problems of foreign residents. During these meetings, "representative" members, who must be at least eighteen years of age and have resided in Kawasaki for at least a year, discuss pressing matters for foreign residents, such as education, community life, and urban improvement.[18] Their discussion, which is conducted only in Japanese, includes debates among members on the proper course of action to recommend to their mayor. At the end of their term, they present their recommendations to the mayor, who then decides how to implement them.

---

15. While foreigner committees in Osaka, Kyoto, and the Hyōgo Prefecture appear to have been established earlier than the one in Kawasaki City, these committees were mostly "Discussion Groups," which also included Japanese members.

16. Interview with Shimohara Hajime, January 20, 1999.

17. Investigative Research Committee of the Kawasaki City Representative Assembly for Foreign Residents, *Kashō: Kawasaki-shi gaikokujin shimin daihyōsha kaigi chōsa kenkyū hōkokusho* [Tentative Name: Kawasaki City Representative Assembly for Foreign Residents—Investigative Report] (Kawasaki: Kawasaki City Government, Citizens Bureau, 1996). Even the name of the assembly is a direct translation of Frankfurt's *Kommunale Ausländervertretung*.

18. Interview with an official of the Kawasaki City Government Citizens Bureau, December 25, 1998; also see Yamada Takao, "Kawasaki-shi gaikokujin shimin daihyōsha kaigi no seiritsu to genjō" [The Establishment and Conditions of the Kawasaki City Representative Assembly for Foreign Residents], in Miyajima Takashi, ed., *Gaikokujin shimin to seiji sanka* [Foreign Residents and Political Participation] (Tokyo: Yushindo, 2000), 39–57; Higuchi Naoto, "Taikō to kyōryoku" [Confrontation and Cooperation], in Miyajima Takashi, ed., *Gaikokujin shimin to seiji sanka* [Foreign Residents and Political Participation] (Tokyo: Yushindo, 2000), 20–38.

The First Representative Assembly (1997–1998) consisted of 26 members: Korean and Chinese immigrant ethnic associations recommended 5 members, while government officials selected the other 21 members from a pool of 258 applications.[19] The number of representatives from each immigrant ethnic group was determined proportionately, based on the number of its members who had registered in Kawasaki City. Each representative member could serve only two terms of office. Lee In Ha, a prominent zainichi Korean, was selected as chairperson of the First Assembly. The First Assembly proposed that the city administrators better assist international students by overhauling the scholarship system. In addition, the Committee on Community Life proposed creating a housing ordinance that included a clause prohibiting discrimination in the private rental market against foreign residents, the disabled, the elderly, single mothers, and families with children. Assembly members urged the city administrators to consider effective methods of abolishing housing discrimination; for example, educating landowners and residential building managers and publicizing the names of those who discriminated. They also asked the city administrators to consider establishing a public guarantor system made up of local governments, real estate agents, universities, vocational schools, and citizens' groups.[20] The Kawasaki City government responded soon after by revising its "Fundamental Plan of Kawasaki Residences" and creating a fundamental ordinance on housing.[21] Moreover, starting in 2000, the Kawasaki City government began offering to sign as guarantor for its foreign residents in renting and buying residences.

Since Kawasaki's experiment, other local governments have established similar foreigner advisory councils in their cities or towns, with varying numbers of foreign members and methods of selection (through application to local officials and/or selection from ethnic groups): the Tokyo Foreigners' Advisory Council (1997), the Kanagawa Foreign Residents'

---

19. The ratio became 3 recommended and 23 selected during the Second Assembly (1998–1999).

20. Kawasaki City Representative Assembly for Foreign Residents, *Kawasaki-shi gaikokujin shimin daihyōsha kaigi nenji hōkoku 1997 nendo* [1997 Annual Report of the Kawasaki City Representative Assembly for Foreign Residents] (Kawasaki: Kawasaki City Government Citizens Affairs Bureau, 1998); also see Kawasaki City Government, *Kawasaki City Representative Assembly for Foreign Residents Newsletter* 1 (March 31, 1997): 5–6.

21. *Asahi Evening News,* October 24, 1999.

Council (1998), the Forum of Kyoto City Policy for Foreign Residents (1998), the Fukuoka Foreign Citizens' Board (1998), the Mino'o City Foreign Residents Policy Council (1999), and the Mitaka International Roundtable (1999). The foreigner advisory councils provide a mechanism for reflecting the voices of resident foreigners in the policy-making process and presenting policy proposals to their local governments. Unfortunately, however, the city administration lacks the authority to enact many of these proposals. An official of Kawasaki's Citizens Affairs Bureau explains, "When they [foreign representatives] talk about their problems, they eventually come up against the wall of national law and visa status. Those problems are difficult for the city alone to solve."[22] On reform of immigration controls, for example, city officials claim that all the mayor of Kawasaki can do is to submit a proposal to the relevant ministry. If the proposal is rejected, officials are "obliged to explain to the council what can and cannot be reflected in policies."[23] In some cases, these foreigner advisory councils fail to offer concrete proposals. The first annual report of the Tokyo Foreigners' Advisory Council, for example, discussed broad and diverse topics, including ways to distribute information to foreigners, human rights, voting in local elections, health, welfare, education, labor, housing, environment, and security, but offered no specific proposals in these areas.[24]

The foreigner advisory councils are further limited by the fact that they are not legislated public entities. As private bodies, they can be changed easily by the council members, for changes require no legislative process. The Tokyo Foreigners' Advisory Council, for example, has not met since 2001, when its members criticized the Tokyo governor, Ishihara Shintarō, for his racist remarks at a gathering of Ground Self-Defense Force troops. Furthermore, private bodies are not places where members make policy but places where members *express* their opinions. For example, the Kanagawa governor Okazaki Hiroshi can only promise to "respect as much as possible" the council's view; like other local government heads, he is not obliged to implement the recommendations of the private panel. In cases where opinions of members are divided, opinions of all sides are included

---

22. Ibid.
23. Ibid.
24. Interview with an official of the Tokyo Metropolitan Government Bureau of Citizens and Cultural Affairs, May 12, 1998.

in the councils' recommendations. In the third session of the Tokyo Foreigners' Advisory Council in May 1998, for example, an apparent majority of the council members supported a recommendation to allow foreign residents the right to vote in local elections and work in local governments. But some North Korean members strongly objected to this recommendation. The Tokyo Metropolitan Government officials then decided not to allow the council to take votes on such issues, fearing that majority decisions could split the council over politically sensitive issues that divide many North and South Korean residents in Japan.[25]

Although the membership of foreign advisory councils reflects the proportion of each immigrant ethnic group in the area, members cannot be viewed as "representatives" of their own ethnic groups, and none claim to be. With the exceptions of the Forum in Saku, whose meetings are open to all, and the Council in Hyōgo, where members are *elected* by their own immigrant ethnic groups, local officials *select* most of these "representatives." Because immigrant ethnic communities and networks among newcomers are not yet sufficiently well-organized to articulate and aggregate their interests at the foreigners' councils, council members represent only their own opinions and not necessarily those of their ethnic communities, perhaps with the exception of the zainichi Koreans and Chinese.[26] Since discussion is held only in Japanese, representation in the councils is also biased by the Japanese language competency of the members. Understandably, zainichi Koreans (and Chinese) dominate most discussion at these councils because they are native speakers of Japanese. A Peruvian representative on the Kawasaki council complained, "I felt that I only came here to warm my seat. Koreans are not the only foreigners."[27] Moreover, the issues raised at these councils, which are usually influenced or controlled by city government officials, are broad and aim to benefit foreign residents in general. Thus, they seldom cover issues of immediate concern for illegal foreigners unless there is an intervention by a Japanese NGO.

---

25. *Japan Times,* August 14, 1998.

26. A Thai representative at the Kawasaki City Representative Assembly for Foreign Residents had tried to encourage other Thais to attend the meeting, but no one showed any interest in participating. Besides, many overstayed foreigners do not have the time to attend, for they must work six days a week and prefer to use their only day off for rest. Interview with Somsee Mochida of the Kawasaki City Representative Assembly for Foreign Residents, October 24, 1998.

27. *Asahi Evening News,* October 24, 1999.

Cooperation between Local Governments
and Immigrant Rights NGOs

Japanese immigrant rights NGOs have had a significant impact on local governments and their efforts to deliver public services to foreign residents. During the 1990s, when officials at various local public entities were just beginning to provide basic services to foreigners and were still inexperienced in assisting foreign residents, they turned to activists at immigrant rights NGOs for help. In order to establish a dialogue with activists and tap their expertise, local government officials invite Japanese activists to give talks in their offices, affiliated institutions, and study groups. Some even join these groups themselves and participate in their activities. Officials from progressive areas have discovered the financial benefit of outsourcing their services and activities to these NGOs, whose work and expertise they quickly come to appreciate. They recognize that the burden on local institutions would be substantially greater without the assistance of NGOs. At the same time, activists may reap some benefits through local government support by organizing toward clearly defined and longstanding goals. Consequently, the *issues* addressed by the support groups tend to be relatively durable, even though these groups may not last long. Cooperation between local governments and NGOs promotes the creation of an innovative institutional environment in which legal foreigners, local government officials, and Japanese activists come together to discuss matters concerning the livelihood of foreign residents and to make policy recommendations to the governor.

Local government officials think highly of Japanese activists and their support groups for foreigners. Some praise their noble effort in helping distressed foreigners, and most appreciate the expert knowledge that these Japanese activists have demonstrated in solving problems for overstayed foreigners.[28] When staff at various international exchange associations in the Kanagawa Prefecture encounter difficult cases involving international marriage, divorce, or domestic violence, they typically refer the foreigners to Mizula or Saalaa.[29] Similarly, an official at the Yokohama Welfare

---

28. Interview with an official of the Kanagawa Foreign Workers Consulting Office, August 27, 1998.

29. Interview with an official of the Kanagawa International Association, May 13, 1998.

Center in Kotobuki-chō often sends foreigners who have come to his center for help to the Kalabaw-no-kai. He explains, "NGOs provide more professional services to foreign workers than do government-run welfare centers. If these NGOs did not exist, local governments would have to do all the work, which means that many of the problems would not be resolved [for foreigners]."[30]

During the 1990s, local officials at International Exchange Associations and international offices in the Kanagawa prefecture admitted that they still lacked the know-how to help foreign residents.[31] In 1996, some of these officials formed the Kanagawa Prefecture Foreigners Consultation Study Group (*Kanagawa-ken gaikokujin sōdan madoguchi kenkyūkai*), which regularly invites members of immigrant rights NGOs to speak at their meetings to share their extensive experience.[32] Invited speakers included activists from the medical group SHARE, the lawyers' group Kanagawa Administrative Lawyer Association—Foreign Negotiation Administrative Research Group, and the women's group Mizula. In educating staff and volunteers of Kanagawa's international offices, these Japanese activists did not restrain themselves from criticizing traditional, discriminatory practices and local government officials' slow response to the needs of distressed foreign residents.[33]

---

30. Interview with an official of the Kotobuki-chō Health and Welfare Center, December 15, 1998.

31. Interview with an official of the Kanagawa Prefecture Government Foreign Affairs Department, December 1, 1998.

32. Interview with a staff member of the Kanagawa International Association and organizer of the Foreigners Consultation Study Group, July 3, 1998.

33. In a meeting at the Kanagawa Kenmin Center on November 27, 1998, for example, the Study Group invited Abe Hiroko of Mizula to talk. Staff and volunteers at the Kanagawa international offices brought up at the meeting difficult cases involving foreign women that they had encountered at their offices. They then asked Abe how to go about resolving them—one case at a time. Abe, who appeared soft and polite at a first glance, spoke fast and loud with great charisma. While advising these government officials, she often mocked Japanese men for their traditional beliefs and attitudes by speaking in a low voice with her lips artificially forced downward while slightly shaking her head like a samurai out of a *jidai gekki* (period) film. When someone raised a specific case involving a troubled, overstayed Filipino woman who was in hiding and showed reluctance to come to the international office for consultation, Abe replied, "That's easy. You...go and meet her. You can decide on a coffee shop or train station or whatever. It would mean that you will have to leave your office in order to meet with her. Go ahead and leave your office, the government can't fire you for leaving your office. You are public officials; you can't be fired!" The participants were embarrassed but all thought that her talk was helpful.

Japanese activists also speak at local government-sponsored forums because they have learned that they can significantly impact policy through local government officials. During her speech at a meeting of the Kawasaki City Representative Assembly for Foreign Residents on June 29, 1996, Miki Emiko of Saalaa expressed her belief that the Ministry of Justice listens more to people from local public institutions (*chihō kōkyō dantai*), who, in turn, respect the opinions of the foreigner advisory councils more than those of lawyers and NGOs.[34] At the Assembly meeting, Miki discussed various problems that arise with each type of visa status and provided concrete examples of problems that foreigners encountered. She also took the opportunity as a guest speaker to discuss pressing concerns regarding medical treatment and health insurance for overstayed foreigners. As she had hoped, the Committee on Community Life announced in the Assembly's newsletter on March 31, 1997, that "[a]ccess to medical care, including the problems faced by people overstaying their visas, will be a topic for future discussion."[35] Because these foreigner advisory councils typically do not touch on issues that concern overstayed foreigners, Miki's presence as a guest speaker at the Kawasaki Assembly was significant in adding this new agenda item for discussion.

Japanese NGOs also impact local government by attracting local government officials to participate in their activities. Some local officials feel so strongly about the purposes and activities of these groups that they have joined them and engage in social activism after work. These individuals call their volunteer work "after five activities," using the English "after five" (*afutā faibu*) and adding the Japanese "activities" (*katsudō*) to form this wonderful phrase. One official explained that local officials like him, who are active in "after five activities," are actually "not important people." He claimed that an official who becomes "important" in the bureaucratic system lacks the freedom to do whatever he pleases. Because as a local bureaucrat, he cannot be fired (unless he commits a serious crime),

---

34. See Kawasaki City Representative Assembly for Foreign Residents, *Kawasaki-shi gaikoku-jin shimin daihyōsha kaigi nenji hōkoku 1997 nendo* [1997 Annual Report of the Kawasaki City Representative Assembly for Foreign Residents] (Kawasaki: Kawasaki City Government Citizens Bureau, 1998), 9–16.

35. *Kawasaki City Representative Assembly for Foreign Residents Newsletter* 1 (March 31, 1997): 6.

he is content not to become "important" inside the bureaucratic system and enjoys meeting many interesting people outside of it. Thus, he devotes his energy to his "after five activities," returning home around 10:30 every night from NGO meetings or study group meetings.[36]

Three prominent "after five" activists work in the Tokyo metropolitan area. The first two, Hatade Akira and Tanaka Kiyoshi (pen names), work at different Tokyo Labor Offices. Hatade is also a member of JCLU and helped found the concerned citizens group Call Network. He then recruited his friend, Tanaka, to join the group. In addition to their articles in the Call Network Newsletter, these two men write extensively, criticizing certain government policies toward foreigners. Hatade has published over ten articles in various books on issues concerning foreign workers in Japan and regularly contributes articles to a newsletter of the Solidarity Network with Migrants Japan (SMJ). His articles reveal the desperate situation and various labor problems that some illegal foreign workers face in Japan.[37] He consistently expresses critical views of the trainee system, the state's construction of negative images of foreigners, and the lack of commitment of the Japanese government and society to protect international human rights.[38] Similarly, Tanaka has contributed articles on foreign workers in Japan to edited books and labor journals, albeit fewer than Hatade. He

---

36. Interview with an official of the Tokyo Labor Office (Shinjuku), December 21, 1998 and June 10, 1999.

37. In particular, see Hatade Akira, "Gaikokujin rōdōsha wo meguru hataraki" [Turning the Work of Foreign Workers Around], in Tanaka Hiroshi and Ebashi Takashi, eds., *Rainichi gaikokujin jinken hakusho* [White Paper on Human Rights of Newcoming Foreigners] (Tokyo: Akashi Shoten, 1997), 75–110; CALL Network, ed., *Anata no machi no gaikokujin* [Foreigners in Your Town] (Tokyo: Dai-ichi Shorin, 1991), 3–10, 161–172. In addition, he has written numerous pieces in the Iwanami Shoten's monthly *Sekai* [World] criticizing the trainee system, government actions against Iranians, and governmental social security for foreigners. See Hatade Akira, "Ginō jisshū seido wa nani wo motarasu" [What Does Learning Skills System Bring?] *Sekai,* April 1993; Hatade, "Jyunbi sareta iranjin tekihatsu geki" [Faking the Arrest of Iranian] *Sekai,* August 1993; Hatade, "Kōtai suru gaikokujin no shakai hoshō" [Retracting Social Security for Foreigners] *Sekai,* June 1994.

38. See Hatade Akira, "Kenshūsei seido no mondai jōkyō" [Problematic Condition of the Trainee System], in Forum on Asian Immigrant Workers, ed., *Okasareru jinken gaikokujin rōdōsha* [Violated Human Rights of Foreign Workers] (Tokyo: Dai-san Shokan, 1992), 295–314; Hatade, *Gaikokujin to kokusai jinken* [Foreigners and International Human Rights] (Tokyo: Kaifū Shobō, 1992), 99–113; Hakoishi Mami and Hatade Akira, "Rainichi gaikokujin no hanzai" [Foreigners Crimes], in Tanaka Hiroshi and Ebashi Takashi, eds., *Rainichi gaikokujin jinken hakusho* [White Paper on Human Rights of Newcoming Foreigners] (Tokyo: Akashi Shoten, 1997), 320–339.

wrote critically about the 1990 reform of the Immigration Control Law and Japan's trainee system.[39] These two officials use pen names for their "after five activities" to avoid possible problems with their work at the Tokyo Labor Offices, where they must interact regularly with Japanese from various labor unions. Although Call Network dissolved in 1996, both continued to attend study groups organized by immigrant rights NGOs in Tokyo and Yokohama.[40]

The third "after five" activist is Ōkawa Akihiro (real name), who works in the Yokohama Welfare Center in Kotobuki-chō and is an executive committee member of the SMJ. Ōkawa regularly participated in the National Forums in Solidarity with Migrant Workers.[41] During the 1999 Third National Forum in Solidarity with Migrant Workers in Tokyo, he and Kawamoto Hiroyuki of the KOSHC led the discussion at the panel on "Support for Migrants' Daily Living and Medical Treatment." During the late 1990s, Ōkawa, like Tanaka, regularly attended the Kanagawa's Occupational Accident Study Group that Kawamoto organized at Miki Emiko's law office. Finding medical services for impoverished residents of Kotobuki-chō to be disappointingly inadequate, Ōkawa believes that the local government should provide medical patrols in the area, as do volunteer medical groups, such as SHARE, to help both Japanese and foreign residents. At the same time, however, he recognizes that local government officials lack the know-how and that their presence would intimidate many overstayed foreigners.[42] As a result, Ōkawa volunteers his time at

39. See Tanaka Kiyoshi, "'Kaisei' nyūkanhō wo kangaeru" [Thinking over the 'Revision' of the Immigration Control Law] *Rōhō Sentā Nyūsu* [Labor Laws Center News] 93 (April-May 1991): 1–12; Tanaka, "Gaikokujin kenshūsei no genjō to mondaiten" [Conditions and Problems of Foreigner Trainees], in Ebashi Takashi, ed., *Gaikokujin rōdōsha to jinken* [Foreign Workers and Human Rights] (Tokyo: Hosei University Press, 1989), 95–119; Tanaka, "Chitsujo aru gaikokujin rōdōryoku no dōnyūe" [Introducing Order to Foreigners Labor Power] *Rōhō Sentā Nyūsu* 112 (April 1993): 1–11.
40. Interview with an official of the Tokyo (Kameido) Labor Office, October 9, 1998.
41. On Ōkawa's role in the First (1995) and Second (1998) Forum, see National Exchange Forum on the Problems of Foreign Workers, *Gaikokujin rōdōsha mondai zenkoku kōryū shūkai hōkokushū* [Report on the National Exchange Forum on Problems of Foreign Workers] (Osaka: Mimeograph, 1995), 42–49; Organizing Committee of the Second National Forum on Migrant Workers' Problems, *Dai-ni kai ijū rōdōsha mondai zenkoku fōrumu hōkokushū* [Report on the Second National Forum on Migrant Workers' Problems] (Nagoya: Mimeograph, 1998), 47–51.
42. Interview with Ōkawa Akihiro of the Yokohama Welfare Center, December 15, 1998.

various immigrant rights NGOs and works to promote their development to better serve impoverished residents.

As the country faces a welfare crisis and international criticism for its lack of legal protections for women, local government officials have felt the need to promote secondary associations in medical and women's issues. Since local governments are legally constrained, however, they cannot assist overstayed foreigners at the same level as can NGOs, even if they are willing to challenge policies of the central government.[43] As a result, they outsource many life-saving services for overstayed foreigners, such as medical assistance and women's emergency shelters, to immigrant rights NGOs. In Tokyo, for example, the Tokyo Metropolitan Government contracted with AMDA to provide medical consultation to foreigners in five languages: English, Chinese, Korean, Thai, and Spanish.[44] In 1994, after a national government study found that foreigners accounted for 80 percent of AIDS patients in Japan, the Tokyo government provided money for AMDA to bring an AIDS specialist from Thailand. (In the Nagano Prefecture alone, 617 out of 679 AIDS patients were foreigners—613 of them were Thais.)[45] In 1996, it funded AMDA to start an AIDS Information Helpline in English and Thai.[46] The women's shelter HELP has also received considerable financial support from the Tokyo Metropolitan Government for its activities in helping foreign women.[47] In 1998, the Tokyo Metropolitan Government also contracted with HELP to publish handbooks specifically for (overstayed) Thai migrants on family life and labor laws in Japan.[48]

In the Kanagawa Prefecture, the Kanagawa International Association initiated the Fund Assistance System (*shikin josei seido*) in 1993 to support international NGOs inside its prefecture. This program provides funding

---

43. On this point see Katherine Tegtmeyer Pak, "Living in Harmony: Prospects for Cooperative Local Responses to Foreign Migrants," in Sheila Smith, ed., *Local Voices, National Issues* (Ann Arbor: University of Michigan's Center for Japanese Studies, 2000), 51–74 (71ff).

44. Interview with an official of the Tokyo Metropolitan Government Policy News Section, May 12, 1998.

45. *Yomiuri Shimbun,* September 29, 1996.

46. *Nikkei Shimbun,* October 24, 1996.

47. In 1996, for example, about 20 percent of HELP's total budget came from the Tokyo Metropolitan Government.

48. The Tokyo Metropolitan Government funded these publications through the Tokyo International Foundation.

of up to three million yen (US$27,500) for projects that have included over-seas development, assistance for resident foreigners, international coopera-tion, NGO promotion, and emergency support for disasters.[49] During the late 1990s, the Kanagawa International Association expressly supported those projects that would enhance the organization of co-ethnic self-help groups. Hence, SOL was able to expand its activities to serve specific groups, such as Koreans, Filipinos, and Latinos, and to hire co-ethnic staff members. The Kalabaw-no-kai similarly organized a Bangladeshi self-help group, most of whose members consist of overstayed foreign workers, with funding from the Kanagawa International Association.[50]

In some places, cash-stricken local governments outsource their activi-ties and services to immigrant rights NGOs in order to save money.[51] Since 1995, when the Yokohama City Government experienced a sharp decline in its budget, the Yokohama Association for International Communica-tion and Exchange (YOKE) has coordinated activities with local NGOs. In 1997, for example, YOKE began contracting with immigrant rights NGOs for the publication of multilingual manuals to provide informa-tion about living in Yokohama. In 2000, YOKE subcontracted Mizula to run its women shelter. It has discovered that partnerships with Japanese NGOs enable the city to offer assistance to foreigners more inexpensively and with greater success. Moreover, this coordination allows YOKE to

---

49. From 1993 to 1997, the Kanagawa International Association gave 35,691,835 yen to NGOs that were involved in such activities. Five Japanese NGOs that were supporting ille-gal foreign workers in the prefecture received 13,933,331 yen (almost 40 percent) of the total amount. The women's shelters Mizula and Saalaa together received over 25 percent of the assis-tance awarded during these four years. Interview with an official of the Kanagawa International Association, May 13, 1998.

50. Interview with Imaizumi Megumi of the Kalabaw-no-kai, March 8, 1998.

51. For example, the Kanagawa Prefecture Government spent approximately 15 million yen per year between 1996 and 1998 to provide information, consultation, and translation ser-vices to foreign residents. In contrast, the Kalabaw-no-kai spent between 6.5 million to 8 million per year during the same period. Kalabaw-no-kai's figure includes rent and administrative staff, whereas the Kanagawa Prefecture Government's figure does not. Moreover, the range and inten-sity of the activities provided by the Kalabaw-no-kai far exceed those of any local governments. Kanagawa Prefecture Government, *Shin-kanagawa kokusai seisaku suishin puran shinchoku daichō* (Yokohama: Kanagawa Prefecture Government Foreign Affairs Division, 1998), 43–44. Figures for Kalabaw-no-kai are from JANIC, *NGO dairekutorī '98* [NGO Directory '98] (Tokyo: JANIC, 1998); JANIC, *Kokusai kyōryoku NGO dairekutorī 2000* [International Cooperation NGO Direc-tory 2000] (Tokyo: JANIC, 2000).

collect far better information on the condition of foreigners in the area. YOKE then uses the information to decide what additional public services for foreigners should be developed.[52] YOKE has also developed an internship program on international volunteer activities for Japanese residents in Yokohama. Three foreigner support groups—Kalabaw-no-kai, Saalaa, and SOL—participate in this program as accepting institutions. The training course lasts from September to January and introduces interns to the activities of these groups.

Local governments have also found that outsourcing services and activities to NGOs allows them to expand services and/or jurisdictions without increasing the number of their officials.[53] In exchange for financial support, local governments can list these groups in their Japanese, English, and other foreign language brochures, pamphlets, and websites as places that provide services to foreigners who live in their areas. For example, in its English guidebook *Living in Tokyo,* the Tokyo Metropolitan Government recommends the women's shelter HELP to foreign women and their children for emergency shelter ahead of its own Tokyo Metropolitan Women's Consulting Center. In fact, some pamphlets read as if local governments are providing the NGO services themselves. For example, at its offices throughout Tokyo, the Tokyo Metropolitan Government distributes a three-by-four inch pamphlet that offers medical services, through the "Tokyo Medical Information Service 'Himawari'"—all of whose telephone numbers go to AMDA.

Although immigrant rights NGOs have forged strong partnerships with local officials in many areas, their impact on local governments is not uniform across geographical regions. In progressive areas or areas with long histories of dealing with foreigners, such as the Kanagawa Prefecture and the Hanshin region, local governments are more innovative in improving the lives of their foreign residents and in cooperating with NGOs. In contrast, local governments in conservative areas and areas with little contact with foreigners, such as the Ibaraki Prefecture, directly provide most services for their foreign residents and typically cooperate with voluntary associations only around the issue of cultural exchange.

---

52. Interview with an official of YOKE, September 24, 1998.

53. In fact, the number of Japanese bureaucrats remains relatively low in comparison to those in other advanced industrial countries.

Institutionalizing Cooperation and Improving
Democratic Representation

After repeated interactions, cooperation between local governments and immigrant rights NGOs is becoming increasingly institutionalized. Until the election of Ishihara Shintarō as governor, the Tokyo Metropolitan Government sponsored multipart seminars to enhance cooperation between its officials and NGO activists. In the 1997–1998 seminar, the Tokyo Metropolitan Government brought Japanese NGO activists and government officials together on February 13–14, 1998, to discuss "International Exchange and Cooperation" for Tokyo, which included such topics as the provision of medical and consultation services to foreigners and Japan's immigration system. Dr. Sawada Takashi of the medical group SHARE participated in a panel on "Health and Medical Treatments for Foreigners," Suzuki Akihiko of the OC-Net in a panel on "Foreigner Consultations and Networking," and Tsunami Kimie of the APFS in one on the "Immigration Control System."[54] There, NGO activists addressed specific problems of overstayed foreign residents and attempted, together with local authorities, to come up with feasible solutions.

The 1998 Nonprofit Organization (NPO) Law, which grants smaller volunteer and other civic groups corporate status, further promotes partnerships between NGOs and local governments.[55] The NPO Law was designed to promote corporate status to small voluntary organizations by eliminating financial requirements and easing the approval process, which dovetailed with Japan's neoliberal reforms at the time. Previously, the criteria for certification of incorporation were too rigid and difficult for many small voluntary organizations, due to a minimum requirement of financial assets and a lengthy approval process. The process was subject to intense bureaucratic scrutiny both during and after the approval process. The NPO

---

54. Tokyo Metropolitan Government, *Tōkyō-to kokusaika suishin shidōsha seminā hōkokusho* [Report on the Leadership Seminar on the Promotion of the Internalization of the Tokyo Metropolitan Government] (Tokyo: Tokyo Metropolitan Government Citizens and Cultural Affairs Division, 1998), 3.

55. Since the passage of the 1998 NPO law, Japan's civil society groups have been growing at an impressive rate, with 22,434 NPO Legal Persons by June 30, 2005. On the passage of this law, see Robert Pekkanen, "Japan's New Politics: The Case of the NPO Law," *Journal of Japanese Studies* 26, no. 1 (2000): 111–143.

law now allows local governments to accept more responsibilities for public welfare and to provide more services to their residents without carrying a heavier financial burden by "inviting" volunteerism from small civil society groups.[56] It has also led to further decentralization of the central government by granting incorporation authority to local government agencies. Under the NPO law, the governor of the prefecture in which an NPO is located (or the director-general of the Economic Planning Agency at the Cabinet Office in the case of NPOs with offices in at least two prefectures) serves as the authority to give a certificate of incorporation if the organization conforms to the guidelines set by the governor (or director-general).

The NPO law does not affect most small foreigner support groups, but it has had a significant impact on the groups, such as medical NGOs and women's support groups, that work closely with local governments to provide social welfare services. Four medical NGOs [AMDA, SHARE, Tokyo Occupational Safety and Health Resource Center (TOSHC), and Multi-language Information Center Kanagawa (MIC Kanagawa)], two women's groups (Mizula and Saalaa), and one faith-based group helping foreign women with AIDS (Āyus) have acquired NPO status. Understandably, those organizations that had already been incorporated as religious corporations, labor unions, medical corporations, lawyer associations, foundations, or social welfare corporations had no reason to apply for NPO status. None of the ideologically concerned citizens' groups, which are not incorporated in any form, have applied for NPO incorporation. They prefer to pressure the central government directly on policies relating to immigration control, such as membership rules and state responsibilities for the welfare of foreigners. In addition, most of these groups do not intend to apply because they fear that incorporation will obligate them to disclose information to local authorities, who also supervise the overall activities of their organizations.[57] Indeed, while institutional capture may have benefits in terms of improved access and be worth the cost of diminished independence, most concerned citizens' groups find this trade-off unacceptable.

56. Akihiro Ogawa, "Invited by the State: Institutionalizing Volunteer Subjectivity in Contemporary Japan," *Asian Anthropology* 3 (2004): 71–96.

57. Interviews with: Imaizumi Megumi of the Kalabaw-no-kai, June 16, 2003; Yoshinari Katsuo of the APFS, June 10, 2003; Yano Manami of the Solidarity Network with Migrants Japan, July 18, 2003.

With the exceptions of TOSHC and Āyus, all foreigner support groups with NPO status perform some services for local governments and receive financial support from them.[58] Although local government officials choose NGOs for partnerships based on their activities/services, they prefer an NPO-incorporated group over a nonincorporated one.[59] On the other hand, they dislike big civic organizations because their large size makes them quite bureaucratic and slow to get things done. As a result, those groups that have acquired NPO status have seen an increase in their operating funds, primarily coming from local governments. For example, between 1996 and 2002, the annual operating funds of the women's group Saalaa doubled, from 18 to 36 million yen (US$165,000 to 330,000) and those of Mizula increased even more, from 21 to 50 million yen (US$193,000 to 460,000). Medical NPOs have also enjoyed more operating funds, but the increase has not been as dramatic as that for the women's groups. Moreover, the newly incorporated NPOs report that it has become easier for them to conduct their activities. For Saalaa, incorporation means that the group can obtain its own bank account instead of using an account of its representative.[60] For TOSHC, incorporation means that small companies are no longer suspicious when its staff asks to assess the environmental conditions in their factories, and government officials are also more willing to cooperate.[61] As a result of the NPO law, the organizational activities of the groups that acquire NPO status have also expanded significantly. Mizula, for example, now runs two additional women's shelters in Yokohama and Yokosuka. The Yokohama City Government also outsources its consulting services for women during the weekends to Mizula. Interestingly, Mizula had already received some financial support from local governments and performed many public services before it was incorporated. In fact, it was Yokohama officials that asked Mizula to incorporate—perhaps to legitimize their decisions to outsource many public services to the group.[62]

---

58. TOSHC hopes to form partnerships with its local government soon.

59. Interview with officials of the Kanagawa Prefecture Government International Division, August 4, 2004.

60. Interview with Niikura Hisano of Saalaa, July 20, 2003.

61. Interview with Iida Katsuyasu of TOSHC, August 8, 2004.

62. Interview with Kikutani Hideko of Mizula, July 16, 2004.

The increase in financial support and organizational activities for those groups with NPO status does not mean that they necessarily fare better than those without it. With an increase in public acceptance and financial resources usually comes greater responsibility. Both Mizula and SHARE report that their financial situations have actually worsened since incorporation. Expenditure on their growing activities and public services has increased tremendously. In addition, SHARE felt the need to improve staff salaries and health insurance coverage after incorporation.[63] Most surprisingly, membership remains relatively the same since incorporation despite the increase in the operating budget and greater ease in organizational activities. Mizula representatives explain that they are overwhelmed with work and now have less time for activities to raise publicity and membership. Since they do not depend on members for funds or legitimacy, they no longer put much effort into attracting new members and retaining old ones.

A landmark institutional experiment that recognized the importance of NGOs in local governance and gave voice to illegal foreigners through Japanese activists was the establishment in the Kanagawa prefecture of an NGO advisory council. In 1998, when it created the Kanagawa Foreign Residents' Council, the Kanagawa Prefecture Government also introduced an NGO advisory council, the NGO Kanagawa International Cooperation Council (NGO *Kanagawa kokusai kyōryoku kaigi*). The idea of creating an NGO advisory council actually came from local government officials at the Kanagawa Prefecture Government Foreign Affairs Division. A Kanagawa official reported that questions were raised as to why the Kawasaki's Representative Assembly for Foreign Residents included only foreigners, when members of immigrant rights NGOs were seen as their local partners. Hence, Kanagawa officials saw the need to create an NGO advisory council alongside the Foreign Residents' Council.[64] The NGO advisory council consists of ten members from different NGOs, who are selected by a four-person Committee of Specialists (mostly university professors). It has four divisions: regional internationalization, international exchange, international cooperation, and peace. For the first

---

63. Interview with Sawada Takashi of SHARE, July 31, 2004.
64. Interview with an official of the Kanagawa Prefecture Government Foreign Affairs Division, December 1, 1998.

NGO advisory council, the Committee of Specialists selected six women and four men, three each for the regional internationalization, international exchange, and international cooperation groups and one for the peace group. One of the ten members in the first NGO advisory council was Ariizumi Keiko of Mizula. The subsequent council included Ueda Yoshitsugu of Kalabaw-no-kai.

The Kanagawa Prefecture Government established the NGO advisory council in order to elicit opinions from NGO members and reflect on them in making the prefecture's international policy. The stated goals of the NGO Kanagawa International Cooperation Council are (1) to promote NGO participation in the policy-making process of the prefecture government on regional international policy; (2) to strengthen cooperation between local governments and NGOs; and (3) to strengthen cooperation among NGOs within the prefecture.[65] The link between the twenty-member Foreign Residents' Council and the ten-member NGO advisory council marked the beginning of institutional experimentation by the Kanagawa government that calls for representation not only from legal residents but also from NGO members who assist both legal and illegal foreign residents. Such institutional innovation at the local level may provide a sort of democratic deliberation to both marginalized Japanese activists and Japan's foreign residents.

To be sure, the NGO advisory council generally cannot extend deliberative opportunities directly to illegal foreigners themselves (otherwise it will undermine its own membership rules); but local governments can improve democratic representation by incorporating these marginalized voices into the council through the representation of immigrant rights NGOs. For example, strengthening and institutionalizing networks of various types of NGOs that assist foreign residents, including those that provide women's shelters and labor consultation to illegal foreigners, would not have been an urgent topic in an advisory council dominated by legal foreigners. However, the inclusion of immigrant rights NGOs in Kanagawa's NGO advisory council directly affects the lives of illegal

---

65. Kanagawa International Policy Promotion Discussion Group, *Gaikokujin kenmin kanagawa kaigi oyobi NGO kanagawa kokusai kyōryoku kaigi* (Kanagawa Foreign Residents' Council and NGO Kanagawa International Cooperation Council) (Yokohama: Kanagawa Prefecture Government Foreign Affairs Division, 1998), 8–12.

foreigners after the council had made this issue its first recommendation to the governor.[66]

Illegal foreign workers in Japan reside in the country and contribute to the economy, but existing policies and prevalent attitudes ensure that their interests are not adequately represented in formal democratic deliberations and outcomes, or indeed in the broader public spheres of artistic and journalistic expression and popular sentiment. Nor is mere ethnic representation sufficient because again, legal foreigners in Japan generally do not share the life experiences of their illegal co-ethnics, and the interests of the former are often inimical to the concerns of the latter. Clearly, those facing persistent marginalization like illegal foreigners have little reason to think that privileged legal foreigners will be willing to adopt their perspective and advance their interests, or even if willing, that these privileged actors will be particularly competent in representing them. When persistent exclusion and marginalization undermine trust and render democratic institutions unrepresentative, as in contemporary Japan, strategies of group representation in legislatures, administrative agencies, and other public bodies may be justified, although these efforts must be carefully tailored to avoid problematic assumptions of group essentialism.

Certainly, the Kanagawa NGO advisory council, which invites a member of immigrant rights' NGOs to participate in the deliberation process, may not appear to be particularly democratic on the surface. However, given earlier reflections on the practical importance of shared experiences to effective representation, we can understand this council as part of a scheme of fair and effective representation: it can certainly better ensure fairness for the foreign community than foreigner advisory councils, which are composed only of legal foreigners. Representatives in the foreigner advisory councils belong only to legal immigrant groups, and aside from the problem of divergent experiences and interests between legal and illegal foreigners, most of these representatives are not even elected by members of their ethnic groups (legal or illegal) but rather are selected by local government officials. In contrast, Japanese activists, who are experienced problem

---

66. NGO Kanagawa International Corporation Council, *21 seiki kyōsei shakai no aratana pātonāshippu no jitsugen* [The Realization of a New Partnership for a Symbiotic Society in the Twenty-first Century] (Yokohama: Kanagawa Prefecture Government Social Welfare Conference, 2000).

solvers for underprivileged people in Japan, may have more in common with illegal foreigners, in terms of their experiences with prevailing public opinion and local authorities. Hence, an NGO advisory council that exists together with a foreigner advisory council like that in the Kanagawa prefecture can improve fairness for the community of foreigners in Japan, by ensuring that the experiences of illegal foreigners do find a voice and receive consideration in a variety of public forums. In contrast to Western countries where the level of official democratic inclusivity is strong and democratic representation in local governments involves mostly representatives of immigrant ethnic associations, Japan has low level of official democratic inclusivity and democratic representation in local governments also includes members from immigrant rights NGOs (Table 5.1).[67]

An outcome of improved fairness for all foreign residents in Kanagawa due to the increased institutionalization of cooperation between local governments and immigrant rights NGOs was demonstrated in 2001, when both the Kanagawa Foreign Residents' Council and the NGO International Cooperation Council made an appeal to improve medical translation services to foreigners.[68] The Kanagawa Prefecture Government responded by gathering a group of medical associations (medical doctor association, dentist association, and pharmaceutical association) and medical NGOs to deliberate with local government officials on the best way to

TABLE 5.1. Democratic Representation of Foreigners in Local Governments in Japan and the West

	Western countries	Japan
Level of official democratic inclusivity	Strong	Weak
Democratic representation at the local level	Direct (through representatives of immigrant ethnic association)	Direct and indirect (through members of immigrant ethnic associations and immigrant rights NGOs)

NGO = nongovernmental organization.

---

67. On Western countries, see Council of Europe, *Political and Social Participation of Immigrants through Consultative Bodies* (Strasbourg: Council of Europe Publication, 1999).

68. Interview with an official of the Kanagawa Prefecture Government International Division, August 4, 2004.

provide all foreigners with people who could translate the statements of medical personnel into a language they understood, with minimal financial burden on government. NGO leaders, led by Hayakawa Hiroshi of MF-MASH and Sawada Takashi of SHARE, recommended the creation of a new NGO that would train volunteers for medical translation. These volunteers would then work with social welfare personnel from the local government and hospital social workers in providing medical translation and social welfare services to foreign patients.[69] Local authorities and representatives of private medical bodies listened seriously to the opinions of these highly educated NGO leaders, who not only demonstrated expert knowledge about the socioeconomic situation of foreigners in the community but also understood Japanese norms of articulation and modes of expression in the deliberation process.

As a result of this deliberation, MIC Kanagawa was established in 2002, with NPO status. It has approximately eighty volunteers, who are dispatched to about thirty public hospitals. These volunteers receive routine training in medical terminology twice a year. They are sent only to specified hospitals that have legal contracts with MIC Kanagawa and have social workers on site. Activists believe that social workers typically provide excellent follow-up services and deal not only with medical problems but also with patients' social and economic problems. Since many foreign patients, especially overstayed foreigners, face medical problems that require extra social and/or economic assistance, officials at MIC Kanagawa prefer to work with hospitals with social workers.

Members of MIC Kanagawa, government officials, and hospital workers understand that this is a back-up system to a professional medical translation service, but it is an inexpensive and full-proof system with NPO volunteers, hospital social workers, and government officials from the social welfare division working closely together. It is a system that connects a network of resources and saves the Kanagawa government a significant amount of money, as volunteers at MIC Kanagawa receive just 3,000 yen ($25) per day for their services—only their travel expenses are paid.[70] In essence, such partnerships between NGOs and local governments allow

---

69. Interview with Sawada Takashi of SHARE and MF-MASH, July 31, 2004.
70. Interview with Tsuruta Mitsuko of MIC Kanagawa, July 23, 2004.

local governments to accept more responsibilities and to provide more services without incurring heavier financial burdens.

Increasingly, local governments in progressive areas are forging partnerships with civil society organizations to provide public services to their foreign residents. Cooperation between local governments and Japanese NGOs has promoted the creation of an innovative institutional environment in which legal foreigners, local government officials, and immigrant rights activists can come together to discuss matters concerning the livelihood of foreign residents and make policy recommendations to the governor. This newly formed institutional environment, which consists of foreigner advisory councils and NGO advisory councils, can potentially yield a new form of democratic governance in Japan, or at least level a real and increasingly institutionalized challenge to strong central government, particularly in the area of incorporation policies toward foreigners. Moreover, the institutional experimentation in Kanagawa, which gives "voice" to illegal foreigners through Japanese activists, can be seen as an innovative and progressive institutional arrangement of multicultural democracy in an advanced industrialized society. Clearly, small foreigners' support groups are exerting increasing influence on government officials and are enabling local authorities to assume broader responsibilities for health care and appropriate medical translation services for all residents. Thus, these civil society organizations are shaping the role of the state through partnership with local governments in actively redefining membership rules and the boundaries of state responsibilities to *residents,* as distinct from citizens.

6

FOREIGNERS IN THE PUBLIC SPHERE

Contesting Prevalent Social Meanings

Of particular interest to students of communicative democracy are the ways in which immigrant rights activists are gaining the attention of the Japanese media. The struggle of NGOs to improve conditions for illegal foreigners has been the subject of much media attention in Japan; indeed, the media increasingly turns to these NGOs for expert information and opinions on overstayed foreign workers. In addition, immigrant rights NGOs play an important role in the political struggle with state actors over the construction of foreigners' images. One major source of information on illegal foreigners for the mass media is the National Police Agency (NPA), which reports criminal activities allegedly committed by foreigners. Although visa violations constitute over half of these crimes, the mass media use the NPA data to focus on violent crime and the overall statistical rise in crimes committed by foreigners. As part of their political strategies to garner political support and/or institutional expansion within the government, conservative government officials take advantage of this slanted foreigner crime data to further construct a public image

of foreigners as "dangerous," with little connection to real events or social situations. Meanwhile, immigrant rights groups also shape public
discourse by supplying to the mass media alternative and sympathetic
information about illegal foreigners. They often portray foreign construction and factory workers as victims of unfair labor practices. Even if
they are not legal immigrants, these workers are entitled by law to receive some benefits, but Japanese employers often ignore workers' rights
because they are in the country illegally. Many workers keep quiet because their employers threaten to report them to the immigration office.
Immigrant rights activists also try to demonstrate that foreign criminals
may have been forced by circumstances to commit the crimes with which
they were charged, such as prostitution or murder. Thus, they create an
alternative narrative that portrays illegal foreigners as victims of Japan's
capitalist society.

This narrative of immigrant rights NGOs serves as an important
counterweight to official portraits of illegal foreigners, as it adds a critical
perspective to newspaper articles on illegal foreign workers in the public
discourse. This perspective is reflexive in its questioning orientation to the
established tradition. As a result of its inclusion in public discourse, cultural
bias is reduced due to consideration of alternative perspectives of educated,
internationally aware, and morally authoritative Japanese activists. In such
a case, a "better argument" can be achieved against people with different
kinds of political power and instrumental motives. In this way, Japanese
activists have the ability to shape how citizens see their own interests and
to make them listen and act accordingly.[1] As a result, these civil society
actors represent an important and influential force in mobilizing public
opinion on illegal foreigners. This opinion mobilization often extends beyond Japan's borders via transnational advocacy networks (TAN) such as
international NGOs and academics.[2] These networks then mobilize their
governments, particularly the U.S. government, to pressure the Japanese

---

1. On the source of power for civil society groups, see Ann M. Florini and P. J. Simmons,
"What the World Needs Now?" in Ann M. Florini, ed., *The Third Force: The Rise of Transnational Civil Society* (Washington, D.C.: Carnegie Endowment for International Peace, 2000), 1–15
(10–11 ff).

2. On TANs, see Margaret Keck and Kathryn Sikkink, *Activists beyond Borders: Advocacy
Networks in International Politics* (Ithaca: Cornell University Press, 1998).

government for policy change. In this sense, Japanese deliberative democrats can be considered to possess "communicative power."[3]

State Construction of Illegal Foreigners As "Criminals"

Japanese leaders such as Ishihara Shintarō, Etō Takami, and officials of the NPA and the Ministry of Foreign Affairs (MOFA) construct and propagate negative images of foreigners, especially illegal ones.[4] Conservative state officials portray illegal foreigners as "deviant" and potentially "dangerous" to the public. They often associate illegal foreigners with crimes beyond immigration violations by taking "official" crime statistics out of their social and demographic contexts. Although illegal foreigners violate immigration laws, this violation alone can hardly be considered a threat or danger to Japanese people. This section presents the official crime statistics from the NPA and focuses on how certain government officials have (mis)used these data to perpetuate an image of illegal foreigners as dangerous criminals.

Official Crime Statistics

An annual NPA white paper, *Keisatsu hakusho,* reports the number of crimes committed by foreigners (Table 6.1).[5] The NPA divides foreigners into "non-Japanese nationals" (mostly *zainichi* or Japan-born Korean and Chinese) and "visiting foreigners" (foreign newcomers, including illegal foreign workers). In the number of cases and of persons, crimes by visiting foreigners have increased since 1995. More than half of crimes by foreigners, however,

<hr>

3. On "communicative power," see Jürgen Habermas, *Between Facts and Norms: Contributions to a Discourse Theory of Law and Democracy* (Cambridge: MIT Press, 1996).

4. Historically, the Japanese elites feared Western Christianity, military and commercial power, and ideology. Moreover, they viewed foreigners as a potentially dangerous force that could undermine their dominance over Japanese commoners. To reinforce the populace's sense of isolation and suspicion of "dangerous" foreigners, Japanese rulers banned certain foreigners from their territory between 1640 and 1853 and severely enforced this ban. The *bakufu* (Tokugawa government) and subsequently the Ministry of Home Affairs have portrayed foreigners as a security threat in order for these institutions to strengthen control over the population and enhance their political power.

5. Keisatsuchō, *Keisatsu hakusho* (Tokyo: Keisatsuchō, annual).

TABLE 6.1. Crime Statistics by Foreigners in Comparison to Those by Japanese, 1993–2005

	1993	1994	1995	1996	1997	1998	1999	2000	2001	2002	2003	2004	2005
Total foreign crime													
Incidents	19,671	21,574	24,374	27,414	32,033	31,779	34,398	30,971	27,763	34,746	40,615	47,128	47,865
Persons	12,467	13,576	11,976	11,949	13,883	13,418	13,436	12,711	14,660	16,212	20,007	21,842	21,178
Penal Code offenses													
Incidents (Japanese)	723,610	767,844	753,174	735,881	759,609	772,282	731,284	576,771	542,115	592,681	648,319	667,620	649,503
Japanese persons	297,725	307,965	293,252	295,584	313,573	324,263	315,355	309,649	325,292	347,558	379,602	389,027	386,955
Incidents (foreigners)	12,771	13,321	17,213	19,513	21,670	21,689	25,135	22,947	18,199	24,258	27,258	32,087	33,037
Foreign persons	7,276	6,989	6,527	6,026	5,435	5,382	5,963	6,329	7,168	7,690	8,725	8,898	8,505
(Illegal foreigners)	1,015	1,215	1,315	1,632	1,317	1,302	1,529	1,603	1,379	1,403	1,520	1,393	1,304
Serious/ Violent cases													
Incidents (Japanese)	10,903	11,103	10,652	11,286	12,366	12,725	14,682	18,281	21,530	22,294	23,971	22,568	20,388
Incidents (foreigners)	218	221	176	162	187	228	267	242	308	323	336	345	315
Population													
Japanese	123,443,252	123,679,989	124,207,629	124,448,864	124,683,293	124,973,884	125,129,887	125,239,556	125,512,538	125,583,242	125,703,970	125,713,253	125,745,260
Foreigners	1,320,748	1,354,011	1,362,371	1,415,136	1,482,707	1,512,116	1,556,113	1,686,444	1,778,462	1,851,758	1,915,030	1,973,747	2,011,555
Illegal foreigners	298,646	293,800	286,704	284,744	281,157	276,541	268,421	232,121	224,067	220,552	219,418	207,299	193,745

Source: National Police Agency, *Crime Statistics on Foreigners* (Tokyo: National Police Agency, various years).

are "special code offenses," such as violations of the immigration laws and alien registration. Penal code offenses, such as burglary, gambling, murder, rape, and robbery, by visiting foreigners (in terms of persons) showed a decline between 1993 and 1998, but a steady increase between 1999 and 2004. While the number of penal offenses by foreigners increased 17 percent between 1993 and 2005, the population of visiting foreigners (including illegals) during this same period increased about 36 percent. In contrast, penal code offenses by Japanese nationals increased 30 percent, from 298,000 people in 1993 to 387,000 people in 2005, although the total number of nationals increased by less than 2 percent. Most important, serious crimes by Japanese increased 87 percent, while those by foreigners rose 44 percent. Most crimes committed by foreigners are of a less serious nature (e.g., fraud and petty theft).[6]

Although the number of illegal foreigners declined from 1993 to 2005 (see Table 6.1), the number committing penal code offenses did not. Crimes by illegal foreigners increased by 28 percent between 1993 and 2005, with the greatest number of penal code offenses (approximately 1,600 people) occurring in 1996 and 2000. Yet violent crimes, such as murder, assault, arson, and rape, saw a more dramatic increase among Japanese than among illegal foreigners. In fact, the number of murders committed by illegal foreigners decreased by 36 percent from 58 to 37 during 1993–2003, while those committed by Japanese increased by 15 percent.[7] Robberies involving illegal foreigners increased by 105 percent, but those involving Japanese increased at a more alarming rate of 200 percent.[8]

Nevertheless, data indicate that illegal foreigners have a higher propensity to commit penal code offenses than Japanese. For example, 1 in 145 to 300 illegal foreigners (depending on the year between 1993 and 2003) commits a penal code offense, in comparison to 1 in 330 to 400 Japanese.[9] In 2003, illegal foreigners committed 16 murders and 145 robberies. Of these, Chinese commit the majority of serious crimes, while Iranians outnumber

---

6. It is possible that the police, knowing that foreign suspects would be deported, charged illegal foreigners with only a violation of the immigration and alien-registration laws instead of larger offenses. To press other, more serious charges would require extra energy and effort on the part of the police. It is also possible that the police found it to their interest to load their uncleared cases on foreigners who would be deported anyway.

7. The number of cases for serious crimes peaked in 2003 and steadily declined thereafter.

8. Keisatsuchō, *Keisatsu hakusho.*

9. Ibid.

other foreigners in drug-related crimes.[10] Although foreign men typically commit four times more crime than foreign women, the gender ratio for Thai and Filipino criminals is about one-to-one.

Three important facts underlie these crime statistics. First, it is well known that the propensity to commit offenses varies considerably for different demographic groups. For example, young people between ages eighteen and forty commit offenses more frequently than older people. Foreign workers in Japan, who are mostly in their twenties and thirties, are thus concentrated in the demographic group that has a higher crime rate. This forces up immigrants' general rate of criminality.

Second, the number of arrests may have increased, but a large proportion of these involve the same people. For example, the Japanese police reported that arrests of foreigners in 1999 increased 8 percent from 1998 to 34,398, whereas the total number of foreigners arrested was 13,436, suggesting the same people were arrested several times. Therefore, the number of foreigners committing crimes increased by only 0.1 percent, from 13,418 in 1998 to 13,436 in 1999, despite the steadily increasing population of foreigners in Japan.

Third, reporting of crimes committed tends to be higher for foreigners than for natives. Foreigners, especially those who do not look like natives, have a higher chance of being suspected and arrested. Moreover, problems involving foreigners, especially those who speak little or no Japanese, are more likely to be reported to the police, whereas many problems among Japanese nationals are not reported when they can settle the issue among themselves.

Manipulation of Crime Statistics by Government Officials

Certain influential and nationalist political leaders, such as Ishihara Shintarō, Etō Takami, Hori Kōsuke, and Satō Hidehiko, use the NPA statistics to propagate an image of illegal foreigners as criminals to garner political support. Tokyo Governor Ishihara Shintarō intentionally used historically

---

10. With the passage of the 1991 Law Concerning Prevention of Unjust Acts by *Bōryokudan* Members (*bōryokudan ni yoru futō no kōi no bōshi nado ni kansuru hōritsu*), there appears to be an emerging pattern of yakuza organizations allowing criminal operations in their territories for a fee, and accepting and increasingly relying on foreigners as street-level drug retailers. Moreover, Iranians are more visible than Japanese or Koreans and operate primarily in public places, such as parks and train stations. See H. Richard Friman, "Gaijinhanzai: Immigrants and Drugs in Contemporary Japan," *Asian Survey* 36, no. 10 (1996): 964–977.

loaded language when he told Japanese troops to keep a close watch on foreigners in the event of a major earthquake, in order to prevent looting and rioting. In his address to Ground Self-Defense Force troops on April 9, 2000, Ishihara claimed that foreigners, whom he called *sangokujin* (third country nationals), were likely to riot and commit crimes due to the breakdown of order.[11] Ishihara later explained:

> People who have entered illegally and who do not have clear identities will certainly cause riots....Crimes in Tokyo are getting more violent. If you ask who is committing them, they are all *sangokujin*. In other words, foreigners... who have entered illegally and remain in Japan are the criminals, is that not so? Are the Snake Heads [Chinese gangs] not like that too?[12]

Ishihara's reasoning is influenced by historical events in Japan during the aftermath of World War II (and probably his acceptance of rumors about Koreans looting, rioting, and killing Japanese during the aftermath of the Great Kanto Earthquake of 1923). In his address, he referred to foreigners as *sangokujin*, which is derived from *daisangokujin*, a term commonly used to describe Koreans, Chinese, and Formosans during the Occupation period (1945–1952).

Ishihara invoked the brutal Snake Heads, which are Chinese gangs that operate in human trafficking of Fuzhounese workers to Japan, to further construct a fearful image of illegal foreigners. The Snake Heads have been active in the entertainment district of Kabuki-chō in Tokyo, where there has been a rise in murders. According to the police, the rise is alarming, not because of the increased number, which remains small, but because most victims of Snake Heads violence have been members of the *yakuza*, who are known for their brutality. An NPA official explains that this is due to a conflict over turf and the low price that Chinese assassins charge for the job. A Chinese gangster will do three jobs for the price a yakuza will charge for one.[13] Ishihara tried to justify his remarks by associating illegal foreigners with ruthless foreign gangsters. By doing so, he instilled greater fear among

---

11. *Asahi Shimbun,* April 10, 2000, 1.

12. *Asahi Shimbun,* April 11, 2000, 38.

13. Interview with an official of the National Police Agency Foreign Crime Division, January 6, 2003.

the Japanese of illegal foreigners as violent and brutal. Ishihara's impact on the Japanese public was evident. Although Japanese newspapers, led by the *Asahi,* denounced Ishihara's statement for being racist, there was an outpouring of public support for Ishihara's position. A survey conducted by TBS radio found that 87 percent of calls to its radio station five days after the address expressed "support" for Ishihara's comments.[14]

Such racial remarks are also heard from more mainstream politicians. In a statement during an opening ceremony for the Liberal Democratic Party (LDP) branch in Fukui prefecture on July 12, 2003, LDP faction leader and former director-general of the Management and Coordination Agency, Etō Takami, stated that "*daisangokujin,* who are staying illegally, rule over Kabuki-chō in Shinjuku. Recently, Chinese, South Koreans, and other illegal foreigners are gathering [there] to commit serious crimes.... In the country, there are one million illegal foreigners, who are committing robbery and murder."[15] Etō deliberately associated illegal foreigners with serious crimes, whereas the 2003 official data indicates that illegal foreigners committed only 145 robberies and 16 murders, in contrast to 4,698 robberies and 1,456 murders committed by Japanese. Moreover, he exaggerated the number of illegal foreigners, which has never exceeded 300,000, in order to exaggerate the seriousness of the situation.[16]

Senior members of the NPA and MOFA also equate foreigners with crimes. When the police apprehended two Japanese men who had kidnapped a young boy in Yokohama, they discovered that the criminals had used prepaid cellular phones, which police were not able to trace calls from. A day after the arrest of these Japanese criminals, the chairman of the National Police Safety Commission, Hori Kōsuke, testified before the House of Councilors that such phones present a threat to public safety because "they can be used easily by foreigners staying here illegally, and they can be used for selling illegal drugs and for other crimes."[17] A high-ranking

---

14. *Asahi Shimbun,* April 12, 2000, 29.

15. *Asahi Shimbun,* July 13, 2003, 39.

16. This association of recent illegal foreigners with negative images can be traced back to 1990. During an inspection in Shinjuku after a police crackdown on Southeast Asian women allegedly engaged in prostitution, Justice Minister Kajiyama Seiroku said, "It's like in America when neighborhoods become mixed because blacks move in and whites are forced out.... Prostitutes ruin the atmosphere in the same way." *Mainichi Shimbun,* October 17, 1990, 1.

17. *Sankei Shimbun,* April 26, 2000, 2.

government official, Hori, made this statement despite the fact that no foreigner was even involved in the incident. During the media hype in early July 2003 over the murder of a four-year-old boy in Nagasaki, the chairman of the NPA, Satō Hidehiko also took the opportunity to link crime to illegal foreigners in the public mind. In that case, although a twelve-year-old Japanese was the prime suspect in the murder, Satō reminded citizens that "our country's security problem consists of juvenile criminals, illegal foreigners, and violent groups (*bōryokudan*)."[18]

Moreover, official Japanese government publications link illegal foreigners with criminal activities. For example, in the section on "Foreigners in Japan" in the *1999 Diplomatic Bluebook,* MOFA states, "many foreigners staying in Japan illegally tend to become involved in crime," without providing any statistical proof or explanation of how it reached such a conclusion.[19] Moreover, police accounts to the public on the rising number of foreigners arrested or held for questioning have created a stereotype that foreigners are prone to criminal behavior. Illegal foreigners have been targets of such association with criminality on the NPA's website as well as in police newsletters.[20] For example, a newsletter issued by a local police box in Kanagawa prefecture announced the following:

> The number of illegal foreigners committing crimes is getting worse and is increasing. Organized groups' illegal immigrant cases and cases

18. *Yomiuri Shimbun,* July 11, 2003, 38.

19. Ministry of Foreign Affairs, *Diplomatic Bluebook* (Tokyo: Ministry of Foreign Affairs, various years). Since 1995 when a section on "Foreigners in Japan" was added, the language regarding illegal foreign workers used by MOFA in the *Diplomatic Bluebook* has changed. Initially, MOFA showed a sympathetic attitude and wrote "illegal workers tend to work under poor labor conditions and with little protection under the Japan's social security system; some cases result in human rights issues" (http://www.mofa.go.jp/policy/other/bluebook/1995/). By 1996, MOFA began to equate illegal workers with criminal activities when it stated that "these illegal workers...tend to get involved in crime" (http://www.mofa.go.jp/policy/other/bluebook/1996/). In 1997, MOFA added that this situation "creates prejudice among some parts of the population against foreigners in Japan" (http://www.mofa.go.jp/policy/other/bluebook/1996/). In 2001, the ministry clarified that "crimes committed by some of these illegal residents present an erroneous image of foreigners living in Japan to the Japanese public" (http://www.mofa.go.jp/policy/other/bluebook/2001/chap4-b.html#5).

20. The website of the NPA in 2000 on foreign crime, for example, has Japan threatened from all sides by an invasion of bad and fearful foreigners (http://www.npa.go.jp/koho2/mado_3.htm [accessed May 9, 2000]).

between Japanese yakuza and illegally staying foreign workers or employers who hire them under severe working conditions are also increasing. . . . Please inform the police office when you see or hear of any suspicious
foreigners.[21]

Here, the police equate illegal foreign workers with "criminals" and being
"suspicious." The police call on the Japanese public to report "suspicious
foreigners," but not suspicious Japanese yakuza or suspicious business-
people employing illegal foreign workers, whom the police actually cite as
being criminal partners with illegal foreigners.

Police posters also associate illegal foreigners with criminality. After an
incident in 1991 that involved money exchange and persons assumed to be
foreigners, the Yotsuya Police Office posted a warning in various super-
markets and stores. The announcement ended with a request: "Please immediately call 110 or report to the Yotsuya Police Office when a foreigner
asks for money exchange even if no damage has been done."[22] According to this warning, any foreigner who asks to exchange money should be
suspected as a criminal and be reported to the police immediately. Here,
the police associated foreigners with criminals and instilled fear of foreigners among the Japanese public.[23] Officials at the Yotsuya Police Office explained that they posted these warnings to prevent the recurrence
of similar incidents.[24] A similar antitheft effort occurred in late November
2000. The Tokyo Metropolitan Police distributed small posters picturing
a young man in a worn-out suit and dirty shoes crouching down while
picking a lock. It also pictured a woman making a phone call. The poster's caption reads: "Apartment break-ins occur frequently. If you think
[the person] is Chinese, call [the police at] 110. If you hear them speaking Chinese...call 110."[25] By focusing on the Chinese, the poster implied
that it is mostly Chinese who break into apartments. Although burglaries

21. Reported in the monthly newsletter of the United Front Japan, *The UFJ* 3, no. 2
(1998): 6.

22. See Hakoishi Mami and Hatade Akira, "Rainichi gaikokujin no hanzai" [Foreigners'
Crimes], in Tanaka Hiroshi and Ebashi Takashi, eds., *Rainichi gaikokujin jinken hakusho* [White
Papers on the Human Rights of Foreigners] (Tokyo: Akashi Shoten, 1997), 320–339 (328–329ff).

23. Ibid., 321.

24. *Asahi Shimbun,* October 4, 1992.

25. *Asahi Shimbun,* December 26, 2000, 15.

involving Chinese have increased, about 97 percent of burglaries in 2000 still involved Japanese.²⁶ After distributing 700 of these posters to police stations, neighborhood associations, and apartment caretakers, the Tokyo Metropolitan Police withdrew them three weeks later after protests from several human rights groups.

Contribution of Immigrants Rights NGOs to Public Discourse

The government does not have a monopoly on influencing public opinion. Immigrant rights activists contribute to the public discourse by providing an alternative source of information about the social conditions of illegal foreign workers. Through direct interaction with foreign workers, activists have gained expert knowledge about their problems and developed an internationalist view of the role of Japan in the world. In addition to providing help to illegal foreigners, these groups have taken up the cause of illegal foreigners by disseminating information about them through newsletters and books. As such, the activities of these immigrant rights groups serve as an important counterweight to official Japan's far more prejudiced activities regarding illegal foreigners.

Immigrant rights groups circulate newsletters and other published works to inform their members and activists in other groups about their activities, as well as to share expertise with them. These publications record detailed individual cases, provide summary statistics of foreign workers the group has helped, and inform members about upcoming activities. Some also disclose the group's financial situation. With the exception of community workers' unions, many support groups publish their newsletters in both Japanese and English. The newsletter for the women's shelter Saalaa even has a Thai-language version. These newsletters bind members together and build networks of Japanese activists who are assisting illegal foreign workers.

Japanese activists usually record testimonial and, at times, strategically exaggerated accounts of illegal foreigners in their newsletters. For example, the newsletter of a women's shelter, HELP, offered the following

---

26. Keisatsuchō, *Keisatsu hakusho* (Tokyo, Keisatsuchō, 2001).

account of a Thai woman who escaped from forced prostitution in Shimodate in Ibaraki Prefecture:

> She...worked as an office worker in Bangkok...[Then] she was encouraged
> to work as an "office lady" in Japan where the pay is better....When she ar-
> rived at Narita,...she was taken to Shimodate and...forced into prostitu-
> tion. She really hated it and her customers complained to her boss that they
> got bad service...[T]he boss bound her feet with chains...and...violently
> abused her....Finally, after three months she was able to escape....A month
> later, the broker, restaurant owner, and other people involved were arrested,
> and this woman's passport and identification papers were returned. When
> the police arrested them, they also found a poster with her picture offering
> a 500,000 yen reward to anyone who could find her.[27]

Occasionally, the testimony on how foreigners' rights have been violated
comes unfiltered and directly from the illegal foreign workers themselves.
A newsletter of the Zentōitsu Workers Union, *FWBZ News,* carries the following remarks by a Bangladeshi. "I was working in 'Kinzok Press' when
I [had] an accident and got my fingers cut. After the accident, my president
opened [a] false bank account in [my] name...without my knowledge."[28]
Although this particular group publishes only Japanese newsletters, the
testimony from the Bangladeshi worker, who spoke English, was written
in English. This increases the creditability of the report and draws new
(English-speaking) foreign workers into the union.

Newsletters of immigrant rights NGOs commonly express compassion for illegal foreigners. The newsletter of the Yamasato Consulting Office, a Christian group, even expresses warmth and sympathy for foreign
criminals. Instead of criticizing the foreigners for the crimes they have
committed, Father Nakaya Isao focuses his criticism on the deplorable condition of Japanese prisons. Of one imprisoned foreigner, Father Nakaya
wrote, "Until we began visiting him, he had not one single visitor, no
change of clothes or personal money, and he had not been able to even
write home."[29]

---

27. *Network News* 32 (May 1998): 1 (English in original).
28. *FWBZ News* 8 (June 5, 1999): 1 (English in original).
29. *Yamazato Dayori* 12 (December 1997): 2 (English in original).

Father Nakaya has also expressed concern with the recent media sensationalism over the rise in crimes committed by illegal foreigners, offering compelling reasons for this increase. First, he downplayed the crime rate by illegal foreigners by claiming that the number of illegal foreign workers in Japan is much higher than the official figure, so per capita crime rate for illegal foreigners should be much lower.[30] Additionally, he argued that foreign workers' illegal status forces them to "always be on guard" and to "live in crowded rooms" with five to six others, and that these conditions lead to quarrels, fights, and even crimes.[31]

Women's shelters, such as Saalaa and HELP, also publish surveys of foreign women who have stayed in their shelters. For example, Saalaa interviewed 160 foreign women who used the shelter from its opening in September 1992 to December 1994. From these interviews, shelter workers have learned how these women came to Japan and how they have been treated since. Their willingness to disclose personal information to Saalaa shows the level of trust the organization has gained. In its January 1995 newsletter (Thai-language version), Saalaa published detailed information on the international trafficking of women from Thailand to Japan. The article discussed some characteristics of Thai prostitutes in Japan and explained the methods used to lure Thai women to Japan. Most interesting about Saalaa's interviews with Thai women was the underground information about the preparation of travel documents and the role Thai brokers played in the process. The newsletter also provided information on the route that these women took to get to Japan:

> After a woman decided she would go to work in Japan, the first person she encountered was the so-called *"nai jang"* (broker), who arranged all the travel documents (passports, Japanese visa) for her. Brokers are usually Thai, but a few were foreigners as well as Japanese.... Of the 132 Thai women, 68 carried real passports while 57 carried fake ones [7 are unknown]. And of these 57 women, 38 entered Japan via an intermediary country, particularly Malaysia and Singapore (17).[32]

---

30. *View from Sanya* 2 (April 1998): 2 (English in original).
31. Ibid.
32. *Jodmaikao "saalaa"* 1 (January 1995): 8.

Finally, the newsletter gave statistical data on the poor living and working conditions of Thai women in Japan.

The surveys of the women's shelter groups demonstrate that far from being the isolated experiences of one or two foreign women, hundreds of women share such experiences. More important, the large sample gives credence to their stories and expertise. Newsletters from other immigrant rights groups contain similar surveys of those foreigners they have helped.

Immigrant rights NGOs also publish books to illustrate the plight of foreigners in Japan. *Letters from Thai Women to the Prostitution Society of Japan (Baishun shakai nihon e, taijin josei kara no tegami),* for example, uses letters written by the three Thai women involved in another incident in Shimodate to reconstruct the morbid conditions that drove these desperate women to murder their Thai boss.[33] The letters, originally written in Thai to the women's families in Thailand, discuss the dreams and aspirations of these women in going to Japan. After they arrived, a Thai boss (named Lek) informed them that they had incurred a debt of 3.5 million yen (US$32,000), which they were to pay back by performing sexual services for Japanese clients at a snack bar in Shimodate. Lek took away their passports and personal identification and placed them in a room with thirty-six other Thai women. Clients paid between 25,000 to 35,000 yen (US$230–320) for the women's services. Of this, 5,000 yen (US$45) went to the snack bar and the rest went to Lek to pay off the "debt." The women received nothing. Lek threatened to kill them if they tried to escape, a threat that appeared real, as the husband of the Japanese mama-san of the snack bar was a yakuza. The book goes on to discuss in detail the murder incident and the court case that followed.

In *A Long Journey with a Burden (Nagai tabi no omoni),* Higashizawa Yasushi of the Dai-ni Tokyo Bar Association Human Rights Protection Committee documents the testimonies of various illegal foreign workers that he has worked with in the past.[34] Similarly, the "Testimonies of

---

33. Shimodate-jiken Tai 3 Josei o Sasaeru Kai, ed., *Baishun shakai nihon e, taijin josei kara no tegami* [Letters from Thai Women to Prostitution Society Japan], (Tokyo: Akashi Shoten, 1995), 14–95.

34. Higashizawa Yasushi, *Nagai tabi no omoni* [A Journey with a Burden] (Tokyo: Kaifū Shobō, 1993).

Foreigners Deported from Japan 1995–97" (*Kyōsei sōkan sareta gaikokujin no shōgen '95–'97*) from the Immigration Review Task Force offers thirteen detailed testimonies of human rights violations committed by agents of the Japanese government against foreigners in Japan. One of these incidents involved two Korean men who were physically assaulted by immigration officers at the Osaka Immigration Control Bureau on June 29, 1994. The incident began when a Korean inmate (Mr. Y), who was annoyed by the cockroaches in the cell, slapped the wall with his slipper in order to kill them. The noise attracted three immigration officers, who then took him to a different room. Soon after, another Korean inmate (Mr. C) heard screams, apparently kicked his cell door, and asked an immigration officer if someone was being beaten. Taken to the room in which Mr. Y was being kept. Mr. C saw Mr. Y lying on the floor, where he had fallen after repeated beatings. Several officers then tried to force Mr. C to sit down with his arms restrained behind his back. When he resisted, he was violently beaten, particularly on his face and arms. The next day, both these Koreans were taken to a hospital, where the doctor reported that Mr. Y had painful wounds on his whole body, while Mr. C had suffered a ruptured eardrum. Without being given proper medical treatment, both were deported to Korea.[35] The Immigration Review Task Force wrote its account of this incident as a first-person narrative from the point of view of Mr. Y., and supplemented it with detailed maps of the Osaka Immigration Central Bureau that showed where the incident took place. The strategic use of writing technique and illustration added credibility to the testimony in the face of repeated denial of any wrongdoing by immigration officers.

Immigrant rights groups also publish surveys, such as the 1992 *White Paper on Foreign Workers' Industrial Accidents (Gaikokujin rōdōsha no rōsai hakusho)* by the Japan Occupational Safety and Health Resource Center and the *Foreign Workers and Labor Disasters (Gaikokujin rōdōsha to rōdō saigai)* by MF-MASH. Some use the cases they worked on to present a better understanding of foreign workers. The Kalabaw-no-kai, for instance, publishes *Foreign Workers—Aren't They Our Comrades? (Nakama jya nai ka, gaikokujin rōdōsha)* with descriptions of representative cases involving

---

35. Immigration Review Task Force, "Kyōsei sōkan sareta gaikokujin no shōgen '95–'97" [Testimonies of Foreigners Deported from Japan '95–'97] (Tokyo: Mimeograph, 1999), 43–48.

foreign workers from its first three years of activity. This work also includes an analysis of the problems of migrant workers from an international perspective, as well as policy recommendations.

Many of these immigrant rights groups publish their books with Akashi Shoten, a liberal, nonmainstream publisher that devotes an entire section of its business to publishing books on foreign workers. Its interest in issues concerning foreign workers evolved out of its past publications on *zainichi* foreigners and the *buraku* liberation movement.[36] The person in charge of the foreign workers' section in Akashi Shoten, Osawa Yoshio, is a former activist with one of the immigrant rights NGOs in Tochigi Prefecture. As an activist, he participated in the 1998 NGO Conference at Atami. He reappeared in 1999 as a representative of Akashi Shoten at the National Forum in Solidarity with Migrant Workers and the symposium of the Asian Peoples Friendship Society (APFS) on the Campaign for Special Permission for Residence, where he had set up a table to sell Akashi Shoten's publications on foreign workers. Akashi Shoten publishes numerous works on foreign workers by prominent Japanese scholars, including Komai Hiroshi, Tanaka Hiroshi, Ebashi Takashi, Miyajima Takashi, and Tezuka Kazuaki. Akashi Shoten publishes six of Komai's most important works on foreign workers. It also publishes translations of classic works on immigration by well-known international scholars such as Tomas Hammar and Myron Weiner. By having their works published at Akashi Shoten, members of these immigrant rights groups gain further recognition as experts in the field. Interestingly, most of these publications appeared before 1997, when the public was still ignorant about the situation of foreigners and the activities of immigrant rights NGOs in assisting them.

In short, Japanese activists have developed expert knowledge of Japanese laws and pressing issues concerning illegal foreign workers through their direct interaction with illegal foreign workers. In their newsletters and books, they often use primary sources, such as conversations or interviews with illegal foreign workers and letters written by them. Although, this information may be exaggerated, it gains credibility and attracts the mass media.

---

36. Interview with Osawa Yoshio of the Akashi Shoten, June 5, 1999.

Contest over the Public Imagination of Illegal Foreigners in the Mass Media

Perhaps the most effective way to shape public opinion on illegal foreigners is through the mass media. Both state and societal actors understand the importance of the media in shaping public opinion. The former, backed by the NPA's foreigner crime statistics, portrays illegal foreigners as criminals. The NPA feeds the media distorted data, which the media print without careful scrutiny. Meanwhile, the rich and, at times, sensational information recorded in NGO publications also attracts the attention of the mass media. As a result, journalists turn to activists for detailed and testimonial information. Newspaper articles that include sources from Japanese activists tend to depict illegal foreigners as victims of Japan's capitalist society. This section explores the contest between state officials and social activists through the mass media over the public imagination of illegal foreigners.

Shaping the Public Sphere: The Impact of State Authority on the Mass Media

Crime data attract journalists; the major dailies assign reporters to the headquarters of the Tokyo Metropolitan Police Department and additional staff to district police offices. The media's main source of information on crimes committed by foreigners comes from the police. Therefore, the content of articles is remarkably similar from one newspaper to another. The main difference between newspapers is the location and character-size of the article. The conservative *Sankei Shimbun* and *Yomiuri Shimbun,* for example, usually print articles on foreigner crimes on the front page and in wide columns. In fact, the *Sankei* sometimes uses foreigner crime as the day's headline. In contrast, the more liberal *Asahi* and *Mainichi* print such articles on back pages and in smaller columns. For example, a headline on May 1, 2000, in the *Sankei Shimbun* read "Foreigner Crimes Rise Again: Six Times from Ten Years Ago" (*Gaikokujin hanzai futatabi zōka: 10-nen de 6-bai ni*). In this same edition, the *Sankei* also ran a special report detailing fearful activities of the Chinese mafia operating in Kabuki-chō. The *Yomiuri* used a similar headline, but in its domestic affairs section. The *Yomiuri's* six-paragraph article announced the 8.2 percent increase from the previous year and stressed the increase in "violent crimes" conducted in groups. A business daily, the *Nikkei,* ran a large headline announcing this increase, but devoted only three paragraphs to its report. However, it added that 60 percent of these foreigner crimes involved "overstayed foreigners." In contrast, the *Mainichi* reported this increase with a much smaller caption in its section on "Society, Interests, People, and Discussion" (*Shakai jiken hito wadai*), which is located in the back of the newspaper. Similarly, the *Asahi* placed this report in the lower corner and toward the end of the newspaper, where it was almost hidden among large corporate advertisements.[37]

The association of particular crimes with particular national groups concurs with reports from the NPA. Japan's five major national newspapers, the *Asahi, Mainichi, Yomiuri, Nikkei,* and *Sankei,* tend to associate Chinese with serious crimes (such as murder, rape, arson, and armed robbery), Thai women with prostitution, and Iranian men with drug-related crimes. Public opinion of the Chinese has worsened dramatically as the number of articles on murder and robbery involving Chinese more than doubled between 2000 and 2003. The number of press reports on foreigner crimes correlates highly with police reports. The main difference is that a newspaper may print multiple articles on an immigrant group and its *alleged* crimes in police reports. Media cover the same crime story more than once as it develops and unfolds. For instance, there were sixteen articles between September and December 2001 concerning a Pakistani man who raped a seventeen-year-old high school girl. Four months of newspaper reports on a single incident can worsen the image of any foreigner group even if that foreign group rarely commits crimes.

During the 1990s, articles on foreigners carried headlines such as: "Violent Crimes by Foreigners Increase Five Times in Five Years," "Foreign Organized Thefts Rise Fivefold" and "Foreigners' Crimes Rise Again."[38] These headlines reflect the first page of the NPA's annual report, which typically highlights the increased crime numbers. Journalists print such headlines without independently checking the statistics given to them by

37. See the May 1, 2000, issues of *Sankei Shimbun,* p. 1; *Yomiuri Shimbun,* p. 26; *Nikkei Shimbun,* p. 34; *Mainichi Shimbun,* p. 22; and *Asahi Shimbun,* p. 26.
38. See respectively *Yomiuri Shimbun,* April 18, 1993; *Daily Yomiuri,* September 4, 1998; *Sankei Shimbun,* May 1, 2000.

the police.[39] Had they done so, they would have realized that the number
of foreigners arrested for committing non–visa-related crimes decreased by
about 5 percent every year between 1993 and 1998.[40] In November 2003, the
cover of the *Yomiuri Weekly* read: "Map of High Risk Foreign Crimes."[41]
The featured article provided a comprehensive list of 103 crimes allegedly
committed by foreigners in Tokyo since 2000 but contained little, if any,
research on what actually happened. Its information came primarily from
the police rather than from trial proceedings.

Although a foreign suspect may not have been found guilty of the crime,
the press often reports his or her illegal status as "visa overstayer." Hence,
these foreigners automatically become "criminals" due to the fact that they
have already violated the law by overstaying their visas.[42] For this reason,
Wolfgang Herbert holds that the media portray illegal foreign workers
as people who are not law-abiding (deviant) and are potentially dangerous.[43] The *Yomiuri Shimbun* illustrates this point: "Although almost all [il-
legals] are serious laborers seeking high wages and therefore often change
jobs, they do get into financial trouble. Cases of criminal involvement, and
crimes committed by illegal workers, happen as often as every month."[44]
This account is strikingly misleading given the fact that crimes committed
by Japanese happen more than eight hundred times per day.

Contesting the Public Sphere: The Influence of Japanese NGOs on the Media

The struggle by immigrant rights NGOs to improve the livelihood of
illegal foreigners (whom they call "overstayed foreign workers") in Japan

39. Interviews with journalists from *Sankei Shimbun,* May 15, 2001, and the *Asahi Shimbun* in Tokyo, May 19, 2001.

40. Keisatsuchō, *Keisatsu hakusho* (Tokyo: Keisatsuchō, 1994–1999).

41. *Yomiuri Weekly,* November 16, 2003, 10–19.

42. Daniel H. Foote finds that the media and the public often regard a suspect, upon arrest, as guilty despite the existence of a presumption of innocence under Japanese law. But fewer
than 5 percent of adults suspected of Penal Code offenses are sentenced to prison. See Daniel H.
Foote, "The Benevolent Paternalism of Japanese Criminal Justice," *California Law Review* 80,
no. 2 (1992): 317–390.

43. See Wolfgang Herbert, *Foreign Workers and Law Enforcement in Japan* (London: Kegan
Paul International, 1996), 262–302.

44. *Yomiuri Shimbun,* May 26, 1988, 31.

has attracted much media attention. The *Asahi, Yomiuri, Mainichi, Nik-kei,* and *Sankei* carried 1,211 articles on these groups and their activities for illegal foreigners between January 1, 1983, and December 31, 2003. The more liberal *Asahi* accounted for 45 percent (549) of these articles, while the conservative *Sankei* accounted for only 5 percent. As Table 6.2 demonstrates, concerned citizens' groups and women's NGOs had 285 and 275 articles, respectively, written about them and their work during this period. The women's shelter HELP alone was the subject of 125 articles—almost as many as the number of articles covering all community workers' unions and twice that for Christian NGOs. Occasionally, a profile of a certain Japanese activist or an announcement of a seminar or symposium is included in these articles. Like book publications, most newspaper articles on these foreigner support groups appeared before 1997 when these support groups had just begun to launch their activities and to gain the interest of the public. One event, discussed below, received considerable press coverage after 1997: the 1999 APFS campaign to grant "special residence permission" to certain families of illegal foreigners who had stayed in Japan for more than ten years.

Newspaper articles commonly explore current trends in the conditions of foreign workers in Japan. For example, the Zentōitsu workers' union reported to the *Mainichi* that

> the situation for foreign workers is getting worse and worse since the recession. Not only are they weak due to their illegal status, the control by the police and the Immigration Bureau is becoming stricter. Illegal foreign workers, some undergoing treatment for their work injuries, are being deported. There are also illegal foreign workers who have been doused with gasoline and lit on fire when they went to their employers demanding unpaid wages.[45]

In this article, the union also mentioned how employers use the names of legal foreigners or Japanese to falsify company documents in order to hide the employment of illegal foreign workers. Some groups quote illegal foreign workers to reveal violations that Japanese employers have committed, such as: "Although I worked, I did not receive pay," and "I am sick, but

---

45. *Mainichi Shimbun,* March 14, 1994, 10.

TABLE 6.2. Articles about Japanese NGOs and Their Activities to Help Illegal Foreign Workers in Selected Japanese Newspapers (1983–2003)

Group	Total number of articles	Newspapers (no.)	Content of article
Christian NGOs	61	Asahi (41), Mainichi (12), Yomiuri (5), Nikkei (0), Sankei (3)	Conditions of illegal foreign workers; activities of group; profile of activists; party announcement
Community workers' unions	139	Asahi (68), Mainichi (25), Yomiuri (21), Nikkei (21), Sankei (4)	Conditions of illegal foreign workers (testimony), activities of group; profile of activists; announcement of union formation, symposium engagements, Philippine's movie
Women's shelters/ NGOs	275	Asahi (128), Mainichi (74), Yomiuri (40), Nikkei (17), Sankei (16)	Conditions of illegal foreign women (testimony); activities of group; symposium engagements; profile of activists; report of their surveys
Medical NGOs	221	Asahi (70), Mainichi (63), Yomiuri (62), Nikkei (18), Sankei (8)	Conditions of illegal foreign workers; activities of group; symposium/ seminar engagements; profile of activists
Lawyer's association NGOs	230	Asahi (102), Mainichi (61), Yomiuri (38), Nikkei (18), Sankei (11)	Conditions of illegal foreign workers; activities of group; symposium/ seminar engagements; profile of activists; Human Rights Prize
Concerned citizens' groups	285	Asahi (140), Mainichi (66), Yomiuri (51), Nikkei (15), Sankei (13)	Conditions of illegal foreign workers (testimony); activities of group; symposium engagements; profile of activists; book announcement

NGO = nongovernmental organization

I don't have money for medical treatment."[46] When these reports are published in the *Yomiuri,* they portray foreign workers as real people and the activities of their support groups as noble.

---

46. *Yomiuri Shimbun,* August 11, 1996, 31.

For some articles, members of immigrant rights groups have supplied journalists not only with direct quotations from foreign workers but also with detailed accounts from the testimonies of specific foreigners. This can be done easily because Japanese activists have recorded such testimonies in their newsletters or books. For instance, LAFLR, a lawyer NGO, offered the following disturbing accounts to the *Mainichi* about a Chinese student in a Japanese police station and an Iranian man in a detention center.

> A Chinese student (age 24), who was suspected of violating the Immigration Control Law, was arrested (the charge was later cleared). This March, he sought compensation from the police department for violence by a number of policemen against him when he was detained inside the police station. Also this June, an Iranian man (age 34), who was arrested, mysteriously died at the detention center during a joint investigation by the National Police and the Tokyo Immigration Bureau.[47]

In some instances, immigrant rights groups call attention to common misunderstandings about labor laws and offer a view sympathetic to illegal foreigners. The concerned citizens' group APFS informed the *Nikkei Weekly* that

> many workers who are injured at the workplace receive neither proper medical care nor their monthly salary or compensation from their employers. Illegal immigrants are usually in a helpless position where they work. Many complain of not receiving any salary for several months. Such workers, even if they are not legal immigrants, are entitled by law to receive those benefits.... But Japanese employers often ignore workers' rights because they are here illegally. Many workers keep quiet because their employers threaten to report them to the immigration office.[48]

The article went on to list the conditions faced by illegal foreigners. Many articles, particularly in the left-of-center newspapers, showcase the progressive vision and extraordinary activities of these immigrant rights groups.

Furthermore, members of immigrant rights groups use the press to criticize the Japanese government and society. Watanabe Hidetoshi of the

---

47. *Mainichi Shimbun,* October 12 1994, 10.
48. *Nikkei Weekly,* July 6, 1998.

Kalabaw-no-kai said that "the police and the government lead in racial discrimination and the media follow that line."[49] He stated the NPA uses unsubstantiated figures, taken out of their social and demographic context, to spread xenophobic propaganda. The lawyers' group LAFLR makes a similar claim in the *Mainichi* that "the government discriminates against foreigners, especially Asians. Immigration officials are rude. Employers consider foreigners as mere labor power."[50] In the same spirit, the women's group Mizula offered harsh remarks about Japanese men in an interview with the *Mainichi*. "Consultations concerning troubles with international marriage have steadily increased. There are many Japanese men who marry overstayed Thai and Filipino women. Why do you think that is so? These women always kindly serve [Japanese men]; they are not [being treated] as partners."[51] Facing such instances of discrimination, Japanese activists turn the situation around and accuse certain Japanese people and government institutions of unethical or illegal actions. By doing so, they raise a critical question among the public: Who are the real criminals?

Activists sometime present their information to the media and public in an exaggerated form. This was exemplified during the 1999 Third National Forum in Solidarity with Migrant Workers in Tokyo, where over eight hundred activists, journalists, and scholars attended. On the second day of the Forum, a lawyer group staged a dramatic and exaggerated skit on the abusive treatment of inmates by immigration officials and police in Japanese prisons. The activists portrayed government officials as arrogant and violent. The skit was followed by a speech of two Iranian children, who spoke in fluent Japanese on being victimized as children of illegal foreigners and their benevolent feelings toward Japan. Their Japanese seemed too perfect and the messages were too mature for their ages. Japanese activists may have assisted or coached these children with their speeches.

The goal of many of these activists is to convince newspaper readers that illegal foreigners in Japan have done nothing wrong. For them, illegal foreigners are not criminals, in contrast to the views of political leaders and the NPA. For example, in an interview with the *Yomiuri,* Temmyō Yoshiomi

---

49. Published interview with Watanabe Hideyoshi, May 1, 2000, at http//www.abcnews. com/.

50. *Mainichi Shimbun,* January 3, 1991, 3.

51. *Mainichi Shimbun* (Osaka evening version), October 2, 1996, 3.

of MF-MASH remarks: "Certainly these working people violate the Immigration Control Law, but...as far as illegal acts are concerned, they have done nothing wrong."[52] In a separate 1991 interview with the *Yomiuri,* Watanabe Hideyoshi of the Kalabaw-no-kai took the argument further, explaining that illegal foreign workers actually help Japanese society by paying taxes and shopping at Japanese stores. He warned that companies "could go bankrupt if there were no foreigners," due to the labor shortage in Japan.[53]

These interviews with members of immigrant rights groups offer the mass media, and thus the public, images of foreigners quite different from those disseminated by political leaders. Readers of these articles have access to descriptions of illegal workers as human beings or victims of Japanese capitalism, and not simply as dangerous criminals. In some instances, immigrant rights groups argue that even illegal immigrants who have committed crimes should not be criticized. They argue that foreigners have been driven by repressive circumstances to commit the crimes with which they were charged, such as prostitution and murder. These immigrant rights NGOs add alternative sources of opinion and have influenced the Japanese in their thinking about the rights of foreigners. Thus, they counterbalance the official Japanese view of illegal foreigners.

Without doubt, Japanese journalists are beginning to see the importance of these immigrant rights groups as dependable, alternative sources of information on illegal foreign workers. In 2003, the *Asahi* awarded its Social Welfare Prize to the women's group, HELP. Similarly, the 1996 Mainichi Prize for International Exchange went to another women's group, Mizula.[54] The *Kanagawa Shimbun* also presented Mizula with the Kanagawa Region Social Work Prize in 1998. When Japan celebrated the fiftieth anniversary of its constitution in 1997, the *Mainichi* provided a list of symposiums that were being held in Tokyo on the Japanese constitution. One of these symposiums was sponsored by the APFS and focused on whether the Japanese constitution protects the human rights of migrant workers in Japan.[55] In May 2001, the Foreign Correspondents' Club of Japan invited Yoshinari

---

52. *Yomiuri Shimbun,* October 3, 1995, 75.
53. *Yomiuri Shimbun,* September 27, 1991, 30.
54. *Mainichi Shimbun,* October 2, 1996, 3.
55. *Mainichi Shimbun,* May 2, 1997, 14.

Kasuo of the APFS to speak to foreign and Japanese journalists about the current situation of illegal foreigners in Japan.

The Impact of Political Struggles on Public Attitudes and Policy

The impact of these newspaper articles on those who read them can only be inferred. In recent years, public opinion appears to have leaned toward official sources as news of foreigner crimes, particularly those committed by Chinese, has escalated dramatically, while reports from immigrant rights NGOs have declined. National surveys reveal that Japanese increasingly fear that illegal foreigners will cause a deterioration of safety and "atmosphere" (living environment) in their neighborhoods. During the early 1990s, roughly two-thirds of Japanese in various public opinion surveys were receptive toward foreigners. By the mid-1990s, however, support for crackdowns against illegal workers had increased dramatically. For example, six out of ten employees working at firms that did not hire foreign workers supported crackdowns.[56] The *Yomiuri Shimbun* reported an increased percentage of Japanese who said they believed that foreigners would cause a deterioration of safety and a worse atmosphere in neighborhoods, from 44 percent in 1993 to 53 percent in 1994. A survey conducted by the NHK (Nippon Hōsō Kyōkai or Japan Broadcasting Corporation) Broadcasting Culture Research Institute in 1995 revealed that 64 percent of Japanese people said they believed that the crime rate would rise if more foreigners sought permanent residence. Only 15 percent disagreed. More recent polls conducted by the Cabinet Office have revealed a similar picture. They have found that the percentage of Japanese who oppose the importation of foreign workers increased from 49.2 percent in 2000 to 70.7 percent in 2004. Of those who opposed foreign workers, 72.5 percent listed the deterioration of safety and atmosphere as their primary reason.[57]

---

56. Hiroshi Komai, *Foreign Migrants in Contemporary Japan* (Melbourne: Trans Pacific Press, 2001), 45–49.

57. These surveys of Japanese public opinion are taken from the Roper Center at http://roper center.uconn.edu/jpoll/home.html. Polling organizations and the release dates of their surveys were: *Yomiuri Shimbun,* March 30, 1993, and March 30, 1994; NHK Broadcasting Culture Research Institute, January 6, 1995; and *Asahi Shimbun,* July 15, 2004.

Paradoxically, another set of survey data shows that a growing number of Japanese supports the rights of foreigners. According to a 1993 survey by the NHK Broadcasting Culture Research Institute, 52 percent support the rights of foreigners to be guaranteed just like those of Japanese people. In a 1997 survey, the *Yomiuri Shimbun* found that 67 percent of Japanese respondents defend the rights of foreigners to be established to meet the needs of an ethnically integrated Japanese society. Surveys conducted by the Prime Minister's Office show a similar pattern regarding equal protection of human rights for foreign residents, with a rise from 61.8 percent in 1988 to 65.5 percent in 1997, but a decline to 54.0 percent in 2002.[58] This set of surveys suggests that Japanese recognize that foreigners do not enjoy the same rights as citizens. In addition, between 1988 and 1997, Japanese increasingly appeared to view foreigners as victims in their society, but this view had dropped in popularity by 2002.

This pattern of public attitudes toward illegal foreigners reinforces my argument that both state and societal actors play an important role in shaping the public views of illegal foreigners. The change in Japanese attitudes toward foreigners during the past fifteen years can be attributed in part to the economic recession of the 1990s, but an economic explanation does not satisfactorily account for the increase in Japanese sympathy for illegal foreigners as victims during the early and mid-1990s when the country was still in a recession. The case of the politics of illegal foreigners elucidates the struggles of both state actors and civil society actors to mobilize public opinion about illegal foreigners. As a result, we can better understand the contradictory pattern of Japanese attitudes toward foreigners during the 1990s and early 2000s: the increasing association of foreigners with criminality throughout this period, the rise in perception of them as victims deprived of basic rights during the early and mid-1990s, and the shift away from an idea of granting foreigners rights similar to those of Japanese since the late 1990s.

Both state and societal actors understand that public opinion is important in policy making. Because the police monopolize "official" information on foreign criminality, they can use the media to shape public opinion and

---

58. These data are also from the Roper Center: NHK Broadcasting Culture Research Institute, July 1, 1993; *Yomiuri Shimbun,* March 19, 1997; Prime Minister's Office, July 1, 1988; July 1, 1997; July 1, 2002.

even to change public policy toward certain groups of illegal foreigners. A high-ranking official from the NPA explained that he had intentionally fed information to the press on criminal activities committed by Iranians during the time when the Iranian population in certain areas of Tokyo became a public menace. He maintains this action changed public opinion toward Iranians from positive or neutral to negative.[59] Indeed, reports in major newspapers on crimes committed by Iranians doubled between 1991 and 1994. More significantly, in 1993 the MOFA eventually revoked its special visa agreement with the Iranian government.

Similarly, the police have contributed to the recent increase in public fear of illegal foreigners, particularly the Chinese. The police pass on information about criminal activities by illegal foreigners to their advantage for expanding their jurisdiction and thereby their funding. Peter Katzenstein finds that "by virtually all measures, police power inside the government has been increasing greatly."[60] He concludes that by the mid-1990s the NPA became one of the top three government agencies, along with the traditionally powerful Ministry of Finance and Ministry of International Trade and Industry. Amplified critiques of foreigner crimes were probably part of a larger set of initiatives or political strategies meant to expand the NPA's coercive abilities.[61] David Bayley observed that "even though foreign residents in Japan committed less than one-tenth of one percent of crimes in 1986, the NPA and the Tokyo Metropolitan Police Department set up special units to deal with the problem because the trend was upward over the preceding decade."[62] The role of the NPA has increased substantially even during the 1990s when it was under fire for corruption and brutality. By focusing the public attention on visible Iranians, subversive North Koreans, or fearful Chinese, the NPA can justify its need for more authority

---

59. Interview with a high-ranking NPA official, December 10, 2000.

60. Peter Katzenstein, *Cultural Norms and National Security: Police and Military in Postwar Japan* (Ithaca: Cornell University Press, 1996), 62–63.

61. In addition to addressing foreigner crimes, the NPA's coercive abilities expanded further during the late 1990s with new authority to crack down on teenage dating services and child prostitution and after 2004 with the government's prioritization to prevent international terrorism. See David Leheny, *Think Global, Fear Local: Sex, Violence, and Anxiety in Contemporary Japan* (Ithaca: Cornell University Press, 2006).

62. David H. Bayley, *Forces of Order: Policing Modern Japan* (Berkeley: University of California Press, 1991), 3.

and funding.[63] In 2003, as part of the government's priority to ensure the security of people and to reduce overstayed foreigners by half, the government authorized the NPA to hire 3,150 new police officers, 451 correction officers, and 56 prosecutors (and the Ministry of Justice [MOJ] to hire 353 new immigration and custom officers). It allocated additional 2.1 billion yen (US$19 million) to enhance immigration control and measures against illegal foreigners. The amount increased 81 percent to 3.8 billion yen (US$35 million) two years later.[64]

Mobilizing public opinion is also critical to NGOs' efforts to counter official attitudes toward illegal foreigners and to influence policy makers. Media attention to their organizations and issues gives activists greater visibility and access to broader audiences. For example, APFS successfully rallied public support through the media for its efforts to convince the MOJ to grant "special residence permission" to twenty-one illegal foreigners who had stayed in Japan longer than ten years. Between the beginning of its campaign in September 1999 and the MOJ's decision in March 2000, APFS contacted the media and was the subject of eighteen newspaper articles. The campaign attracted scholars in- and outside of Japan, who signed a petition in support of the APFS efforts. As mentioned earlier, the MOJ eventually granted special permission to these twenty-one overstayed foreigners. The Ministry's decision was also reflected in the 2000 Basic Plan for Immigration Control, which requires authorities dealing with overstayed foreigners to consider their ties with Japanese society. Since 2000, the MOJ has taken various factors, such as the rights of children, into account when reviewing "special permission" applicants that have "ties with Japan." Between 2000 and 2004, the MOJ has granted special permission to over 40,000 overstayed foreigners.[65]

Another major policy victory for immigrant rights NGOs involves the criminalization of transnational human traffickers and protection for victims of trafficking. A political opportunity opened up for immigrant rights

---

63. On the importance of social impact in indictment or prosecution, see David T. Johnson, *The Japanese Way of Justice: Prosecuting Crime in Japan* (Oxford: Oxford University Press, 2001). On the criminalization of Iranians, see Friman, "Gaijinhanzai."

64. Ministry of Finance, [Annual Budget] (Tokyo: Ōkurasho Insatsukyoku, various years).

65. Ministry of Justice, *Shutsunyukoku kanri* [Annual Statistics on Immigration Control] (Tokyo: Ōkurasho Insatsukyoku, 2005).

activists during the early 2000s after the U.S. government enacted the Trafficking Victims Protection Act of 2000. Since then, the U.S. State Department has begun to monitor countries around the world on its efforts to stop trafficking in persons. Its annual *Trafficking in Persons Report* places each country into one of three tiers (with the highest, tier 1, considered acceptable) based on sources from foreign governments, NGOs, news media account, U.S. embassies, and official visits. Since 2001, the State Department has consistently weighed its opinions on the NGOs' side and placed Japan in tier 2—the only developed country in this category. In 2004, it downgraded Japan to a new category within tier 2, Watch List, which consists of countries in danger of falling to tier 3. Japan received this embarrassing evaluation despite having signed the Protocol to Prevent, Suppress, and Punish Trafficking (also known as the Palermo Protocol), which supplemented the UN Convention against Transnational Organized Crime in 2002. The 2004 Report stated that the Japanese government "needs to increase its efforts to combat severe forms of trafficking in persons, including increased investigations, prosecutions and convictions of trafficking crimes and better assistance to victims."[66] The Director of the Office to Monitor and Combat Trafficking in Persons, John Miller, explained that there is a tremendous gap in Japan "between the size of the problem and the resources and efforts devoted to addressing the problem.... When the victims number in the thousands, I found only two small shelters...willing to take trafficking victims.... We [also] looked at the prosecutions, the arrests and convictions.... The sentences appeared to be relatively light."[67] In fact, prior to 2005, there were no cases in which human traffickers were punished under the Criminal Code. All human trafficking crimes were prosecuted and punished as violations of the Immigration Law or Employment Security Law, which carried lighter punishments and fines. In 2003, for example, the leader of one of Japan's largest human trafficking rings, Koichi "Sony" Hagiwara, was found guilty of brokering several dozen Colombian strip dancers and was sentenced to twenty-two months in prison along with a 300,000 yen (US$2,750) fine. In other countries with

---

66. See http://www.state.gov/g/tip/rls/tiprpt/2004/33191.htm (accessed January 28, 2006).
67. See http://www.state.gov/g/tip/rls/rm/33532.htm (accessed January 28, 2006).

antitrafficking legislation, a crime of this nature would typically result in a prison sentence of ten years or more.

In 2004, Japan was aggressively seeking a permanent seat in the Security Council of the UN, and the perception of the U.S. State Department that Japan was soft on addressing serious human rights crime within its borders represented an obstacle to that effort. Therefore, the Japanese government quickly responded by inviting members of the Japan Network against Trafficking in Persons (JNATIP) to its study groups, as mentioned earlier. In December 2004, the Inter-Ministerial Liaison Committee (Task Force), comprised of members from the Cabinet Secretariat, the MOJ, the NPA, the MOFA, and the Ministry of Health, Labor, and Welfare (MHLW), adopted the National Action Plan. Most interesting about this Action Plan was a noticeable change in officials' attitude toward overstayed foreign prostitutes, whom they had previously viewed as "criminals." Moreover, the language in the Action Plan was remarkably similar to that of immigrant rights NGOs. For instance, the opening sentence of the Action Plan reads "Trafficking in persons is a grave violation of human rights and requires a prompt and appropriate response from a humanitarian perspective, as trafficking in persons causes serious emotional and physical pain for the victims, especially women and children, and recovery from such damages is very difficult."[68]

Members of the JNATIP expressed concern that the original Action Plan focused mainly on the punishment of perpetrators. Like the APFS campaign to grant "special residence permission" to certain illegal foreigners, the JNATIP collaborated with academics and lobbied the government to also consider the protection of victims and assistance in their rehabilitation. Before the Diet approved the conclusions of the Palermo Protocol in June 2005, the government revised its Penal Code to criminalize the buying and selling of persons. The revision also granted victims special residency status to protect them even if they had overstayed their visas so that they could receive treatment before returning to their countries. As a result, the number of victims protected at the government-run Women's Consulting Offices has increased, and the Immigration Bureau granted seventy-four special

---

68. See http://www.mofa.go.jp/policy/i_crime/people/action0508.html (accessed March 14, 2008).

residence permissions to victims in 2005 and 2006. Starting on April 1, 2005, the government budgeted around US$100,000 per year to private shelters. Between 2005 and 2007 the MOFA has funded approximately US$844,000 for repatriation assistance to 126 victims through the International Organization for Migration (IOM).[69] In 2006, the MHLW started budgeting medical costs for victims. The government also provides examinations by physicians at the Women's Consulting Offices. Meanwhile, the Task Force has sent directives on how to protect victims to relevant offices throughout Japan. As a result of these directives, police at the *kōban* (police box) no longer treat trafficking victims (mostly overstayed foreign prostitutes) as criminals, and immigration officials do not automatically deport them. More interesting, the government has launched an aggressive public relations campaign through television and radio broadcasts, newspapers, and magazines as well as the distribution of multilingual leaflets and posters. The NPA even produced and distributed a Japanese-English-Spanish video and DVD called "Trafficking," featuring an interview with Otsu Keiko of HELP. Ironically, this public awareness campaign now depicts those illegal foreign women, previously associated by the authorities with active criminals, as passive "victims."

As new arrivals from Asia enter Japan to seek work and stay past the expiration of their visas, certain nationalistic political elites twist official figures by taking them out of their social and demographic context to portray illegal foreigners as criminals and dangerous. Such behavior is not unusual in Western countries, where right-wing politicians exploit the public sentiments on widespread fear of foreign criminality and bogus asylum seekers. Japanese activists, with their cosmopolitan views, have competed for the public imagination of illegal foreigners by supplying alternative but educated information that depicts these illegal aliens as victims. These activists increasingly play a role in transforming prevalent social meanings and serve as an important counterforce to Japan's official position on, and far more prejudiced activities toward, illegal foreigners.

The growing attention in the Japanese media to immigrant rights NGOs and their issues certainly increases the amount of publicly available

---

69. Ibid.

information on illegal foreigners, gives activists greater visibility, and affords them access to wider audiences. What impact this trend will have on public perceptions and political attitudes more broadly is, as yet, unclear; obviously this is a speculative matter. Nonetheless, it is plausible that by giving voice to marginalized residents and providing alternative sources of information to the media, these activists may well be shaping public discourse in Japan, especially on matters relating (however indirectly) to issues of immigration as well as Japanese citizenship. This public discourse has already had a considerable impact on a number of public policies regarding membership rules, foreign relations, domestic violence, and human trafficking.

7

Conclusion

Foreigners and Democracy

The presence of foreigners challenges democratic ideals. On the one hand, democracies set clear criteria for membership and presuppose a minimum of shared values among members of the political community. On the other hand, they require a respect for individual political rights and for differences in culture (beliefs and identities) between individuals and groups. The question, then, is how do different advanced industrialized countries deal with foreign migrants, and where does Japan fit in this comparative matrix? This book offers a theoretical contribution to comparative immigration politics by examining Japan's policy response to the challenges of rising numbers of foreigners to democratic ideals.

This book also offers a theoretical contribution to how strong states are understood by showing how foreigner support groups assist in organizing Japan's civil society. Unquestionably, Japan has been a case of state-dominance, in which truly autonomous associations have in the past found it difficult to function but are now, gradually, gaining a foothold. Therefore, we would not expect to find much institutional innovation aimed at more responsive and inclusive democratic governance at the local level, least of all to accommodate foreign workers. Yet, perhaps more than other civil society organizations, support groups organized by Japanese citizens on behalf of overstayed foreigners demonstrate how civic groups in Japan can exert influence on state actors.

Immigration Politics: Japan in Comparative Perspective

The findings of this book contribute to the growing field of comparative immigration politics, particularly the challenges of foreigners to democratic ideals. In response to labor migration across Europe, North America, and, increasingly, Asia, governments struggle to reinterpret or reform existing immigration laws and entitlement schemes in light of both changing economic and demographic realities and, as important, shifting public sentiment.[1] Two approaches to immigration policies emerge from the responses by governments in Western and Asian countries. Most Western governments view immigration in terms of permanent settlement and work to improve their integration policies. In contrast, governments in Asian countries see immigration in terms of temporary workers and try to devise effective immigration control policies. Japan is ambivalent in how it draws from these two ideal types. On the one hand, Japan is an industrial democracy ("Western") and could be expected for economic and developmental reasons to follow policies somewhat like those of the European Union or the United States. On the other hand, Japan is geographically located in Asia and has been influenced by many of the social and cultural norms of the region, particularly regarding migrants.

Common to both industrialized Western societies and developing Asian countries, regardless of their restrictive immigration policies and rigorous border controls, is the presence of illegal foreigners.[2] All advanced democracies must address the question of how to deal with illegal foreigners: round them up and deport them; ignore their existence and refuse them

---

1. Takeyuki Tsuda, ed., *Local Citizenship in Recent Countries of Immigration: Japan in Comparative Perspective* (Lanham: Lexington Books, 2006).

2. Global Commission on International Migration, *Migration in an Interconnected World: New Directions for Actions* (Geneva: SRO-Kundig, 2005).

their social and political rights; or recognize their existence and work to turn them into legal and productive members of society. The Japanese experience offers one possible solution.

Most governments in Western countries view immigration as permanent settlement; therefore, they have coherent and comprehensive policies on immigration and foreign labor that guarantee certain rights and privileges to foreign residents, including illegal foreigners. They lay out categories of residence and an explicit process for changing one's resident status. They also tend to have liberal naturalization policies that clearly state the criteria for becoming a permanent resident or naturalized citizen. In these countries, the requirements for naturalization typically include (1) a certain period of continued residence, (2) language competence, (3) knowledge of the country's history and constitution, (4) loyalty to the political ideology of the state and to the state itself, (5) a good moral character (i.e., absence of criminal convictions), and (6) an intention to stay permanently in the country.[3] Naturalization has become a somewhat routine matter.[4]

Once immigrant workers have been in the host country for a specific number of years, foreign workers in Western Europe are accorded progressive socioeconomic rights that approximate those of native workers.[5] Many Western governments also encourage immigrants to participate in cultural, civic, and political activities (such as joining trade unions and political parties) with the same rights and obligations as the rest of the population. Many even offer them voting rights in local elections. Notably, immigration policies in Europe and the United States deal explicitly with the integration of immigrants into their societies. Such policies, which extend citizenship rights to immigrants, typically entail sustained efforts to secure for immigrants equal social conditions and opportunities by reducing various social and economic disadvantages through legislation against

---

3. Tomas Hammer, *Democracy and the Nation State* (Aldershot: Avebury, 1990), 76. People who belong to the same ethnic groups or speak the same language as natives may be given a fast-track to naturalization.

4. OECD (SOPEMI), *Trends in International Migration* (Paris: OECD, 2002).

5. Mark J. Miller, *Foreign Workers in Western Europe: An Emerging Political Force* (New York: Praeger, 1981), 16. For an excellent general comparison on the provision of socioeconomic rights to migrants in France, Switzerland, and Germany during the 1970s, see Mark J. Miller and Philip L. Martin, *Administering Foreign-Worker Programs: Lessons from Europe* (Lexington: Lexington Books, 1982), 184–185 (appendix I).

racism and xenophobia and language programs for newly arrived immigrants. Integration policies in most Western countries also include linguistic and cultural rights as well as the cultivation of ethnic solidarity.[6]

In contrast to Western immigration policies, those in Asia are designed to deal with workers—not immigrants.[7] In general, Asian governments welcome and encourage highly skilled foreign migrants but discourage or closely control unskilled workers.[8] Some countries, such as South Korea, Taiwan, Singapore, and Malaysia, have employment permit systems that allow the entry of unskilled foreign workers but limit the number admitted, the sectors in which foreign workers can be employed, and the terms and conditions of their employment. Asian countries tend to have restrictive naturalization policies whereby transition to permanent settlement is rarely possible except through marriage with a national.[9]

Since they do not actively seek immigrants, most Asian governments do not extend the benefits of citizenship to legal foreigners. These governments usually do not offer foreign workers citizenship or linguistic and cultural rights. Neither do legal foreigners have the right to vote in local elections. Immigration policies in Asia are based on the assumption that the employment of foreign workers is a temporary measure, so little attempt has been made by national governments to integrate the foreigners. Free public medical services and free public education are typically not offered to foreign workers. Responsibility for integration activities in Asian countries typically falls onto civil society groups and local governments. The exclusion of legal foreigners from social security and other entitlements

---

6. Some of these rights were curtailed in many Western countries after September 11, 2001.

7. There are some exceptions. Singapore and Hong Kong had investor programs that granted permanent residence to rich foreigners who wanted to invest large amounts of money in their states. Malaysia had a "silver hair program" that encouraged rich foreigners above the age of fifty to reside in the country. In the late 1990s, Thailand actively sought to assimilate long-term migrants from Vietnam.

8. OECD, *Migration and the Labour Market in Asia: Recent Trends and Policies* (Paris: OECD, 2003).

9. Through these interracial marriages and/or birth of foreigners' children in their countries, a multiethnic society with a system of "graduated sovereignty" emerges. Under this system, the government subjects different segments of the population to different regimes of valuation and control. In Malaysia, for example, the government constructs six differentiated zones of laws in accordance to race, gender, and nature of work and attempts to discipline each group according to these laws. See Aihwa Ong, *Flexible Citizenship: The Cultural Logics of Transnationality* (Durham: Duke University Press, 1999).

in most of Asia can be seen as another measure by their governments to discourage settlement. Only Japan offers access to public schooling for the children of foreigners. Legal foreign workers in Japan also enjoy medical care, sickness, family, and maternity benefits.[10] Japan's social insurance schemes also include unemployment and old-age benefits; it is the only East Asian country where legal foreign workers receive equal treatment with nationals regarding these benefits.

In Western societies, governments typically guarantee illegal aliens basic rights and social services regardless of their legal status.[11] The Social Charter of the Council of Europe grants illegal immigrants and their children entitlement to public medical assistance.[12] Children of illegal immigrants, in particular, are ensured medical assistance beyond an immediate threat to life with no minimum residence requirement. In the United States, illegal aliens are eligible, often indirectly, for social insurance programs and workers' compensation. They can receive welfare benefits on behalf of their U.S.–born children, including food stamps and cash assistance through the Temporary Assistance to Needy Families (TANF) and Supplemental Security Income (SSI) programs.[13]

Whereas illegal foreigners in Europe and the United States have basic rights and entitlements to critical welfare programs, those in Asia are less protected. As mentioned above, all foreigners remain excluded from social security and welfare programs in Asia. In most countries, illegal foreigners do not remain illegal indefinitely. In the United States, amnesty programs

---

10. International Labor Organization, *ILO Migration Survey 2003: Country Summaries* (Geneva: ILO International Migration Program, 2004).

11. Yasemin Nuhoglu Soysal, *Limits of Citizenship: Migrants and Postnational Membership in Europe* (Chicago: University of Chicago Press, 1994), 131.

12. See http://www.coe.int/T/E/Human_Rights/ESC/7_Resources/factsheet_migrants.pdf (accessed March 25, 2006).

13. Hospitals can cover the costs of care for illegal aliens from several federal funding sources, such as Medicaid coverage for emergency medical services (including those associated with childbirth), supplemental Medicaid payments to certain hospitals serving a large number of low-income patients, funds ($100 million) available to twelve states in fiscal years 1998 through 2001 for emergency services furnished to undocumented aliens under the Balanced Budget Act of 1997, and funds ($1 billion) in fiscal years 2005 through 2008 for payments to hospitals and other providers for emergency services furnished to undocumented aliens under the Medicare Prescription Drug, Improvement, and Modernization Act of 2003. See http://www.gao.gov/highlights/d04472high.pdf (accessed March 26, 2006); Peter H. Schuck, "The Status and Rights of Undocumented Aliens in the United States," *International Migration* 25 (1987): 125–139 (131ff).

gave permanent legal status to millions of illegal aliens. An increasing number of countries in the Organization for Economic Cooperation and Development (OECD) have also implemented programs to regularize (or to grant temporary legal status to) illegal foreigners who meet certain criteria and/or follow a specified procedure.[14] Often, regularization in Europe is granted based on prior work and a demonstration of continued formal employment, while amnesties in the United States cover persons who have been present in the country for a certain period of time. In Asia, some countries have also instituted procedures for regularizing the status of illegal migrants. However, regularization programs in Asia are intended to give legal status for illegal migrants to work in the country for a specified number of years while restricting their permanent settlement. Only Japan provides legal channels for permanent residency to illegal foreigners. Since 2000, regularization has taken place in Japan on a limited case-by-case basis for foreigners who have lived in the country for more than ten years and have established ties with Japanese society. Between 2000 and 2004, Japan had granted special permission of permanent residence to over 40,000 overstayed foreigners.

In sum, how Japan treats foreigners officially involves an ambiguous response to two very different Western versus Asian models—though Japan clearly comes down being more Asian than Western. This is because Japanese government officials' desire for social stability and racial homogeneity coincides with its concern for economic productivity and tax revenue amidst labor shortages and rising welfare spending in an aging society. As a result, they have decided to bring foreign workers into the country but with restrictive immigration policies and inadequate welfare provisions. To preserve their national identity, they prefer to have these foreigners looking like Japanese (hence, their preference for nikkeijin) and limit their integration policy to this group.

Foreigners, Associative Activism, and Civil Society

The inadequacy of government policies and state welfare has prompted ethnic, religious, and activist communities to organize paternalistic,

---

14. OECD (SOPEMI), *Trends in International Migration* (Paris: OECD, 2002), 90.

nonstate institutions that offer various forms of assistance to foreigners in Japan. An examination of institutional arrangements for foreigners extends our understanding of the organization of Japan's civil society. Scholars have consistently characterized political life in contemporary Japan as consisting of a strong central government and influential economic elites; thus, much of Japanese behavior and civic activities can be interpreted as the result of state efforts.[15] Foreigner support groups in Japanese civil society, however, are still able to influence more inclusive democratic governance.

This influence in the context of a strong Japanese state is unexpected. Robert Pekkanen, for instance, contends that the state shapes civil society by selectively promoting certain civil society organizations and allowing them to expand, while regulating others that may undermine its power and making it difficult for them to survive or flourish.[16] According to Pekkanen, who points to the existence of few large civil society organizations and numerous small ones, the Japanese state provides preferential treatment to those civic organizations that are useful to the state, such as neighborhood associations, promoting their growth before eventually exerting influence over them. In contrast, the government makes it difficult for issue-oriented organizations, such as environmental NGOs, to expand, because it fears that these organizations may undermine its power. Pekkanen interprets the impressive increase of civil society organizations in Japan during the past few decades and the passage of the NPO law as continued efforts by the state to control and to shape civil society organizations. Akihiro Ogawa argues further that the NPO law can be seen as an invitation from the government to civil society organizations to participate in activities that support state's goals, thereby institutionalizing volunteer subjectivity.[17]

These interpretations of state–civil society relationships highlight the dominant role of the state and, consequently, portray Japan as having a

15. For such characterizations, see inter alia Chalmers Johnson, *MITI and the Japanese Miracle: The Growth of Industrial Policy, 1925–1977* (Stanford: Stanford University Press, 1982); Kent Calder, *Strategic Capitalism: Private Business and Public Purpose in Japanese Industrial Finance* (Princeton: Princeton University Press, 1993).

16. Robert Pekkanen, "Molding Japanese Civil Society: State-Structured Incentives and the Patterning of Civil Society," in Frank J. Schwartz and Susan J. Pharr, eds., *The State of Civil Society in Japan* (New York: Cambridge University Press, 2003), 116–134.

17. Akihiro Ogawa, "Invited by the State: Institutionalizing Volunteer Subjectivity in Contemporary Japan," *Asian Anthropology* 3 (2004): 71–96.

dependent civil society. As illustrated in chapter 3, however, the state neither promoted nor discouraged the development of zainichi Korean and
Chinese ethnic associations. These associations grew large as a result of in-
tergroup competition stemming from ideological differences and divided
imaginations of their homelands. Furthermore, the impact of the NPO
law on small foreigner support groups has been limited to a handful of
women's support groups and medical NGOs, groups that provide social
welfare services and whose agenda supports government interests. But
rather than being a passive partner or co-opted by the state, these groups
are pushing local governments to accept broader responsibilities in caring for their foreign residents. Increasingly, local governments in progressive areas are forging partnerships with these small NGOs as evidenced
by Mizula and Kalabaw-no-kai in the Kanagawa NGO advisory council,
and MF-MASH and SHARE in the creation of MIC Kanagawa. Local
governments seek institutional ideas and innovation from these NGOs
and work closely with Japanese activists in implementation. In this way,
instead of the state molding the civil society, civil society organizations
are shaping the role and responsibilities of the state.

Indeed, Japan's civil society appears small in comparison to those of other
developed countries and its Asian neighbors.[18] Moreover, there seems to be
a noticeable decline of large social movements and protests as witnessed in
the 1960s and early 1970s, such as the anti-U.S. Security Treaty (*anzen hoshō
jōyaku* or ANPO) protest, the environment protests, the student protests,
and the Narita protest.[19] However, this should not lead us to prematurely
conclude that Japan's political environment has become less pluralized or
that these small organizations lack political influence. This book demonstrates that it is precisely these small, issued-oriented groups, rather than

18. Susan Pharr and Robert Putnam, *Disaffected Democracies: What's Troubling the Trilat-
eral Countries?* (Princeton: Princeton University Press, 2000); Multhiah Alagappa, "Civil Society
and Democratic Change: Indeterminate Connection, Transforming Relations," in Multhiah
Alagappa, ed., *Civil Society and Political Change in Asia: Expanding and Contracting Democratic
Space* (Stanford: Stanford University Press, 2004).
19. On large social movements and protests of the 1960s and 1970s, see Ellis S. Kraus, *Japanese
Radicals Revisited: Student Protest in Postwar Japan* (Berkeley: University of California Press, 1974);
David E. Apter and Nagayo Sawa, *Against the State: Policies and Social Protest in Japan* (Cam-
bridge: Harvard University Press, 1984); Frank Upham, *Law and Social Change in Postwar Japan*
(Cambridge: Harvard University Press, 1987).

large, identity-reproducing ethnic associations, that increasingly are having an important policy impact and advancing social democracy in Japan. The Asian Peoples Friendship Society (APFS), with assistance from their epistemic communities, has successfully pressured the government to grant certain overstayed foreigners "special residence permission," while others have challenged the government to extend national health insurance (NHI) to certain unqualified foreigners. Mizula also played a significant role on the 2001 passage of the Domestic Violence Prevention Law. Similarly, the Japan Network against Trafficking in Persons (JNATIP) was influential in getting the government to adopt an action plan in 2004 to combat human trafficking and to implement legal changes such as amending the Penal Code to make human trafficking a crime.

One mechanism through which this influence is exerted, a process I call *associative activism,* highlights the creativeness of activists in working with existing legal and social institutions. Associative activism emphasizes the ways in which the motivations of local activists are defined through a range of professional activities. Of particular importance is the establishment of flexible associations aimed at solving specific problems faced by illegal foreign workers, and exchanges of information and strategies among activists. Through these associations and activities, the motives of activists are shaped into a coherent vision of a more inclusive democratic society, a vision that is pursued not through existing mechanisms of political representation, but through innovative institutions and activities, carried out largely in the informal public sphere.

In other Asian countries, civil society organizations grew rapidly only after the fall of their authoritarian governments.[20] The Japanese case reaffirms that a vibrant and relatively autonomous civil society can and often does coexist with a strong and active state, although we may have to look carefully at previously overlooked activities and spaces to identify and analyze such organizations. Richard Samuels and Daniel Okimoto have demonstrated a reciprocal relationship between state and business actors

20. See inter alia Sunhyuk Kim, *The Politics of Democratization in Korea: The Role of Civil Society* (Pittsburgh: Pittsburgh University Press, 2000); Juree Vichit-Vadakan, "Thai Civil Society: Exploring a Diverse and Complex Landscape," in David Schak and Wayne Hudson, eds., *Civil Society in Asia* (Aldershot: Ashgate, 2003), 87–102.

in contemporary Japan.[21] Sheldon Garon has extended this argument to Japanese civil society groups that are self-organized and operate within the public sphere. He documents the ways in which state actors historically mobilized citizens and fostered certain key propensities in the process of modernization during the Meiji period.[22] He describes the extraordinary efforts of bureaucrats, sometimes in response to and contingent on the demands and efforts of certain nonstate actors, to transform or to mold the minds of the Japanese people into active participants in the state's various projects through moral suasion campaigns.

With the increased importance of party politics in Japan, we might expect that reforms would come about through established parties adopting issues—such as the plight of foreign workers—for the purposes of challenging the ruling party.[23] There has arguably been some movement in this direction, but even these recent overtures have been limited for the most part to the issue of voting rights for legal resident aliens in local government. In 1998, the Kōmeitō (Clean Government Party) proposed a bill to grant voting rights in local elections to permanent foreign residents, but it and other opposition parties have not been able to successfully convince the Liberal Democratic Party (LDP) to introduce the bill in the Diet for deliberation. The LDP has consistently placed issues concerning foreigners as a low priority, even after the Kōmeitō had joined the ruling coalition in 2000.[24] This may change in the near future due to recent developments, including the incorporation of foreign workers into the centralized labor unions Rengō and Zenrōren in 2006 and the 2007 electoral success of the Democratic Party of Japan (DPJ) in the Upper House. Because Rengō and Zenrōren are central political supporters of the DPJ and the Japan Com-

---

21. Richard Samuels, *The Business of the Japanese State: Energy Markets in Comparative and Historical Perspective* (Ithaca: Cornell University Press, 1987); Daniel I. Okimoto, *Between MITI and the Market: Japanese Industrial Policy for High Technology* (Stanford: Stanford University Press, 1989).

22. Sheldon Garon, *Molding Japanese Minds: The State in Everyday Life* (Princeton: Princeton University Press, 1997); Garon, "From Meiji to Heisei: The State and Civil Society in Japan," in Frank J. Schwartz and Susan J. Pharr, eds., *The State of Civil Society in Japan* (New York: Cambridge University Press, 2003), 42–62.

23. See J. Mark Ramseyer and Frances Rosenbluth, *Japan's Political Marketplace* (Cambridge: Harvard University Press, 1993).

24. Interview with Tōyama Kiyohiko of the Kōmeitō and the House of Councilors, August 4, 2007.

munist Party, respectively, issues concerning foreigners are likely to be placed high on their priority lists.

Without voting rights, however, foreigners in Japan have little opportunity for political engagement in formal democratic organizations. I suggest instead that the extent of multicultural democratic transformation through associative activism by Japanese on behalf of illegal foreigners is deeper than any changes associated with party politics, and far greater than proponents of the strong Japanese state would have predicted.[25] Indeed, the transformation toward a multicultural democracy is occurring in what has traditionally been viewed as a highly centralized polity, where any hope for democratic reform would be top down. This makes my findings surprising, to say the least.

Even more surprising is that most of these foreigner rights NGOs were established by Japanese citizens, a fact that challenges our understanding of the Japanese people and their political culture. Japan's culture and politics have historically been less than accommodating to foreigners, and its people insular and suspicious of foreigners. This suspicion has deep roots in Japan's culture and history. To reinforce the populace's sense of isolation and suspicion of outsiders, Japan's rulers banned foreigners from 1640 to 1853 and severely enforced this ban. In present-day Japan, police and immigration officials frequently receive anonymous calls about "suspicious" foreigners. The Immigration Bureau in Tokyo receives approximately 20,000 letters and telephone calls per year denouncing foreigners. Moreover, media portrayals of illegal workers—as in several other industrialized democracies—exacerbate the public's suspicion and fear of these foreigners. Nevertheless, Japanese citizens have formed numerous local associations to assist illegal foreigners. This unexpected fact suggests that the Japanese suspicion of foreigners and/or racism is due not only to their geographic insularity but also to political constructions by certain government elites.

---

25. Moreover, the inclusion of foreigners in electoral politics does not necessarily constitute a sufficient condition for democratic action. On this point, see Renato Rosaldo and William Flores, "Identity, Conflict, and Evolving Latino Communities: Cultural Citizenship in San José, California," in William Flores and Rina Benmayor, eds., *Latino Cultural Citizenship: Claiming Identity, Space, and Rights* (Boston: Beacon Press, 1997), 57–96.

Associative Activism and Its Future

Foreigners historically played an important role in the founding of Japan's democracy. The arrival of Commodore Matthew C. Perry's black ships in 1853 prompted a regime change. The new ruling elites abolished the unjust feudal system and fashioned a constitution, a parliamentary system, and other political institutions after Western models in order to impress the West that Japan was democratized and so should be free of the unequal treaties that granted special privileges, such as extraterritorial rights on Japanese soil, to Westerners. After World War II, the United States pressured Japan to adopt a more democratic and progressive constitution that gave sovereignty to the people, guaranteed personal liberty and freedom from the state, and protected individuals from discrimination.

By the end of the twentieth century, Japan had reached a mature and advanced stage of welfare democracy and faced vulnerable moments as the country began to encounter economic and social problems associated with an aging population, labor shortage, and financial troubles. At this point, foreigners again had an important role to play in helping to revitalize the slow economy and expanding Japanese democratic ideals and institutions. Fortunately, the influx of foreigners into Japan from developing and newly industrialized countries in search of economic opportunity over the past two decades has not only helped alleviate some concerns over these problems but also stimulated associative activism, civil society, and social democracy. The ethnic associations, schools, and media of legal foreigners have generated civic activities among their members, especially activities linked to their homelands. But these groups, ideologically divided and socially segmented, have contributed in only a limited way to the furtherance of multicultural understanding and trust within Japanese society. Rather, it is the new, and especially illegal, foreigners whose presence has reinvigorated Japanese activists and civil society. Foreigner support groups and local networks formed by Japanese citizens have stimulated activism and public discussion about the marginalization of certain ethnic groups. In addition to helping solve problems for illegal foreigners, Japanese activists seek to transform public attitudes about, and official treatment of, illegal foreigners. These activists have forced government officials to reflect on Japan's national identity and to negotiate a new social contract with citizens on agreed rules, procedures, and responsibilities for all those who reside on their islands.

It is a basic principle of democracy that all members of a political community should have a share in its decision-making processes. In other words, everyone whose basic interests are affected by public policies should be included in the process of making them. Those groups that are easily oppressed and exploited in society ought to receive special representation rights. Foreigners, especially illegal foreign workers, arguably are the most easily oppressed and exploited in advanced industrialized societies. Unscrupulous employers have refused to provide workers' compensation or to pay minimum wage or time-and-a-half overtime to immigrants, who may be required to work between sixty and eighty hours per week. Female illegal immigrant workers have complained of being sexually harassed by their bosses but have kept quiet out of fear that their bosses would report them to immigration officials. Many illegal foreigners are placed in this situation because of their accident of birth in poorer countries and a human desire to improve their economic situation and help their families. If a minimum level of justice is to be applied to nonmembers of a society, some sort of representation rights must be considered for illegal foreigners. Indirect representation through immigrant rights activists, as illustrated in the Japanese experience, provides one plausible solution. Although the Japanese government does not grant political rights to foreigners, immigrant rights NGOs can influence the political process on behalf of illegal foreigners. Furthermore, immigrant rights' activists who encourage institutional experimentation aimed at fairer schemes of political representation for illegal foreigners at the local level promote a more just and humane Japanese society in general.

In recent years, Japan has achieved a relatively high degree of humanitarianism in its accommodation of foreign workers, including illegal ones, due not to government efforts but to the associative activities of Japanese activists. These activists ensure that globalization works for the most disadvantaged by fighting energetically for the protection of their rights and the provision of welfare services to all foreign workers. In this way, associative activism is helping to further Japan's progress toward a more democratic society. Once again, foreigners are playing a key role in Japan, as they help the country solve some of its domestic problems while advancing social democracy.

In sum, the influx of foreigners has stimulated public discussion, respect for differences in beliefs and identities among individuals and groups, political participation of marginalized groups, and institutional experimentation in search of more just and humane treatment of foreigners in Japan. Surprisingly, it is illegal foreigners who sparked associative activism among Japanese activists that appears to protect the most disadvantaged and to promote democratic multiculturalism. Associative activism by Japanese citizens, however, can only be a temporary solution to resolve some of the problems that recent foreigners face. The demand for political rights and social welfare provision will surely increase as the children of these recent arrivals grow up. Just as illegal foreigners place serious welfare constraints on Western governments, Japan will likely encounter similar welfare problems caused by foreigners. At that critical moment, Japanese policy makers will have to renegotiate a new social contract with their citizens and come up with a responsible solution to meet such demands from the children of foreigners. Throughout that process, Japanese activists will certainly continue to invoke international norms, monitor the government's responses, and provide new ideas.

Appendix

Foreigners' Support Groups in Tokyo and Kanagawa

Group Name	Location	Year Began	Ethnic Groups Served
Faith–based organizations			
Catholic Tokyo International Center (CTIC)	Tokyo	1990	Filipino, Nikkei Peruvian
CTIC—Meguro	Tokyo	2000	Filipino, Nikkei Peruvian
Society in Solidarity with Foreigners in Japan	Tokyo	1983	Filipino
Christian Coalitions on Refugees and Foreign Migrant Workers (Nankiren)	Tokyo	1989	Filipino, North Korean
Yamasato Consulting Office	Tokyo	1988	Chinese, Iranian
Society to Struggle Together with Asian Workers in Japan	Tokyo	1989	Filipino, Korean
Kapatiran—Nihon Sei-Ko-Kai	Tokyo	1987	Filipino
Makoto Kaibigan	Tokyo	1990	Filipino
The Philippines Center	Tokyo	1992	Filipino
Āyus	Tokyo	1999	Thai, Korean, Chinese
Pastoral Center for Migrants (PACEM)	Kanagawa	2002	Filipino, Korean, Peruvian

Group Name	Location	Year Began	Ethnic Groups Served
Yokohama Diocese: Solidarity Center for Migrants (SOL)	Kanagawa	1992–2002	
Korean Desk	Kanagawa	1992–2002	Filipino
Philippines Desk	Kanagawa	1994–2002	Korean
Latin Desk	Kanagawa	1994–2002	Nikkei Peruvian
Yokosuka Citizens Group to Think about the Philippines and Japan	Kanagawa	1983	Filipino

Community workers' unions

Group Name	Location	Year Began	Ethnic Groups Served
Edogawa Workers' Union	Tokyo	1988 (1984)	Iranian, Pakistani, Bangladeshi
Keihin Union	Tokyo	1992	Bangladeshi, Iranian
Sumida Union	Tokyo	1991	Filipino
National Union of General Workers-Tokyo South	Tokyo	1974 (1960)	Chinese, (American, European)
Foreign Workers Branch of Zentōitsu	Tokyo	1992 (1960)	Indian, Bangladeshi, Pakistani, Indian
Foreign Laborers' Union (FLU)	Tokyo	1992–2001	Bangladeshi, Nikkei, Indian, Pakistani
Tokyo Union	Tokyo	1989 (1979)	
Japanese Language School Teachers Union	Tokyo		
Nerima Part-time Workers' Union	Tokyo	1992	
Toshima Union	Tokyo	1992	
Fureai Koto Workers' Union	Tokyo	1988	Bangladeshi, Iranian, Pakistani
Hachioji Union	Tokyo	1988 (1984)	Iranian
Santama Joint Labor Union	Tokyo	1991 (1977)	
Hokubu Part-time Workers' Union	Tokyo	1998 (1990)	
Labor Union of Migrant Workers	Tokyo	2001	Bangladeshi, Filipino
International Labor Union Bright	Tokyo	1993	Iranian, Chinese, Pakistani, Filipino
Kanagawa City Union	Kanagawa	1990	Nikkei Peruvian, Korean
Yokohama City Union	Kanagawa	1997	Indian, Korean, Bangladeshi
Yokohama Workers' Union	Kanagawa	1991 (1986)	Korean, Chinese

Foreign women's support groups

Group Name	Location	Year Began	Ethnic Groups Served
Asia–Japan Women's Resource Center	Tokyo	1995 (1977)	Asian Women
Friends of Thai Women Association	Tokyo	1991 (1989)	Thai
Group Akakabu	Tokyo	1992 (1983)	Thai, Filipina
Women's Shelter HELP	Tokyo	1986	Thai, Filipina
International Movement Against All Forms of Discriminations and Racism (IMADR)	Tokyo	1988	Asian Women

Group Name	Location	Year Began	Ethnic Groups Served
Kanagawa Women's Space "Mizula"	Kanagawa	1990	Thai, Filipina
Women's Shelter "Saalaa"	Kanagawa	1992	Thai, Filipina, Chinese, Peruvian
Kalakasan	Kanagawa	2002	Filipina
Medical NGOs			
AMDA International Information Center	Tokyo	1991	Thai, Chinese, Indian, Filipino
SHARE	Tokyo	1991 (1983)	Thai, Filipino, Peruvian
Kameido Himawari Clinic	Tokyo	1990	Indian, Bangladeshi, Pakistani, Filipino
Tokyo English Life Line—TELL Filipino Line	Tokyo		Filipino
Santama District Occupational Safety and Health Center	Tokyo	1992 (1985)	
Tokyo Occupational Safety and Health Resource Center	Tokyo	1998 (1989)	Pakistani, Bangladeshi
Japan Occupational Safety and Health Resource Center	Tokyo	1990	
Health Insurance to All Foreigners! Committee	Kanagawa	1990	All "illegal" foreigners
Esperanza-no-kai	Kanagawa	1993	Nikkei, Filipino, Indian
MF-MASH	Kanagawa	1991	Filipino, Iranian, Korean, Pakistani, Bangladeshi
Minatomachi Clinic	Kanagawa	1991	
Jujo-dori Clinic	Kanagawa	1991	
Yokosuka Chuo Clinic	Kanagawa	1991	
Isezaki Women's Clinic	Kanagawa	1995	
Imai International Clinic	Kanagawa	1995–1998	
Kobayashi International Clinic	Kanagawa	1991	Peruvian, Thai, Filipino
Sabay	Kanagawa	1993	Filipina, Thai
Kanagawa Occupational Safety and Health Center	Kanagawa	1990 (1980)	Thai, Peruvian
MIC Kanagawa	Kanagawa	2002	All Foreigners
Lawyers' groups			
Lawyers Association for Foreign Laborers Rights (LAFLR)	Tokyo	1990–2000	Filipino, Chinese, Iranian, Peruvian
Immigration Review Task Force	Tokyo	1994	Bangladeshi, Thai, Korean
Tokyo Bar Association—Center for Protection of Foreigners' Human Rights	Tokyo	1989 (1946)	Chinese
Japan Legal Aid Association	Tokyo	1995 (1952)	Chinese, Iranian, Korean, Filipino
Lawyers Association for Foreign Criminal Cases (LAFOCC)	Tokyo	1992	Chinese, Iranian
Dai-ichi Tokyo Bar Association—International Human Rights Section	Tokyo	1989	Chinese, Filipino, Iranian, Korean

Group Name	Location	Year Began	Ethnic Groups Served
Dai-ni Tokyo Bar Association-Human Rights Protection Committee	Tokyo	1993 (1990)	Chinese, Iranian, Bangladeshi
Japan Civil Liberties Union (JCLU)/Foreigners Rights Sub-committee	Tokyo	1988	All foreigners
JCLU Social Rights Sub-committee	Tokyo	1998	All foreigners
Yokohama Bar Association: Legal Consultation for Foreigners	Kanagawa	1991	Chinese, Thai, Peruvian, Korean
Kanagawa Administrative Lawyer Association—Foreign Negotiation Administrative Research Group	Kanagawa	1998	Chinese, Peruvian, Korean
Concerned citizens' groups			
Ōta Citizen's Network for Peoples' Togetherness (OC Net)	Tokyo	1992	Pakistani, Bangladeshi
Shibuya-Harajuku Group to Gain Life and Rights (Inoken)	Tokyo	1993–1998	Iranian
Call Network	Tokyo	1988–1995	Iranian, Filipino, Thai
Asian Peoples Friendship Society (APFS)	Tokyo	1987	Bangladeshi, Pakistani
Solidarity Network with Migrants Japan (SMJ)	Tokyo	1997	All foreigners
Forum on Kanagawa's Foreign Workers Problems	Tokyo	1997	
Kalabaw-no-Kai	Kanagawa	1987	Bangladeshi, Pakistani
Sagamihara Solidarity with Foreign Workers	Kanagawa	1991	Filipino

INDEX